THE RISE OF MODERN ASIA

THE RISE OF MODERN ASIA

IAN THOMSON

PITMAN PUBLISHING CORPORATION

New York · Toronto · London

Library of Congress Catalog Card Number 58–6406

CONTENTS

Contents

Contents

Contents

ILLUSTRATIONS

Illustrations

MAPS

The author is grateful to Miss Bip Pares and the Observer
*for permission to adapt the map of Korea on p. 168 from
Miss Pares' original.*

INTRODUCTION

In the last ten years an entirely new perspective has appeared in history and world affairs. European domination has been challenged throughout the world, and Europe is no longer a power house generating and manipulating vast empires as of old. Most of her past empires have completely changed in pattern and texture during recent decades, whether they were Spanish, Portuguese, Dutch, French, British, Belgian, German, Italian, or Ottoman. Some, decadent and redundant, collapsed internally. Others became weak and were dismembered or vanquished. Only one of the great empires can claim to have been relatively successful in adapting itself in time to the new age and in retaining goodwill. The remarkable constitutional experiment carried out by Britain —from the old conception of centrifugal Empire into a genuine partnership of free nations—is one of the most notable developments of the twentieth century, both a symptom and a symbol of an organic change that cried out to give birth to something new.

In many respects Europe can no longer claim to be the world's political centre of gravity as once she was. The European family of nations has been a quarrelsome one, its members continuously at loggerheads; though creative, vigorous, rich in thought and insight, the crucible of precious inheritances, it has consistently been fractious and divided. Europe has forfeited her leadership by her quarrels—recently, by promoting two world wars.

Out of this turbulence two rival conceptions of life have emerged, both of which now hold the field and claim the attention of the world. Each uses the same language of peace, liberty, equality, democracy, and economic freedom, and each denounces the same principles of Imperialism, slavery, injustice, and exploitation. But each interprets these words in its own way, and the interpretations are wide of each other. Each conception has found its champion—

xi

one in Russia, or, more widely, Asia, the other in the United States of America. Thus has the modern world developed two centres of gravity instead of one—Asia and America, in place of Europe.

A rough and ready focus of these two rival conceptions is contained in two historic events, widely separated in time but in significance closely linked—the voyage of the Pilgrim Fathers on the one hand, and the October Revolution of 1917 on the other. Each was in its way a venture of faith, and in each case the prime movers were historic pioneers, but their beliefs were at variance, and as a result the world stands now divided into two main camps.

Fundamentally, the issue is neither political nor diplomatic, neither economic nor military, though these are all intrinsically bound up with it. The clash is ideological, concerning quite different ways of living, and stemming from quite different assumptions. All talk of 'peaceful co-existence' is a tacit acknowledgement that the differences are real and mutually incompatible, and most of the work of statesmen and protagonists on both sides is conditioned by an awareness that this is so.

The pressing need is to understand the issues involved, and to know something of the background of those countries through which the particular forces of this century have been working and are still at work. It is with this in mind that this short book is offered. Not to know about Asia is to be out of touch and out of focus, in fact to be asleep at a time of great happenings. In the past the impact of Europe upon Asia has been indirectly and unintentionally to arouse her from slumber, and the pace of the awakening has varied from place to place. But no one can doubt that Asia, as a continent, is wide awake today and has assumed a strength and a greatness unforeseen even fifty years ago.

As for the fascination of the period, what of the vision and tenacity of Sun Yat-sen? Mazzini pales in comparison. For the embodiment of a struggle, who can touch Gandhi? And what an enigma he was. For scale of operation and length of tenure in office, Stalin can rival Napoleon. If, as Voltaire and Rousseau indicate, thought precedes action in social change, then Tagore is one of the Eastern sages to whom we may look. That one generation can produce such a range of exceptional political architects as Kemal Ataturk, Ibn Saud, Chiang Kai-shek, Weizmann, Jinnah, Nehru, Mao Tse-tung and Ho Chi Minh is remarkable enough in itself quantitatively. Qualitatively, these same individuals rank high in terms ranging from ruthlessness to glamour, scholarship to astuteness.

In fact, most of these leaders were moved far more by the local forces of patriotism and nationalism than by the struggle between Communism and Western Democracy. So nationalism adds a third factor to the scene. And nationalism in some quarters speaks with a desire not to take sides with 'East' or 'West', but to remain aloof or neutral, allied only with the 'uncommitted', or with some other alignment, be it Arab League, or more internationally, the United Nations. Here, the principle of discussion and arbitration and the rule of law must somehow win the day.

Meanwhile, cutting clean across all frontiers and human alliances there remains the religious impulse. The soul of Asia hitherto has been nurtured in one or other of several religions, and in due course her struggle may eventually come to a head between those who hold life to be a sacred trust and those who deny the reality of the eternal.

* * * * *

This book is divided into two parts. The first attempts to trace the main outline—and it is no more than an outline—over the period from approximately 1900 to the end of the Second World War. The second concentrates on post-war developments, and is, therefore, a summary of some of the tremendous events that have occurred in the creative decade 1945 to 1955. Both periods are momentous.

In the first part we see how Asia became infused with new or revived vitality; during this period the old way of life and thought were challenged by contact with the West more deeply, more drastically and more extensively than in previous generations. For us the only possible way of dealing with so vast a subject is to take it piecemeal, area by area, for the situations and problems were nowhere quite alike or exactly contemporary; some countries set the pace, others were content to follow. To pick out an outline which can be said to be factual and balanced is a delicate task. The temptation to pass too many judgements must be resisted. In any case we are still too close to many of the events to be able to view them dispassionately or in proper perspective. Time will

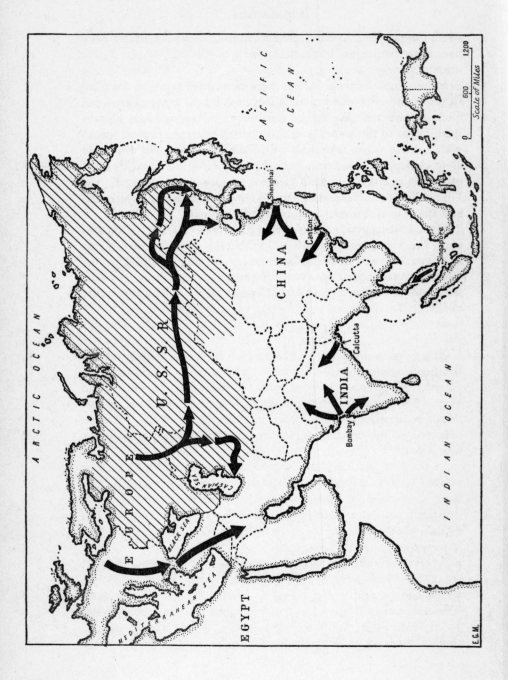

Introduction

give grounds for sounder judgements, and these may come later in another book or from another pen.

But the purpose of this initial survey is to acknowledge that the new perspective—the rise of modern Asia—has appeared, and that all the world must sooner or later take it into consideration. Unfortunately, however, inhibitions abound on every side, and prejudice distorts all reason. Probably, for a long time to come Asians will regard Europe as the wolf of the past, as an object of apprehension, once harassing and at present held at bay. Centuries of European domination cannot be forgotten overnight. Many Asians will look back on the period of 'Europe in Asia' with accusation, complaint, and censure, breeding an ill-will which can be as harmful and unwholesome to Asia as to Europe. But the burden of self-government will not be eased by recrimination, however justified any resentment may be. In Europe there will for a time persist a legacy of mild regret, the inevitable consequence of retrenchment after 'loss of Empire'. Both of these must pass, for we are moving into a new era, international in scope and morally and economically more interdependent. The rule of law is more than holding its own against the rule of might, underlying the years of struggle and liberation, jubilation and self-government; and this is significant and heartening.

I.T.

Old Plumtrees
Headcorn
Kent

August 1957

WESTERN APPROACHES TO ASIA—BY LAND AND BY SEA

German aspirations—Berlin to Baghdad railway—Russian advance—Trans-Siberian railway—the Maritime Nations (British, European and American)—advance by trade, chartered companies, settlement, extra-territorial concessions and development, from bases such as Bombay, Calcutta, Singapore, Canton and Shanghai

PART ONE

The End of
'Europe in Asia'

THE RISE OF MODERN TURKEY

1. THE BREAK-UP OF THE OTTOMAN EMPIRE

THE rise of modern Turkey is largely the story of one man—
Kemal Ataturk. Under his leadership Turkey became one of the
first countries in Asia to arise from the embers of an old Empire
and attain fulfilment as a nation. Of the crop of dictators produced
by the first half of the twentieth century Ataturk was certainly one
of the most successful, and most ruthless, and his work has been
most enduring. He has escaped much of the odium that attaches
to the memory of Hitler, and never quite suffered the same degree
of misplaced megalomania that afflicted Mussolini.

History so far has treated Ataturk generously, and to understand
his career one must try to see how it was that a movement in favour
of constitutional reform and social progress came about in Turkey.

Abdul Hamid II promised at the beginning of his rule (1876–
1909) to abide by certain liberal forms of government, including
the fair treatment of Christian minorities, but afterwards made no
genuine attempt to honour his promises. Indeed the characteristics
of his reign are cruelty, incompetence and harshness at every turn.
In 1901, when a revolt broke out in Macedonia, his repressive
measures brought about a reign of terror, and even such autocratic
nations as Austria and Russia advocated restraint and tried to
suggest reforms. Their advice was not heeded. Meanwhile, liberation movements were at work in Serbia and Bulgaria. The more
enlightened of a younger group of Turks known as the 'Committee
of Union and Progress', with their headquarters at Salonika,
pressed the Sultan to restore the constitution of 1876, a constitution which embodied the principle of Parliamentary Government,
with deputies elected by the people. Almost to the surprise of the
Young Turks themselves this pressure was successful and the so-
called Revolution of 1908 took place peacefully in Constantinople.

The End of 'Europe in Asia'

In the autumn of the same year Bulgaria struck out for independence from Turkish suzerainty; Bosnia and Herzegovina were annexed by Austria; and Crete began to look to Greece as her guardian against Turkish savagery. Serbia was indignant at Austria's sudden stroke. Albania was already disaffected, and Greece had an eye on Macedonia. Austro-German infiltration into the Balkans was unpopular, suspect and precarious. Everywhere there was a feeling of crisis.

In the following spring, April 1909, the more conservative politicians in Turkey reacted against the Young Turk revolution, but failed in their designs. The Sultan, Abdul Hamid, was deposed, and his brother Mohamed V succeeded him to the throne. So weak was the Ottoman Empire at its centre that it could do nothing to prevent Italy capturing the villayet of Tripoli in North Africa three years later, and the Sultan was forced to acknowledge this defeat and loss by the treaty of Lausanne in October 1912.

Meanwhile the disaffection throughout the Balkans had resulted in the first Balkan war. Trouble began in the most distant province of Montenegro, which declared war against the Ottoman Empire. Without hesitation Serbia, Bulgaria, and Greece threw in their lot with Montenegro. An armistice was declared in December and the treaty of London attempted to settle the Balkan problem. So unsatisfactory, however, were the arrangements made for various frontiers that in the following year Serbia declared war on Bulgaria, and the second Balkan war flared up. The war was short-lived, and an International Commission which set out to apportion the responsibility for it declared that equal blame rested on every country concerned.

Thus by the outbreak of the First World War the Ottoman Empire in Europe had been folded back to Thrace and all but squeezed out of Europe. Italy had advanced to Libya. Egypt was far beyond recovery, as far as Ottoman authority was concerned, having come under British influence. Turkey was gradually being committed to an alliance with Germany. Ironically, a British Admiral was reorganizing the Turkish fleet in 1914 while a German General, Liman von Sanders, was training the Turkish army. It was still just a question as to whether the Ottoman Empire would come in on the side of the Triple Entente, or with the Central Powers, in the event of war. There were strong arguments either

4

way: the Young Turks, German-trained, were confident of German victory; and responsible Turkish politicians feared partition if the Entente Powers won. Their fears were justified. Eventually Germany offered a military alliance which was accepted on 2 August 1914, and the Ottoman Empire was ranged against France and Britain in the Eastern Mediterranean. The situation had changed completely.

During the course of the war partition suggestions were circulated amongst the Entente Powers. As early as April 1915 Russia was promised Constantinople and the Straits. Britain by a later plan was to gain Mesopotamia, the Tigris and Euphrates area from north of Baghdad to the Persian Gulf, together with a sphere of influence reaching westwards to the Mediterranean. France was to have a zone that extended along the Levant coastline from Beirut northwards covering the Lebanon region and South-East Asia Minor, and a sphere of influence that ran from Damascus two-thirds of the way to the Caspian Sea. But these were private and preliminary ideas anticipating victory.

On 30 October 1918, the armistice of Mudros marked the collapse of the Ottoman Empire, and the threat of impending partition. The Peace conference at Versailles confirmed the principle of partition, and embodied the various suggestions, reconsidered, in the treaty of Sèvres of August 1920. The Turks were practically excluded from Europe, and confined to an area that extended from the Sea of Marmora to Armenia, and from the Black Sea scarcely to the Mediterranean.

Allied forces were still entrenched along the Dardanelles. Italy was given a chain of islands from the Aegean to Rhodes. France claimed the south-eastern province of Asia Minor as a kind of buffer state between French Syria and the new Turkey. Greece desired an area of Western Asia Minor, by way of paying off old scores, together with the valuable sea-port of Smyrna as the local capital. Such a territorial settlement could never be accepted for long.

On 28 January 1920 a National Pact was proclaimed in which the inseparability of all territory inhabited by an Ottoman Turk majority was reaffirmed. This was in accord with the spirit of President Wilson's 'Four Principles', the third of which stated that 'Every territorial settlement involved in this war must be

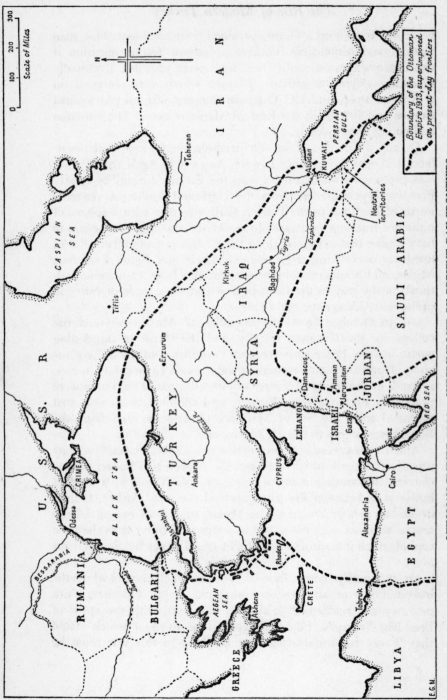

OTTOMAN EMPIRE 1913—SUPERIMPOSED BY PRESENT-DAY FRONTIERS

Boundary of the Ottoman
Empire 1913, superimposed
on present-day frontiers

Scale of Miles

0 100 200 300

N

I R A N

Teheran

CASPIAN SEA

Tiflis

PERSIAN GULF

Abadan

KUWAIT

Neutral
Territories

SAUDI ARABIA

Erzurum

Kirkuk

I R A Q

Baghdad

Tigris

Euphrates

U. S. S. R.

Crimea

Odessa

BLACK SEA

T U R K E Y

Ankara

S Y R I A

Damascus

LEBANON

Amman

Jerusalem

JORDAN

Gaza

ISRAEL

RED SEA

Suez

CYPRUS

Cairo

Bessarabia

RUMANIA

Danube

BULGARIA

Istanbul

AEGEAN SEA

Athens

GREECE

Rhodes

CRETE

Tobruk

Alexandria

E G Y P T

LIBYA

E.G.M.

made in the interest and for the benefit of the populations concerned, and not as a part of any mere adjustment or compromise of claims among rival states' (President Wilson's speech of 11 February 1918). The injustice of the treaty of Sèvres called for urgent redress. A leader was needed to voice the national indignation and to resist the process of partition. Mustapha Kemal, later known as Kemal Ataturk, turned out to be the man.

2. KEMAL ATATURK—HIS RISE TO POWER

Born in 1881 and brought up in Salonika Mustapha was destined for a military career and, in the usual way, passed through a cadet school, a senior military academy, and eventually the Vatan, the Staff College in Constantinople. Even as a young officer he disliked intensely the infiltration of German influence in Turkey, but he never failed to admire the German commander, Liman von Sanders. Mustapha hoped to rise to power on his return to Constantinople at the end of the war, but failed to find a position or a patron. Nevertheless his services as a soldier were suddenly needed to quell a nationalist rising in a remote northern province, and in May 1919, as Inspector-General of the Army of the north, he was sent to restore peace in that area.

Far from quelling the insurgents, he took over the leadership of the forces already gathered and began to use them for his own political ends. His early political moves were at Congresses demanding the ejection of French, Greeks, British and Italians from Turkish soil, and the restoration of Turkish sovereignty. In January 1920, a Turkish Parliament had been elected and assembled in Constantinople, but it only survived till March. In April a grand National Assembly was convened and met for the first time in Ankara, which from then on became the political centre, and later capital of the country, removed as it were from all the memory of slight and failure which Constantinople represented.

Mustapha Kemal now organized and trained an efficient Turkish force to meet the Greek Army entrenched on the Turkish mainland. Clever strategist that he was, he made no attempt to go to the Greeks, but left them to choose their own moment to come to him. As they marched into Central Turkey and extended their lines of communication they merely walked into disaster. When within striking distance of Ankara, Kemal suddenly swooped and the Greeks were driven helter-skelter back to the coast. With no reluctance they surrendered Smyrna and their hope of remaining in Asia Minor. The Greek occupation of Smyrna and the surrounding district had been short-lived.

As a reward for that dramatic military success, Mustapha Kemal was given the title of Ghazi, the destroyer of Christians. Meanwhile the allied troops guarding the Dardanelles were withdrawn and European statesmen were quick to realize that the treaty of Sèvres could never be enforced and was already out of date. Thus in July 1923, a new treaty was made at Lausanne, by which the extent of Turkey was internationally acknowledged to be in effect Asia Minor and the foothold in Europe around Constantinople.

3. THE TURKISH REPUBLIC AND DICTATORSHIP

In 1922 Mustapha Kemal had organized his People's Party, promising sweeping reforms and social progress, and making a direct appeal to Turkish patriotism. Meanwhile European statesmen were watching with interest Turkey's struggle to set herself up on a sound footing and free herself of foreign influences— Greek, Italian, British and French. Fortunately Turkey had little to fear from the north, for the new Communist régime in Russia had problems enough of its own. Soviet Russia was in the same position as Turkey in that it was the heir of a decadent imperialism, which it had denounced and partially overcome. In March 1921 Turkey and Russia had concluded a treaty which reciprocated recognition.

On 29 October 1923 Turkey became a Republic, and Kemal was appointed President. The new republic ratified the treaty of Lausanne, which gave Turkey much fairer treatment than had ever been intended under the terms of the treaty of Sèvres. Five years after the armistice of Mudros Turkey was salvaged, and unified under a powerful leader—whose measures were to be more drastic and determined than even the Turks anticipated.

Mustapha Kemal pledged himself as much to peace as to reform, but it was a peace which had to be maintained by military preparedness and strict discipline. His reforms were rapid and ruthless, and were deliberate breaks with the past. He was determined that the new Turkey should be abreast of the times, a democracy with an elected assembly, educated out of its illiteracy, and thoroughly secularized. He abhorred the backwardness of the people, the lack of industrial development and proper communications. He deplored the lack of intellectual criticism, and the subservience of the people to the unchallenged authority of the Koran. Every custom, convention and authority was subjected to his scrutiny and consideration.

The secularization of the State came first. The Caliphate was abolished in 1924, and the abolition of the fez followed the next year. Mustapha Kemal well knew how fanatical Moslems could be, and how much many of them detested his overthrow of the Caliphate. The fez was the traditional headgear, of a shape that enabled every true Moslem to touch his forehead to the ground as required when he prayed five times a day. Deliberately to encourage men to wear peaked caps, Western fashion, was to hit at Moslem discipline and devotional practice. In fact, devout Moslems entered the mosques in Western headdress and turned the peaks of their caps round to the back of their heads and were still able to touch the ground in obeisance when they said their prayers. Nevertheless, the fact that the fez was abolished undermined the sense of obligation to worship and began to weaken the spiritual authority of Islam. In 1928 Mohammedanism was no longer recognized as the official State religion.

From the new capital at Ankara reforms were passed and implemented with relentless zeal. In 1926 a new civil code, based on the Swiss model, was accepted. In 1928 an attempt was made not merely to dispel illiteracy, but even to replace the Arabic script by the Latin alphabet, and to persuade even adults to return voluntarily to evening classes and schools as a means of re-educating the nation as a whole. The new spirit of nationalism engendered by Kemal lent support to many of these reforms, but it was inevitable that the rapidity with which the changes were announced and the dutiful response expected of the populace should also have generated resistance and rebellion. The government, therefore, accompanied the process of change with strict censorship of the press and frequent purges. Few dictators have ever been as ruthless as Kemal in the execution of their policies. On one occasion he invited scores of foreign diplomats to an evening banquet at his farm outside Ankara. Early next morning as they drove home they saw nearly seventy of Kemal's political opponents hanging at intervals along the main road into the capital. It is surprising that he was not assassinated. The outside world knew of his tyrannies and could do little about them, apart from lodging protests. Inside the country Kemal liked to claim that he had unqualified popular support, that he was initiating the principle of personal freedom and that his subjects were free from oppression. He tried to demonstrate this by pretending that it was safe for him to roam through the streets of Istanbul or Ankara at will. Kemal could sometimes be seen, and liked to be seen, ostensibly enjoying the leisure of a statesman, basking in the sunshine on the pavement outside a café in Istanbul for choice. But even a casual observation would reveal that no ordinary customers were in the immediate vicinity of the café. The other outwardly carefree loungers sipping drinks were the strong personal bodyguard which made assassination difficult. The façade of personal freedom masked a despotic will.

The problem was not so much how to revolutionize and Westernize the nation; dictatorship was the means to that end. But dictatorship was not the end in view. Modern Turkey was officially a democracy, and Kemal was determined to turn the theory into reality. It was desperately important for the people to learn to think for themselves and to be willing to shoulder responsibility, and this in turn involved a need for discussion and debate and practice in taking decisions. But this was not what the Turks expected. The nation had so acclimatized itself to the notion of direction from above that the idea of any alternative policy or opposing theory had been virtually dismissed. Kemal himself was aware of this, and saw the difficulty.

In 1930, therefore, the President tried to introduce into the National Assembly the principle of responsible opposition, at least in debate. One-party rule had at this time become the accepted system, but Kemal persuaded his old friend Fethi and some of his own followers to stage a genuine debate along Western European lines. The Prime Minister, Ismet, and Fethi realized what was required of them and debated well. Kemal himself presided over the proceedings. Members of the Assembly were aghast to see politicians disagreeing in public and arguing with one another in what looked like the beginnings of political friction and trouble.

So when Ismet and Fethi left the Chamber arm in arm and obviously still friends the members were even more bewildered. How could one disagree in public and yet not break fellowship? The idea proved to be too new and the experiment failed for the present. Kemal was forced to admit that his own personal authority and the rule of his People's Party were seemingly so secure that the people in general wished for nothing better.

But this does not mean that the nation was not constantly surprised, alarmed, and even antagonized by the welter of reform. One measure that caused serious heart-burning was the drastic policy pursued with regard to the status of women. No longer were they required to be veiled. In future they were to take their place in national life, not in accordance with the patriarchal view that man is everything and woman of little account, but on the supposition that women were to be partners with men in the making of the new country. Women, therefore, were included in the battle against illiteracy. They, too, were to be educated, and counted worthy of civil rights. But the emancipation of women was more easily catered for in legislation than carried out in practice. Many women had no wish to change their lot, and Kemal met the full force of an inarticulate resistance in this as in other matters. Only a strong-minded man with a very clear sense of mission and policy could have continued true to his purpose against such forces of habit and custom. Kemal was not deflected.

By chance, the various crises or misunderstandings of his career often synchronized with Kurdish revolts. Each time this occurred Kemal had to turn his attention to quelling the revolt, and usually the nation became unified under his personal leadership. Thus crisis after crisis passed safely and the prestige of Kemal rose proportionately. In 1934 he was given by the Assembly the title of Ataturk, 'The father of the Turks'.

We must now turn to the question of Kemal's foreign policy. The first necessity was to ensure the territorial solidarity of the whole of Asia Minor under the sovereignty of Turkey. This first involved repelling the Greek invasion, expelling British units, and frustrating French and Italian designs. The treaty in March 1921 with the new Soviet Government in Russia offset any immediate prospect of danger from that quarter. In 1923 the Lausanne Treaty superseded the partition terms of Sèvres, assuring the integrity of

Turkey. In March 1924 friendship with Germany was sealed by treaty, and the two countries, temperamentally somewhat akin, leaned to each other once again.

By December 1925 the new Turkish Republic was sufficiently sure of itself to cast its eyes on Mosul in Northern Iraq, then a new mandate of Britain. Mussolini, anxious to limit any expansion of Turkey and with his own eye on the whole Eastern Mediterranean situation, threatened to invade Anatolia if Turkey dared to go to war over Mosul and the matter was dropped. For the next few years domestic reforms and internal security more than occupied the attention of the government.

A change of policy came in 1932. The invasion of Manchuria by Japan, the rise of National Socialism in Germany, the consolidation of strength in Russia, and the mistrust of Italy, whose occupation of Rhodes put her all too close, may all have been contributory reasons. Turkey turned to the principle of collective security, and joined the League of Nations in July. By September 1933 she had resolved her differences with Greece and concluded a Graeco-Turkish Treaty. In February 1934 Turkey was a party to the Balkan Entente, a step which was interpreted by the Turks as evidence of their new prestige in the international sphere and a recognition of their peaceful intent. A semi-permanent seat on the League Council followed soon afterwards. In March 1934 Mussolini began to hint at war. His speech about Italy's 'historic mission in Africa and Asia' sounded ominous, and Turkey kept a wary eye on the Dodecanese Islands which had become Italian in 1923.

In 1935 Britain supported Turkey in the matter of a naval agreement, and in July 1936 the Turkish Republic rejoiced at the revision of the Straits Convention at Montreux, which was a measure of international trust in Turkey's ability to ensure the protection and security of the Dardanelles and the Bosphorus. But her foreign policy was not only concerned with relations with Europe and the West, or the League of Nations. Three other countries to the East—Iraq, Persia (Iran) and Afghanistan—were as ready to find security in a regional pact as Turkey was, and the idea of a friendship and non-aggression treaty was initialled in Geneva as early as 1935. This Eastern Pact, or Pact of Saadabad, was signed in July 1937, and provided the basis of the subsequent alliance which was loosely or conveniently called the 'Northern

Tier'. In the late 1930's relations between Turkey and Russia steadily cooled, in spite of accords in 1925, 1931 and 1933, and at the same time relations between Turkey and Britain improved. Britain had supported Turkish rights in the Straits, and granted a loan of £16,000,000 for industrial expansion. In 1939 France conceded the territory around the port of Alexandretta, and Turkey thus recovered a small portion of the lost Ottoman Empire.

Meanwhile, on 10 November 1938, worn out by responsibility and struggle and with his vitality sapped by physical excesses, Kemal Ataturk died. He had lived long enough to see the Republic through its first fifteen years of life, and to see it firmly established on entirely new lines. Though he had looked to the West for many of his ideas of government and social change, the country over which he had ruled, so far from being any longer a part of Europe, was now almost totally in Asia. The choice of Ankara as capital in preference to Istanbul (Constantinople) had been a symbol of the new orientation.

Kemal Ataturk's successor as President was Ismet Inönü who had been Prime Minister from 1925 to 1937, and who was very much in sympathy with the guiding principles laid down by Ataturk.

4. TURKEY 1938–45

Within seven weeks of the outbreak of the Second World War—in October 1939—Turkey signed a treaty of alliance with Britain and France at Ankara. This did not involve Turkey in the war. From 1939 till August 1944 Turkey managed to remain neutral, and refused to be drawn in by one side or the other, although both the Western Allies and the Axis Powers bid hard for her alliance and co-operation. It paid Turkey to be neutral, and to become one of the main thoroughfares for spy traffic and communication. By the spring of 1944 the German forces were pushed back far enough from Turkey for the Axis menace to be negligible. At this point Britain and the United States began to induce Turkey to come in on the side of the Western Allies.

In August 1944 Turkey broke off both diplomatic and economic relations with Germany and similarly with Japan in January 1945. Meanwhile, steps were being taken to launch the United Nations

Organization and the inaugural Conference was to be at San Francisco. Invitations to this conference were only to be granted to nations which were at war with the Axis Powers on 1 March 1945. On 23 February, therefore, the Grand National Assembly of Turkey made the necessary formal declaration of war, and made sure of her place in the United Nations.

In March 1945 Russia renounced her treaty of Neutrality and Non-Aggression with Turkey, and the steam-rolling of Eastern Europe by the Russian armies filled the Turks with apprehension. Russia began to renew her claims upon Kars and Ardahan and to ask for a revision of the Montreaux Convention, and the effect of this was to drive Turkey to look elsewhere for friendship and assistance in a consolidation of the Eastern or Saadabad Pact, and later a link with Western Europe.

As the Second World War came to an end in Europe Turkey was busily engaged on a mass Land Reform scheme dividing up large estates into new holdings for the benefit of landless peasants. The urge for reform was still alive.

The modern Turkey of 1945 bore little resemblance to the Ottoman Empire of 1918. The Sultanate and Caliphate had been eclipsed by a more enlightened despotism, but these were only the first steps in the creation of one of the most stable democracies of modern Asia.

II

ARAB ASIA

1. POLITICAL VACUUM IN THE MIDDLE EAST

WITH the collapse of the Ottoman Empire between 1900 and 1920, all semblance of unity in the Middle East disappeared. The vast area that extended from the Black Sea to the Red Sea, from Armenia to Abadan, and from the Mediterranean to the Persian Gulf was suddenly open to fortune. The Arab world in general was slow to take advantage of this, but several European nations were ready to step in—and the result was a final resurgence of Empire-building and colonial trusteeship.

Interest in the Levant had been longstanding, counted not in decades but in centuries. The Crusades, involving a host of Christian principalities, the rights of pilgrims, Orders of chivalry supporting hospitals and other works of mercy, had all contributed to the pattern of interest and had established ancient connexions. But in modern times contacts with the Levant had multiplied and an element of vested interest began to creep in. The growth of the East India companies, English and European; Napoleon's expedition and Nelson's opposition to it; the Straits Convention; Disraeli's personal tour; the cutting of the Suez Canal; the possession of Cyprus; the occupation of Egypt; and the more cultural pursuit of archaeology; all were indications of growing interests—particularly British and French—in the future of this extensive territory. At the turn of the nineteenth century Sultan Abdul Hamid II had ruled despotically over a population of some twenty-five million, mostly in Turkey and the Balkans, and his writ also ran weakly in the more distant parts of Arabia and Africa. In the double capacity of Caliph and Sultan, the spiritual head of the Moslems as well as the political head of an Empire, he exercised an indirect influence over at least a further eleven million subjects, chiefly in Africa. Thus at one and the same time he was an

15

Oriental potentate, an ecclesiastical patriarch, and one of the crowned heads of Europe, an incongruous emblem of archaic prestige and waning authority. But by 1924 the old Ottoman Empire had disappeared from the map and had been completely replaced by new states. As we have seen, the new republic of Turkey—secular, Western, and progressive, and with the exception of a foothold in Europe restricted to Asia Minor—was beginning to take shape in place of the picturesque, retrograde, and effete Sultanate. The remainder of the Ottoman Empire broke up into a collection of small independent states, mostly under the protection of either Britain or France.

Germany hoped also to benefit from the change, but failed in her bid, though not for want of trying. The energetic Emperor of Germany, William II, had thought of using the Ottoman Empire as a means of extending his own. He had visited the Sultan, flattered him, and promoted himself as the friend and patron of the Moslem world. He had planned a railway to run from Berlin to Constantinople and on to Baghdad as part of his 'drive to the East' (*Drang nach Osten*). He had dreamt of these three cities as his capitals in Europe, the Near East and Asia respectively, a Germanic Empire thrusting through the Balkans and overlaying Arab Asia. He obtained the co-operation of the Turks in this innocent-looking railway scheme. The Emperor even induced some Germans—nobles, merchants, and engineers—to anticipate the successful conclusion of these plans by building for themselves residences appropriate to their station in the more fashionable quarters of Pera and along the banks of the Bosphorus. For a time Constantinople boomed with all the outward evidence of prosperity. The population increased to over a million. But it was a German pulse that beat within the Turkish vein, and Constantinople lost its power when Germany lost the war. Britain and France were left as the chief contenders for leadership and control in this part of Western Asia. The way to the East was vital to the governance of great empires.

2. THE RISE OF HUSSEIN AND IBN SAUD

The primary objective of the Allies in the Eastern Mediterranean zone during the First World War was to ensure the safety and security of the Suez Canal, and to prevent Germany from gaining a foothold round either the Red Sea or the Persian Gulf. To do this Britain had to be able to depend on local support. Her first step was to declare a protectorate over Egypt in December 1914, and this continued until February 1922. Egypt was thus lopped from the Ottoman Empire for reasons of military and strategic necessity. But there remained the urgent question as to how many of the Arab tribes and rulers would react to the Ottoman Sultan's demand for help. Had the bulk of Mohammedan tribes gone to the assistance of the Caliphate the outcome of the war might have been very different, but events were to take the opposite course. A spirit of revolt was already at work and the British obtained the support of Hussein, Sherif of Mecca, in the war against the Turks. Hussein was subsidized in return for this co-operation during the war, and was promised further compensation in the form of political advancement after the war. These 'promises', contained in correspondence between Sir Henry McMahon, the British High Commissioner in Egypt, and Sherif Hussein, were given in general terms which were to lead to considerable misunderstanding in later years. At the time, Hussein pinned his hopes on the creation of an independent Arab state which would stretch from Arabia to Syria. It was an ambitious dream.

Sherif Hussein fell in with the British in 1916, and supported them when driving out the Turks in 1917. In 1919 he was represented at the Conference of Versailles by his son Feisal, and had hopes of becoming the supreme head of the Moslem world in due course. Feisal became Emir of Syria for a short time in 1920, and the dream began to come true. When in 1924 the Caliphate was abolished in Turkey Sherif Hussein was persuaded to assume the title of Caliph. Another son, Abdullah, had been established as Emir in Trans-Jordan, and the Hashimite family of Hussein was everywhere in the ascendant. Family fortunes had moved northwards from Arabia in the wake of the British, and the dream was becoming reality. But Hussein had to reckon with a more capable and more illustrious rival—Ibn Saud.

Ibn Saud was the ruler of Nejd, the vast central area of the Arabian peninsula. Hussein, besides being Sherif of Mecca, the spiritual centre of Islam, was also ruler of the Hejaz, the territory bordering the Red Sea from north of Mecca to the Sinai Peninsula.

Between these two rulers there was no love lost, yet Britain had gained the co-operation of both. Ibn Saud was leader of the Wahabis, a virile and powerful tribe, who had recently been through the revitalizing period of a religious revival. They were ready to face any challenge, including war, and they had been most efficiently organized in colonies which were both military and agricultural settlements. Ibn Saud bided his time. He had personal grievances against the Sherif of Mecca which he waited to settle. Eventually, in 1924, when the Sherif's sons were taking over control of Trans-Jordan and Iraq as protégés of the British Mandate, Ibn Saud struck, and in less than two years overthrew Hussein. In January 1926 he was proclaimed King of the Hejaz, in addition to King of Nejd and its Dependencies. By 1932 his control was so unquestioned that the kingdom took his name and became Saudi-Arabia—one of the tokens of revived Arab power.

Behind the story of the rise of new Arab nations lies the personal influence of countless British Arabophils. The strong British characteristics of individuality, eccentricity, administrative genius and pioneer instinct were very much to the fore in the Middle East. No organization sponsored them. No policy was dictated to them. Yet all over the Arab world individuals from Great Britain had roamed and settled and learnt the language. They came to know and love the Arab, and their trust was reciprocated. It may be no exaggeration to say that the Arabs only maintained their good faith with the West, especially during the First World War and just afterwards, because of the wise, statesmanlike and patient influence of such people as Miss Gertrude Bell, T. E. Lawrence, George Lloyd (the future Lord Lloyd), Colonel Leechman, and many another. Yet it must be remembered that it was in the hope of gaining independent sovereignty for themselves that the Arabs supported the campaign of 1917 in which General Allenby succeeded in driving the Turks northwards from Palestine.

One alarm nearly wrecked this relationship of trust and co-operation. The Arabs discovered that a secret agreement with the intention of partitioning the Levant had been reached between Britain and France (the Sykes-Picot Agreement of May 1916). Incorporated in this same agreement was an understanding that Russia was to acquire much of Armenia. But the overthrow of the Turks was the first requisite for any settlement, and this had not

at that time been achieved. The Arabs meanwhile did not lose
faith in the British. Their aspirations were encouraged by their
successes against the Turks, especially the capture of Damascus in
1918, and by the pledges and overtures of Lawrence. Their hopes
of one or two Arab kingdoms arising out of ex-Ottoman territory
were later dashed by the decisions of the Versailles conference
when mandatory responsibility in that area was divided between
Britain and France. The Sykes-Picot Agreement proved to be no
empty dream. The Russian claim to Armenia was forfeited by the
Bolshevik renunciation of all treaties previously contracted by the
Tsarist regime. The Arabs had to possess themselves in patience
before their hopes began to take shape in the creation of Iraq
and (later) Jordan.

3. ZIONISM

An even more serious alarm hit the Moslem and Arab world in
November 1917, for another political star rose above the horizon.
In December 1917, one month before the capture of Jerusalem,
the Jews were given an assurance—the Balfour Declaration—that
Britain would 'view with favour the establishment in Palestine of a
national home for the Jewish people'. The Arab world was
astounded. True there had always been some Jews in Palestine,
content to live as a minority in their Holy Land, but the majority
lived scattered all over the world. True the principle of Zionism—
return of the Jews to Palestine—had recently become a living
force, which was continuously pressed upon the attention of statesmen of all countries. Various other parts of the world had been
suggested to the Jews as possible places for settlement, but all were
equally unacceptable. Successive waves of anti-semitism and racial
persecution had sensitized the conscience of the civilized world
and generated a sympathy for the Jews.

Furthermore, in 1917 the Allies could ill afford to lose the varied
support which Jews in many countries were giving to the war
effort. But any serious attempt to turn a tolerated minority into a
racial group with territorial rights was a very different matter. The
person who turned the issue to good account was a Jewish scientist,
Chaim Weitzman, who had done valuable work for the British
Admiralty. The day came for some reward. With characteristic
modesty and opportunism Weitzman declined any personal gain

or distinction, but pressed the Zionist cause—begging that the Jews might build a home for themselves from the ruins of the Ottoman Empire.

This assurance was given in the Balfour Declaration. It is, therefore, to the British that the Jews chiefly owe their national home, although the British never went so far as to promise a state or a country. But it is also to the British that the Arabs owe several of their new nations. Both were made possible by the collapse of the Ottoman Empire. Antipathy between Jew and Arab manifested itself in heightened nationalism on either side. The tension thus created was to become a major world problem.

4. THE MANDATES—SYRIA AND PALESTINE

At the end of the war, the liberated Turkish Levant fell into the hands of neither Arab nor Jew. The country was divided by the newly created League of Nations into two territories, to be governed by Mandate from the League. Palestine, from Galilee to the Egyptian border, came under British administration. Syria, including the Lebanon, was entrusted to France. Historically both Britain and France had deep-rooted interests in the Levant and their political administration in the area could thus be justified on strategic grounds. But in another sense this might be considered as a final stage of territorial advance on the part of the great Imperial Powers, and for the time being it checked the newly roused Arab nationalism from developing.

Palestine suddenly came to life after 1920. Until then the country had been backward and had developed very slowly. The population had been less than a million, made up of innumerable sects and communities, Christian, Moslem and Jew. But a new vitality came in with the British administration. Haifa was developed as a modern harbour and became the terminus of a pipe-line bearing oil from Mesopotamia to the Mediterranean. Previously, pilgrims and tourists had travelled in discomfort, now communications improved out of recognition. Jerusalem grew in size and prosperity. Justice, education and medical services, all took on a new lease of life.

It was a bold step when Britain appointed as her first High Commissioner in Palestine a prominent Jew, Sir Herbert Samuel.

As it turned out, no one could have been more impartial in his management of affairs, so much so, that when his term of office came to an end the Arabs were anxious to keep him, while the Jews in general felt he had been too impartial for their liking.

In the early 1920's model Jewish settlements began to spring up everywhere in Palestine. Side by side with Jaffa there grew up the new Jewish metropolis of Tel Aviv. In Jerusalem there developed the Hebrew University and the Hadasseh Hospital, and to the west of the old city the new Jewish quarter of Rehavia. No one particular portion of the country was allotted to the Jews. Rather did they begin to settle in many districts and develop the beginnings of their own national life. To these settlements came Jews from every corner of the world and it was quite common to see professional men—doctors, lawyers, professors—trying their hand at agriculture in order to convince the world that the Jew could revert to the land.

The enigma of the situation lay in the difference between the progressive attitude of the Jew and the lethargy and bewildered consternation of the Palestinian Arab who lived beside him. It was no rarity to see modern machinery being used by a Jew in some model settlement, a few hundred yards from an Arab ploughing his furrow with a wooden ploughshare drawn by a camel. The juxtaposition was peculiar if not pathetic, yet the Arab in most cases was content to carry on as of old and had little or no desire to change.

On the other hand, in the schools of Jerusalem, Arabs, Greeks, Armenians, Cypriots, Syrians and many other nationalities met and got to know one another, and the brighter Arab students soon began to pursue their studies at Middle Eastern Universities, such as Beirut and Cairo, and even penetrated to European and American Universities. Thus they in turn came back to take their place in the professional life of the Levant, side by side with their Jewish counterparts.

All this presented a problem. What hope was there of Jew and Arab learning to live alongside? The Mufti in Jerusalem represented the keenest national and religious fervour of the Arab and Moslem populace. The Jewish Agency represented the equal desire of Zionism to root itself in its new home. Prosperous as the country became in many respects with this new lease of life, it was not without anxiety to the British administration. There were repeated outbreaks of trouble, as in 1929 and 1935, and a prolonged military struggle from 1937 to the outbreak of the Second World War. British troops were always available in the Canal Zone to safeguard life and property when occasion required, but the friction between both Arab and British, and Arab and Jew, clearly indicated that a time of reckoning would one day come. The British administration did, however, guarantee a period of reasonable stability for all the minor sects whose existence had in the past been tenuous.

Meanwhile in the north the French were also facing acute difficulties and seemed to approach them in the wrong way. From the outset there was an element of mistrust, for they divided the country into five military areas and ruled them repressively. In this way they forfeited a large measure of potential harmony and co-operation. Whereas in 1920 it had looked as if Damascus might one day become the capital of a separate Arab kingdom ruled by Feisal, the second son of the Sherif of Mecca, the French riveted their control by severe administration and military coercion and for the time being any hope of Arab sovereignty was lost. Nor did the small number of responsible posts given to Arabs suggest the French had any confidence in their ability.

And on the Mediterranean coast the district of Lebanon, lying as it does in a narrow strip between the mountains and the sea, was an equally difficult problem. A high percentage of the population was Christian, not Moslem, and these Christians were a mixture of Eastern Orthodox, Maronite, Presbyterian, and a few Anglican. It was doubtful whether a Catholic French Government would readily understand or sympathize with such a mixed populace. It certainly did not help matters when Senegalese troops were brought in to quell riots. Nor did it restore confidence when able Lebanese or Syrians discovered that preferential treatment was invariably given to Frenchmen in order to superimpose upon these territories what the French thought to be their greatest export— French culture. True, the French language and way of life were partially accepted, but not without a feeling of impatience and antipathy. The French occupation of Syria certainly was not the best example of Colonial Government. In the end it was to prove fatal, and the French had to go.

22

Arab Asia

5. IRAQ AND TRANS-JORDAN

We must now turn our attention to the Tigris and Euphrates valleys—formerly known as Mesopotamia—a district strategically important because of its geographical position and which became economically valuable after the discovery there of oil. For some time this area had owed its order to the Indian Civil Service and the Indian Army. But after the Bolshevik Revolution of 1917 there was always the fear that Russian influence might at any moment want to penetrate into Mesopotamia, as well as neighbouring Persia, and this, of course, would have been a threat to Afghanistan and India. Britain could not afford to lose her influence in that part of the world. After escaping from Turkish sovereignty in 1921 Mesopotamia, now Iraq, came under the rule of the Emir Feisal. In 1923 a treaty with Britain guaranteed a continuance of British influence, putting airfields at Britain's disposal and granting her the right to defend the country if danger arose. For strategic reasons Britain was content. Three years later, Mosul in the north, the centre of valuable oil fields, became a part of Iraq; in 1932 Iraq became independent and a member of the League of Nations. In 1935 there was further development in the supply of oil through a new pipe-line and prosperity began to flow into the country.

To return to 1919, the fate of the country east of the river Jordan was entirely undecided, until Abdullah, the other son of the Sherif of Mecca already mentioned, moved with a considerable force northwards towards Damascus, but halted at Amman, where he decided to stay temporarily. The British determined to use this Emir as the local ruler in Trans-Jordan and this country soon became a British Protectorate. The compromise suited both sides. Abdullah proved loyal to the British, and the British in turn seconded British Officers to train his Arab Legion.

Though economic and commercial prosperity never really grew in Trans-Jordan to any great extent between the two great Wars, the country nevertheless became a recognized sovereignty, and in return for support in the Second World War was eventually raised to the status of kingdom. As Iraq and Jordan were ruled by members of the same Hashemite family Abdullah began to dream of a Greater Syria which would connect the Tigris and the

Euphrates, Damascus and Jordan, a revival of the ancient 'Fertile Crescent'. The dream did not materialize.

A thorn in the flesh of the British protection of Palestine was Italy's insidious campaign to succeed Britain as the mandatory power. Mussolini's imperialism of the 1930's sought steadily to increase the Italian sphere of influence in the Eastern Mediterranean. He had developed Libya, he already possessed the Island of Rhodes, he had plans for Abyssinia. He well knew to what extent some Arabs resented the British occupation, and offered to be their protector in very much the same way that both Napoleon and the Kaiser had previously set themselves up as champions of Islam. He directed a powerful propaganda in Palestine through radio and press. He offered free education for Arab students in Italy. He also knew that the Papacy would probably support any attempt to bring the Holy places within the closer jurisdiction of Italian control.

Another surprise was the unexpectedly rapid change brought about in Palestine by the influx of Zionists. Accepting the new opportunity offered by the Balfour Declaration thousands of Jews poured into the country and began to transform it. The valley of Esdraelon, lying between Haifa and the river Jordan, was turned from a neglected plain into a fertile area, and Tel Aviv outbid Jaffa as a commercial centre on the coast. This modern city with its modern buildings and facilities began to steal trade from the more leisurely Arab merchants. But the very success of the Jews in establishing so firm a footing in so short a time, and with such spectacular vigour and promise, only served to arouse Arab nationalism where hitherto it had scarcely existed. The Arabs had lacked political coherence, but were now beginning to feel their way towards the creation of an Arab League, in which all the Arab countries—Syria, Saudi-Arabia, Trans-Jordan, Egypt and Iraq—might draw together defensively and politically. However, there was no effective political force behind this movement until the Second World War.

Meanwhile, the comparatively new doctrines of Marxism found little sympathy or response in the Eastern Mediterranean. It was fondly imagined by many that the strength of religious faith—Moslem, Jewish and Christian—would be sufficient to hold at bay any likelihood of Communism gaining acceptance or taking root.

As Communism was avowedly anti-religious and materialist it was thought to be beyond the pale in the religious atmosphere of the Middle East. But this resistance began to wear thin in many quarters. However real the antipathy was up to the end of the Second World War it was certainly not as potent afterwards. Compromise was on the way, stimulated by nationalism, anti-Western resentments, and economic change.

6. THE SECOND WORLD WAR AND THE LEVANT

The outbreak of the Second World War brought once again an immediate threat to Allied influence in the Middle East. It was in Mussolini's interests to conquer Egypt, hold the Suez Canal zone and cut off French and British reinforcements to and from the Far East. In Syria, rebellious influences were at work and a separate campaign had to be fought; likewise in Iraq. Palestine at first remained outwardly loyal, but both Arabs and Jews well knew that the immediate aftermath of war for each would be a critical period. Meanwhile the Italian thrust along the North African coast towards Egypt was met by General Wavell, and the two subsequent German attacks were met by Generals Auchinleck and Montgomery. Had the Germans broken through on the Russian front at Stalingrad and forced a passage through the Caucasus to Syria, and at the same time won the Battle of El Alamein, this gigantic pincer movement might well have ended the War. But their failure did not make it any easier for France and Britain to maintain their positions in the Middle East.

Western European countries now met the full force of a re-created Arab nationalism. The impact of war drew the Arab nations more closely together, and especially after 1942 when the likelihood of an Axis victory seemed less. In December 1943 the French were forced to promise independence to Syria and the Lebanon, an assurance which brought momentary satisfaction but no lasting confidence. American leaders vied with each other in the protestations of support for Zionism, and these pronouncements were echoed elsewhere, particularly in South Africa. In September 1944 the Arab nations of the Middle East, convened at the instigation of Nuri es Said of Iraq and Nahas Pasha of Egypt, met at Alexandria to discuss matters of common concern, and, most important, the future of Palestine after the war. From 1945 onward acts of terrorism mostly Jewish increased alarmingly. Extremist Jews organized in terrorist gangs such as the Irgun and Stern gangs began to intimidate moderate Zionists into fighting for complete independence. Even before the end of 1944 Lord Moyne, the British Minister Resident in the Middle East, had been assassinated in Cairo by two Jews.

In February 1945, on their way back from conference with Marshal Stalin at Yalta, President Roosevelt and Mr. Churchill each met King Farouk, and before the end of the month Egypt had officially declared war against the Axis. The Egyptian Prime Minister, Ahmed Pasha, who made the announcement was shot and fatally wounded by a fellow Egyptian a few minutes afterwards. The situation in the Middle East was becoming explosive. Egypt declared her wish to revise the 1936 treaty with Britain, and began her bid for the Sudan. Trans-Jordan demanded territorial sovereignty. Saudi-Arabia began to emerge from her seclusion, and her princes began to be seen in the West as emissaries. General de Gaulle boasted of France's 'predominant position' in Syria and the Lebanon 'which she will retain', and sent military reinforcements to Beirut. The least tortured by political complications was Iraq. The end of the European war in 1945 brought no return to stability in the Middle East, but left the area in a state of flux.

III

INDIA

1. THE PATTERN OF LIFE AND BRITISH RULE

IN 1900 India was a glittering jewel in the British crown; and there were good reasons for this sub-continent of Asia with its teeming millions to be the pride of Britain. Three-fifths of the vast area of India was under British rule and the remaining two-fifths, made up of a collection of innumerable states ruled by their own Princes, was in general willing to be advised by the British. Yet up till the nineteenth century no one had seriously considered that India could be given any lasting unity. How could one expect to unify such a huge territory, with its amazing mixture of creeds, races, customs and languages and its complicated jigsaw of states?

Yet some degree of unity had emerged and it was largely due to three factors: first, the Indian Civil Service, which gave India the blessings of good government; secondly, the Army in India, British and Indian—usually with no more than 50,000 British and 150,000 Indians—which guaranteed peace and order and main-tained the Pax Britannica amongst a population of nearly 400,000,000; thirdly, the vision of statesmen who thought in terms of developing the country and advancing the welfare of her people.

There was hardly a family in Great Britain in Victorian times that did not owe something to this distant part of the Empire—whether it were cotton, tea, rice, or some other essential. Everyone knew of India's poverty and splendour, the beauty of her archi-tecture, the dignity of her Princes; of tiger hunts, the dangers of the North-West Frontier, the sanctity of cows, monkeys and peacocks; of the Kashmiri Love Song, the house-boats on the Jhelum river, the Shalimar gardens, and the Indians' devastating aptitude for cricket. All this played on the imagination and the memory to produce a colourful, alluring picture; and it all made for pride of possession.

The 'benefits of civilization' were first and foremost, relative peace and security, and a government and administration which was objective and therefore impartial, delegated and therefore both personal and responsible. The government set itself to fight disaster and lessen the possibility of every form of calamity, from epidemics to famines and disorders. Social reforms were also encouraged, although the government was always careful to recognize that no change ought to come suddenly if customs were time-honoured and served their purpose. The government of the country was tolerant and sensitive, and generally speaking it was both just and efficient. Secondly, there was the advantage of a single common language, English, which served as the medium of education as well as a medium of government. English was imposed by necessity; no one native language was in a position to be universally accepted, and the Indians apparently had no difficulty whatsoever in acquiring a command of the English language. Thirdly, India was soon linked together by a railway system extending for 42,000 miles, and by a canal system of 75,000 miles, which irrigated over thirty million acres, and brought hope and prosperity to regions that had been barren. All this and more was to the credit of Britain.

But in spite of it all was not well. India was reacting to tutelage. The intellectual youth of the sub-continent, having gained educational opportunities hitherto unknown, were coming to wish for a share in their own affairs. From government and mission schools they passed on to Universities in India, in Britain and elsewhere. They became conscious of India as a subject country, and this condition of occupation irked them and was to become the basis of resistance and contention. The India which on the surface looked quiet and submissive began to feel an urge to be itself—Asian, not Western; respected, not controlled; free, not ruled. But the road to freedom was not easy.

The Indians were themselves forced to admit that many of the most difficult and complicated problems were indigenous and traditional, and in no way connected with British rule. The age-long caste system by which an Indian remained for ever in the social caste in which he was born, was proving a barrier to progress in an age of enlightenment. Rigid conventions with regard to marriage, the preparation of food, and occupation in life, riveted

India

the hold of caste upon the people of India. Family life was close knit, and village life made for a strong sense of community.

Religion, whether Hindu, Buddhist, Muslim,* Parsee or Christian, brought not merely spiritual comfort but also a sense of resignation, and resignation was an antidote to the sufferings of millions. Indians beyond number lived on the verge of starvation. It is said that millions lived on one meal a day. The margin between life and death was tragically precarious, and undernourishment was a fundamental problem. Poverty, debt and a fantastically rapid rise in the population provided three other problems that cried out for attention.

Not all of India was a glittering jewel. The parched places and hungry faces told another tale. It was not that the government or the Princes were unaware or callous or inactive in these matters of deep concern, but that the scale of the problems was so immense and took so long to deal with. One thing at least can be said. Whenever flood or famine, so common in India, did strike a district, the government sent immediate relief, which certainly had not been forthcoming before the days of British administration.

Railways and better roads had made travel and communication easier and brought the states into closer touch with one another. So long as British rule was sensitive, fair and benevolent, resistance to alien rule was dormant or unspoken, but it only required one ill-advised action to unleash a tide of nationalism.

This came in 1905. The Viceroy, Lord Curzon, considered that Bengal was too big a province to be governed as a single unit. He therefore decided to divide it, and in October 1905 this involved the detachment under separate government of an area of 106,000 square miles, affecting a population of eighteen million Muslims and twelve million Hindus. Temperamentally the Bengalis are peace loving, but this was too much for them and the indignation spread as a grievance from Bengal throughout India and embittered the relations between the Viceroy and his people. The arbitrary partitioning of Bengal intensified the urge towards nationalism.

In November 1905 the Prince and Princess of Wales arrived in India for a four months' tour and the Prince himself (the future

* Throughout this chapter the word is spelt thus to conform to current usage.

29

King George V) recorded his observations. He wrote: 'I could not help noticing that the general bearing of the European towards the native was, to say the least, unsympathetic'; 'the ruling Chiefs [the Princes] ought to be treated with greater tact and sympathy, more as equals than inferiors. Why not a Council of all the Chiefs, presided over by the Viceroy, which would bring them together and enable them to know each other's views?'

Here was Royal insight. The analysis was correct, the direction indicated, a solution offered, but the instinct of the Prince of Wales was not heeded. Steps were taken in 1909, 1919 and 1935 to build a working partnership in which British and Indian administrators might co-operate together for the good of India, but at each stage the method suggested was cautious, feeble and too much of a compromise. National feeling raced ahead of British willingness to share or shed responsibility.

During this same tour the Prince of Wales had met Gopal Gokhale, the President of the Indian Congress Party, and was left in no doubt as to the extent of the desire on the part of Indians to have some responsibility in the administration of their own country.

A natural leader was on the horizon—Mohandas Gandhi (1869–1948). Born a medium-caste Hindu, he had qualified as a barrister in England, and had already shown that a quick and virile mind could take advantage of every opportunity for advancement. He came to know Britain and the British and was at first a loyal subject of the Empire. From 1893 to 1914 he harnessed his energies to the cause of the Indian community in South Africa, where the claims of three races, white, brown and black, constantly competed. During the Boer War his humanitarian instinct led him to work for the Red Cross. In working for others he found himself.

Gandhi's apprenticeship in defending his compatriots against injustice, therefore, began outside his own country; he became aware of the extent to which the coloured races can be despised or down-trodden where their interests clash with others. While he was in South Africa some of the first attempts were being made to bring about constitutional reform in India. In 1909 the India Councils Act embodied certain recommendations which had been made by the Secretary of State, Lord Morley, and the Viceroy, Lord Minto. These provided for the enlarging of the legislative

India

Councils so that they could be more fully representative of the nation, the encouraging of debate in these Councils, and the introduction of elections. These changes may seem half-hearted to us at this distance, but they were at least a start in the right direction.

Even the Indian National Congress was so satisfied as to send a deputation to the Viceroy to voice their appreciation and gratitude. The very fact that these reformed Councils contained increasing Indian representation meant that the road to self-government was being carefully laid. It was the beginning of the transfer of power.

King George V, on his own initiative, decided to visit India soon after his coronation at Westminster in 1911. At a Coronation Durbar held outside Delhi he received homage of the rulers of India, distributed largesse and boons, and announced several important changes. Delhi was to be the new capital of India instead of Calcutta. Bengal was to be reunited and the status of certain princely states was to be raised. The Royal visit stimulated tremendous loyalty and was an unqualified success. It made India feel that the King-Emperor genuinely considered himself the ruler of India as much as of England, and knew and understood their problems. In a way they felt that he was more sympathetic to their aspirations than any official government of the country.

This was fortunate for many reasons. Russia's defeat at the hands of Japan in 1905 had enhanced Asian self-confidence. For the first time the East had overwhelmingly defeated a European power, and this was itself a step in the undermining of any feeling of European superiority. Secondly, in 1911 China overthrew an outworn dynasty and became a republic, which meant that monarchy as such was no longer a *sine qua non* of national sovereignty. Third, and not least important, insidious propaganda was at work in India planning a break with the United Kingdom if she should become involved in war.

The War indeed came, but India in 1914 remained loyal. When Turkey joined Germany it was hoped by the Germans that Indian Muslims would decide for solidarity with their Turkish co-religionists, but it was a forlorn hope. Britain still meant too much to India to be left in the lurch. Indian troops fought for the allies on many fronts and it was a remarkable tribute to confidence that

31

during the First World War the garrison force in India was reduced at one time to a mere 15,000 men, barely enough to cope with a provincial emergency had there been one.

2. NATIONALISM AND ATTEMPTS AT REFORM

Notwithstanding their loyalty at the outbreak of war, members of the National Congress, who were mostly Hindu, and of the Muslim League, soon decided that the moment was ripe to agitate for home rule. At a meeting in Lucknow in December 1916, the Congress and League agreed to sink their differences and work together for the common goal of Indian self-government. This agreement became known as the Lucknow Compact. It was perfectly clear now that nationalism was a force to be taken very seriously by the British Government, and that India was unlikely to rest until she had her way.

From 1916 the struggle was on. Lord Chelmsford, who succeeded Lord Hardinge as Viceroy in 1916, realized that the nationalist undercurrents would only be controlled if it was made known officially that the ultimate aim of the Parliament at Westminster was to grant India responsible self-government. A declaration to this effect was eventually made in the House of Commons by the Secretary of State for India, Mr. E. S. Montagu, on 20 August 1917. It reads:

> The policy of H.M. Government is that of increasing the association of Indians in every branch of the administration and the gradual development of self-governing institutions with a view to the progressive realization of responsible government in India as an integral part of the British Empire . . . progress in this policy can only be achieved by successive stages. The British Government and the Government of India, on whom the responsibility lies for the welfare and advancement of the Indian peoples, must be the judges of the time and measure of each advance, and they must be guided by the co-operation received from those upon whom new opportunities of service will thus be conferred, and by the extent to which it is found that confidence can be reposed in their sense of responsibility.

The declaration held out a clear enough promise, but it was shot through and through with caution, which was only too easily interpreted as a policy of delay. It was to be another thirty years

32

before the hope became fulfilment, and the stages in between were frequently painful, with repeated loss of goodwill.

Lord Chelmsford and Mr. Montagu issued a report in July 1918, and on the basis of their recommendations amendments were to be made to the Government of India Act. Most unfortunately, before the new constitution could be passed, three major setbacks occurred.

The political situation in India was felt to be so delicate and acute that a Bill was passed in England designed to give emergency powers to the Governor-General in Council in case of any incitement or disorder. Superficially, it appeared to authorize the power to arrest and imprison without warrant or trial and was, therefore, immediately represented as an attack on personal liberties and the beginnings of calculated oppression. In actual fact this Rowlatt Bill provided for the trial of seditious crime by no less than three judges of the highest status and the setting up of committees to investigate internment. However, suspicion grew into alarm, with the result that disorder broke out in some districts.

Tragic to relate, in April 1919, the military were called in by the civil authorities of Amritsar in the Punjab to deal with a mob that was holding an unauthorized assembly in the city. General Dyer dispersed the mob, but 400 people were killed in the process. Public opinion in India was immediately inflamed and the nationalist demand for home rule was redoubled.

The Rowlatt Bill with its firm emergency powers cut clean across Indian peoples' confidence in British justice. Rowlatt was a Judge, and the principles embodied in the Bill that bore his name were now to be contested and challenged by a trained and practised barrister—M. K. Gandhi—the same Gandhi who had been the friend of Britain, called to the Bar in London, and who understood the meaning of freedom in England. He now became hostile to imperial domination and gradually assumed the role of architect of Indian independence. His methods were unusual and largely unanswerable; he fought the case for India not on the battlefield, nor by foreign alliances, nor even chiefly in the law courts, as one might have expected of a barrister. The slogan of his campaign was Swaraj—demand for self-government. His weapon was the opposite of aggression and ultimately more effective: Satyagrapha, a stubborn, passive resistance. It entailed both a refusal to co-operate in any way, and harmless forms of obstruction.

In practice this spiritual principle—for its roots lay deep in Indian religion—demanded a refusal to support any activity thought to be wrong, and involved immense self-control. It produced an attitude of obstinacy, but was comparatively harmless in itself. In order to hit at British rule all British goods were boycotted, a serious blow to trade. For instance, Gandhi's action on hearing of the Amritsar massacre was to invite all Indian shops to close for a day as a token of mourning, lamenting the Rowlatt Bill. By such actions the people of India made their feelings of indignation and resistance perfectly clear, but abstained nevertheless from violent retaliation, at least for the time being. Gandhi had experimented with this type of passive resistance already in South Africa. He was now to develop it into an art as a political weapon. The British described his campaign as 'Civil Disobedience' and this behaviour became the greatest possible embarrassment to the Government of India.

Throughout 1919 the recommendations of the Montagu-Chelmsford Report of 1918 were being codified at Westminster as amendments to the Government of India Act. The Act was finally passed in December. The people of India were being taught to clamour for home rule, but they were actually being offered only a fraction of their hopes.

In the new constitution the Viceroy remained supreme, with an Executive Council which usually included two or three Indians. The Central Legislature was revised and 70 per cent. of its members were to be elected by an extended franchise. In the provinces a new system of delegation was introduced. Agriculture, education, public health and public works were transferred to Indian Ministers who were to be responsible to their local legislative assemblies. It was the beginning of a partnership in Government, and in an atmosphere of good will it might have worked well.

But this system of divided rule in the provinces, known as Diarchy, was too great a compromise to satisfy Indian expectations. Moreover the British had financial control and were therefore in a position to say the final word on almost any issue. Britain thought that she had been generous in the measure of reform granted; Indians felt they were not trusted. The gulf was widening and resentment grew. Thousands of British-educated students returned to India determined to fight for freedom from the British Raj.

India

By 1920 there was already ample proof that India was rapidly acquiring a new status—mature and international—in the eyes of the world. India was represented at the Versailles Conference in 1919, was a signatory of the Peace Treaty and a foundation member of the League of Nations. But her constitutional status, subservient to Britain, bore little relation to this wider development. Tutelage persisted.

3. INDIAN POLITICAL PROGRAMME

A campaign of passive resistance or civil disobedience was in itself so unproductive that it could not really be expected to be anything more than a nuisance. Indian politicians gradually became aware that they would only be able to justify their claim for home rule if they were able to draw up a clear programme of constructive reform, and this they did, basing it upon five main principles.

The first need was an economic one. India was a small industrial producer and depended very much on goods from overseas. It was essential, therefore, that somehow or other she should become economically more self-supporting, or at any rate capable of producing more for the home market. Apart from the resulting decrease in the volume of imports and reduction of prices this would encourage a pride in her own self sufficiency.

Thus there came about a revival of village cotton spinning and cloth making, which provided a livelihood for many families in thousands of villages. In many cases it saved the village community from mere marginal existence, and Gandhi himself set an example by his own spinning and by wearing homespun. Of course the British cotton and textile industry—in particular Lancashire— was affected unfavourably, and this delighted the Indians.

One of the less noble features of European civilization in the past has been the consumption of alcoholic liquor and the toleration of drug traffic, which naturally has weakened the moral fibre of any peoples which fell addict to either drug or alcohol. Gandhi and others made their second main principle the destruction of this trade and persuaded Indians to abstain from either form of indulgence. It was virtually a temperance movement, but it was also another element in the principle of boycott.

Thirdly, they set out to raise the status of women, who were then considered to be lowly and servile. Two manifestations of this attitude were purdah, the seclusion of women, and child marriages, which were common practice. Whatever complaint India might have had about British domination she had nothing to boast about in her own treatment of Indian women. Gandhi and many others set about to rectify this failing. It was good that the move should have come from Indians themselves.

One of the perennial problems in India had always been the friction between Hindus and Muslims. Over seventy million Muslims were living amongst a population of over 200 million Hindus and bloodshed had been frequent in the past. Congress, hitherto predominantly Hindu, now began to welcome more and more Muslim members into the Congress Party and Assembly, realizing that it was the only possible way of demonstrating some kind of solidarity among Indians. This was their fourth principle; they hoped that by lessening sectarian rivalry and showing that they could live together they would have a strong argument for levering the British out of India. The impulse was worthy, though the process itself was not always successful.

A further fault in the Indian structure of society was the existence of the Untouchables, a mass of over fifty million Indians who were outside caste—despised, avoided, ostracized. Their lot was pitiable in the extreme and a disgrace to India. As his fifth task Gandhi set himself to remove the stigma of 'untouchability' and managed to persuade Congress to accept this course as policy. At last the problem became the political concern of some of India's leaders.

With these five clear principles to work for, India began to acquire a more widespread national conscience, and the Congress Party, together with the Muslim League, began to speak in a more representative way. Opposition to the Raj now became more organized, as well as more vocal. From now on suspicion coloured politics and even genuine attempts to pave the way to independence were all too readily misunderstood.

Throughout the British Empire country after country had been granted full Dominion status—Canada in 1867, Australia in 1901, New Zealand in 1907 and South Africa in 1909. Clearly India thought her time was due. Gandhi had been in South Africa when she had become a self-governing Dominion. He asked the same for India, whose native population had a nobler culture and great dignity. Indians resented alien occupation. To Gandhi self-government seemed a reasonable demand.

The next blow occurred in 1926 over a matter of currency reform. The value of the rupee was raised to 1s. 6d. from 1s. 4d. This was to the advantage of British trade and investment and to the disadvantage of India. Once again there was ill-feeling.

The 1919 India (Amendment) Act provided that within ten years a statutory Commission should report on the working of the new constitution. When the Commission was appointed in 1927 not a single Indian was chosen to serve on it. This was regarded as a deliberate affront, and Sir John Simon's Commission embarked on a thankless task, knowing full well that they would meet with misunderstanding and lack of co-operation at every turn. The Commission began its investigation in 1928 and issued its report— thorough, sensible and progressive—rather belatedly in June 1930.

4. GANDHI AND THE STRUGGLE FOR SELF-GOVERNMENT

By this time Gandhi had launched another Civil Disobedience campaign and was at the height of his popularity, and at his most effective as a nuisance. He had become an enigma and a problem. As a token of his disgust with everything Western, he had deliberately reverted to an oriental simplicity of life of his own choosing. A thin, wizened and bespectacled figure wearing nothing but a loin-cloth, much of the time he controlled the minds of millions, and not least the general policy of Congress. To India he became Mahatma—the Holy One.

Sometimes appearing to be half saint and mystic, he remained an uncommonly astute statesman playing at power politics. Imprisonment was useless, it only enhanced his prestige. His repeated efforts to fast to death bewildered the British conscience and were frequently effective in bringing about an easing of the situation or a change of heart among his followers.

Fortunately for Britain the Viceroy from 1926 to 1931 was a man of saintly character. Sincere and a man of prayer, Lord Irwin, later Lord Halifax, was quickly trusted by Muslims and Hindus alike and was a man after Gandhi's own heart. His wisdom, sympathy, and integrity probably saved India from open revolution.

The End of 'Europe in Asia'

The report of the Simon Commission in 1930 had its repercussions—good and bad. On the one hand it gave the British public a knowledge of India and her affairs as no other single document had ever done and thus aroused widespread interest. On the other hand it gave yet another boost to the Indian demand for home rule. The Report had proposed that India should eventually become a Federation of self-governing provinces, rather on the model of Canada, but that critical matters such as Foreign Policy, Defence and Finance should continue to be vested in the Viceroy in Council. Once again this fell a long way short of independence.

In November 1930, discussions were opened in London on the future government of India, and continued till January 1931. At this Round Table Conference some progress in the direction of Federal Government was made and on the strength of this encouragement Lord Irwin and Gandhi reached an agreement. Gandhi undertook to lift his Civil Disobedience campaign and the Viceroy promised concessions in the salt areas. Gandhi even attended the next sittings of the Round Table Conference held in the autumn of 1931. From his point of view this may have been a mistake, for he held greater prestige when at a distance from Westminster than he did when sitting as an equal among negotiators.

The Conference dragged on slowly. The Muslims led by Mohammed Ali Jinnah were convinced that they would be submerged by the Hindus. The Princes consented to come into the scheme for federating the States and Provinces, but unfortunately Congress thought that the Indian Princes were in league with the British Government—privilege with privilege—and that the proposal would merely perpetuate British rule. In 1932 the British tried to solve the dilemma of the Hindu-Muslim deadlock by a constitutional safeguard, the 'Communal Award', a kind of proportional representation. Each community was guaranteed a block of seats in the provincial legislations. The Muslims were given a sop, but Jinnah was wary of the implications.

At long last, after yet a third Conference, a Report was issued in November 1934 and on this basis India was given another new constitution. Gandhi, disappointed with the discussions in London, stirred up further Civil Disobedience and had to be imprisoned. There also emerged a 'Men of God' movement, which aimed at a kind of Communism, based somewhat on the Russian model.

Nevertheless the Government of India Act was passed in 1935, and by this Act a central Government was to be created; the eleven Provinces were to be given full self-government; and India was to become a Federation.

The conciliatory attitude of Lord Irwin was desperately needed to give effect to such an Act, but he had already been succeeded by Lord Willingdon, whose firm and uncompromising rule added fuel to the embers. Once more India became engulfed in the fires of nationalism. The more the nationalist movement was restricted or prohibited, the more it was driven underground and flourished. Merely by sitting in the middle of main roads, crowding railway platforms and even sitting down on railway tracks, thousands of Indians disrupted civil life and the normal course of law and order. Lathi charges were made by the police to disperse crowds, but this kind of treatment merely intensified the growing bitterness. At the same time trouble continued on the North-West Frontier and the Indian Army was kept constantly on guard to stave off danger from that quarter.

British administration was put to a severe test at the outbreak of the Second World War in 1939 by the prevalence of political disaffection. For twenty years Indians had hoped for self-rule and from time to time Commissions, Reports and Acts of Parliament had led up to the idea of independence by the gradual processes of dyarchy and the prospect of dominion status, but the British pledges of self-government were still too gradual and out of step to satisfy Indian aspirations.

One particular action offended many. On the outbreak of war, the Viceroy himself, Lord Linlithgow, declared war against Germany in the name of India without so much as consulting the Legislative Council. This was autocracy itself, a mode of Government which India well knew in her own past, but which was not in tune with the principles of Parliamentary democracy which the British themselves had so generally practised and instilled into the Indian mind. Parliamentary democracy, as Pundit Nehru himself later protested, suited India well, and Indians had now reached a stage where they were quite convinced that they were well able to manage their own affairs.

On the outbreak of the Second World War a Commonwealth Defence Council had been formed to support the war effort.

Indian troops took part on many fronts against the forces of Fascism and Nazism, whether Italian, German or Japanese. They covered themselves with glory and proved once again their brilliant military capacity. Twenty-eight Indians, including Gurkhas, gained the V.C. for outstanding valour.

In a remarkable way, at a time when the tide of public opinion in India, especially in political circles, was demanding the right of self-determination and a wave of nationalism was sweeping the country, Indian troops remained almost wholly loyal to the British, whose leadership in the army they had come to respect. The only real exception at a later stage in the war was the treachery of Subhas Chandra Bose, who formed an Indian National Army to fight alongside the Japanese in the campaigns in South-East Asia. Many of his supporters were Indian prisoners of war whom the Japanese had captured, and who were persuaded by Subhas Bose to fight with the Japanese.

Meanwhile, even during the war, the process of Indianization was speeded up in the army and hundreds of Indians became commissioned officers as a step towards eventual leadership.

By 1943 there were in fact more Indians in the Indian Civil Service than there were British. In that year the Indian Civil Service, which normally totalled 1,200, was made up of 629 Indians to 560 British. Indeed, at one stage during the Second World War the Viceroy's Executive Council, which was composed of fourteen members, besides the Viceroy himself and the Commander-in-Chief, contained no less than eleven Indians.

By 1940 the Congress Party, realizing how deeply committed India was to war, began to mistrust British promises of independence and opened a campaign for individual Satyagraha—refusal to co-operate with the civil authority. This was open revolt, as Mahatma Gandhi himself admitted. The central government proceeded, therefore, to imprison the Congress Working Committee, and it is estimated that upwards of 24,000 Indians were at one time or another imprisoned for reasons of revolt.

Meanwhile the Muslim League, which ever since 1937 had been anxious about its survival as a minority, seemed likely to be swamped by the creation of a Hindu state and began to put forth a new idea of a Muslim country arising out of the embers of the dying Indian Empire. By 1940 this idea had crystallized into the conception of Pakistan—a separate country in which Muslims would predominate and govern themselves. Once envisaged, the pursuit of this goal became a powerful force which alienated itself more and more from the Congress Party. It added to the complexity of the situation.

In April 1942, the British Cabinet, fully aware of the dangerous situation that had developed in India, sent Sir Stafford Cripps to Delhi to try to reach some satisfactory reconciliation. Sir Stafford, well known as a negotiator and a man of peace, tried to convince India that the old conception of imperialism was now dead and buried in the minds of British statesmen and that Britain no longer looked upon India as a country which they expected to hold in subservience. He made an offer on behalf of the Cabinet of self-determination for India and promised that at the end of the war a constitutional assembly would be convened to draw up the necessary instrument of government.

It had been hoped that Sir Stafford Cripps and Mahatma Gandhi would be able to trust each other and come to some mutual agreement, for both in their different ways were devout and practical. But the Cripps Mission was followed by a new wave of terrorism and open revolt. Gandhi declared that the only thing which would satisfy India was an immediate transfer of power, but in the British view this was out of the question; Japanese forces were already in Burma, advancing dangerously in the direction of Assam and Bengal. The threat to India was serious.

This advance of the Japanese, with their dramatic occupation of so much of South-East Asia, led many Indians to hope that British influence in places like Hong Kong, Singapore, Malaya and Burma would never be restored. Indeed if any major outbreak of civil war in India had occurred simultaneously with the Japanese advance in Assam, British rule might then have been made impossible, but the common sense of the majority of Indians held firm and this particular crisis never came. What did happen was a serious famine in Bengal which occupied the attention and energy of the central government.

In August 1942 the All India Congress Committee took up the cry of 'Quit India' at a conference in Bombay and for the next three years one of the main problems was the maintenance of civil order. The Viceroy throughout the second half of the war was

The End of 'Europe in Asia'

Field-Marshal Lord Wavell, the conqueror of the Italians in North Africa, a great statesman and man of letters, and also a friend of India.

In 1943 and 1944, as the Japanese were pushed back in South-East Asia and the Pacific islands, and as allied victory became increasingly certain, nationalist propaganda in India never relaxed its insistence upon home rule. By May 1944 the general situation was sufficiently eased for Gandhi to be released and in the following spring a meeting of all the main political leaders was held at Simla in order to work out a constitutional solution.

The British still hopefully imagined that India might be kept intact as one great union or dominion within the Commonwealth, but the Simla Conference was final proof that any such hope was vain, for the Congress Party and the Muslim League could not in any way be brought together. The only possible solution appeared to lie in the principle of partition.

IV

JAPAN

1. SUDDEN RE-BIRTH

THE entry of Japan into world politics was meteoric, a calculated threat to every country that bordered on the Pacific. A small island kingdom had become a mighty Empire in little more than two generations; her actions were to shake the whole of modern Asia into a new way of thinking.

The secret of this extraordinary re-birth of Japan lay as much in the people as in the new social, economic, and industrial system they were to evolve. The Japanese proved themselves to be capable of accepting entirely new ideas and harnessing them to their own needs, and the system upon which their national life was built was powerful, controlled from the centre and depending upon loyalty and submission. Disciplined, patriotic and industrious Japan was soon in a position to outmatch the very countries which she had so quickly emulated.

It is not possible to understand the growth of this Empire without a knowledge of the way Japan first took her place among the nations of the world. Until 1850 Japan was largely cut off from the rest of the civilized world—isolated, unvisited and mysterious. She had no wish to mix or trade with other countries. But the Western nations were making a bid for trade posts in the Far East. Britain had forced China to open up five great ports and in 1842 had acquired the island of Hong Kong by treaty concession. The United States felt strong enough to issue a similar challenge and in 1853 Commodore Perry appeared off the Japanese coast in a warship and demanded that Japan should open her ports likewise to foreign trade. Against superior military might there was no alternative but to give way, and at the point of the pistol Japan was forced to take note of the family of nations and surrender her policy of isolation.

This step divided the nation. Ruling families which had held the country in their grip for generations lamented it as a betrayal and surrender. They were supported in this view by conservative forces in the Army and in the higher levels of the feudal system. But others in tune with the times recognized the futility of any further seclusion; the time for change had come, however unwelcome or disturbing it might prove to be. The progressives managed to assert themselves and in 1868 Japan entered a new phase of political and national development which is now known as the Meiji Restoration. Hitherto many an Emperor had been little more than a figurehead or a puppet, but now the Emperor, Mutsuhito, took his rightful place at the head of the nation. Mutsuhito's reign (1867–1912) was to coincide exactly with the re-birth of the nation.

The oligarchy of nobles that had ruled Japan for centuries was deposed and the Tenno (or Emperor) ruled in its stead. He was not a despot or an autocrat, for from the first he governed through advisers; later, a Parliamentary system was inaugurated, first Liberal, then Conservative, but always intensely nationalist.

In one way Japan as an island kingdom stands to the Continent of Asia very much as Britain stands to Europe—detached, yet belonging; sentinel, yet independent. From small beginnings each island became the centre of a vast Empire, but whereas Britain accumulated hers by the most gradual processes the Japanese Empire was a more necessary and deliberate expansion.

In Japan a growing population in a very limited space constituted a real problem, but it also gave a sense of unity to the island, and made it necessary for every individual to be an integral part of the whole. Consequently, Japan was very closely knit: it had to be. Other factors also strengthened this unity. An instinctive love of nature; the traditional ancestor-worship; a strong family sense; worship at the Shinto shrine; and above all, the veneration in which the person of the Emperor was held, all contributed to an inherent and internal solidarity.

The structure of society was clearly stratified. After the Royal family came the aristocracy, Daimios, then the warriors, Samurai, an hereditary caste, and finally the commoners. In this feudal structure everyone knew his place and authority was easily recognized and followed. The military held a place of honour, in complete contrast to the situation in China, where, generally speaking, the soldier ranked very low.

Once awakened by the action of Commodore Perry, the Japanese did not take long to find out what had given Western countries their superiority over other nations. They sent missions all over the world to investigate systems of education, military training, government and all aspects of public service and scientific development, in order that they might choose for themselves which to copy and which to ignore. There was no limit to their determination to adapt themselves to modern methods and to copy anything which might advance their own development. It is doubtful whether any nation has ever been so thorough in investigating how other nations lived.

For example, in the matter of education they chose to follow the rigid French pattern of curriculum, but the German model of educational hierarchy based on the unquestioned authority of superiors. In other words the Japanese adopted an educational system which tended to be inflexible and authoritarian, but at the same time systematic and very thorough. But this foreign importation, in which every hour of every day was meticulously planned, and where the authority of the professors and lecturers and teachers was taken for granted, was overlaid by the Japanese with something of their own tradition. It may be summed up in the word Shushin, which means something like duty, and is based firmly on the virtues of respect, loyalty and obedience.

In 1890 an Imperial Rescript on education was issued and this was read five times a year at every school in the country. Although the Rescript was couched in general terms and explained the purpose of education, there was behind it an implicit assumption that high authority would always be obeyed. Indeed the tone of it was so authoritarian that it contained the germ of a totalitarian state. It was made clear that all children were destined to serve the best interests of their country, and this led to a heightened patriotism, which eventually became almost fanatical.

One of the most extraordinary examples of their capacity for copying was the new terminology the Japanese adopted for the nobility, modelled largely on the English pattern. During the period of restoration and rejuvenation we find the Japanese taking on titles such as Viscount and Marquess and decking themselves out in frock-coats and top hats—a drastic change from an almost medieval society. Nevertheless the change had this advantage; that the Emperor was able to create new nobles from wealthy and intelligent families which had every right to assist in the progressive development of the new Japan. They would never have been able to be at ease among the old nobility: new ideas required new people.

So far as the armed forces were concerned training was rigid and old fashioned and weapons were completely out of date. Swords were obviously no match for rifle-fire, so the army had to be thoroughly overhauled. As for the navy, none existed in any modern sense until Queen Victoria gave Japan her first war vessel and British officers were sent out to train the new Japanese navy.

These are but three illustrations of the way Japan was adapting herself to the future. There was still no political enfranchisement nor were there yet any real glimmerings of democracy. Japan's industrial revolution was only just starting, but the whole machine was very quickly speeded up. Yet in spite of all these radical changes which were bound to benefit the country an important minority among the leaders of Japan continued to regret the opening of Japan to foreign influences, though even their conservative views could not prevent them taking pride in the progress of the country.

External events and a growing need to expand forced Japan to look beyond her island kingdom. She was faced with three challenges. The first came from Russia, encroaching steadily eastwards across Siberia. This tremendous imperial power in the north-west was likely before long to become a serious threat to Japan if not resisted. In 1891, when the Trans-Siberian railway was started, Japan became acutely alarmed. The second challenge lay in the internal decay of China behind the façade of effective government at the time of the Dowager Empress Tzu Hsi. Japan knew that incompetence was sapping China's vitality, and such weakness on the mainland was a great temptation for Japan to test her new-found strength. Thirdly, European infiltration along the coastline of Eastern Asia was resented as bitterly in Japan as in China. Germany, Britain, France, the United States and Portugal all had their bases or international settlements firmly established in Canton, Macao, Shanghai and elsewhere, and quantities of foreign capital were being poured into China to develop her industrial life and public utilities. China was showing herself incapable of resistance, and she was in danger of being economically partitioned and brought under European control. If this happened in China it might also happen in Japan. It was clearly in the interests of Japan to acquire in due course what part of the mainland she could, not merely for the settlement of her surplus population, nor primarily for the extension of commerce, but also to guard against further penetration by Europeans and Americans.

2. PROOF OF POWER

Japan's first trial of strength came in her war against China in 1894-95. To the surprise of many nations the small island kingdom, which most people so far had tended to disregard, had no difficulty in overcoming her massive neighbour. The Chinese forces suffered humiliating defeats by land and sea, and the Japanese were quick to press home their advantage by invading Manchuria, attacking Port Arthur, and menacing other parts of China. China's military and administrative weaknesses were soon exposed. By the Treaty of Shimonoseki (1895) China was forced to cede to Japan the island of Formosa (Taiwan) and other islands off the China coast, and to acknowledge the independence of Korea. The islands were to serve as stepping-stones to a greater Empire. This was the new Japan's first victory, and it was significant; the nation was elated by success. Three years later Germany acquired Kiaochou, a base with considerable territory on the Chinese mainland opposite Korea. When in 1900 Germany declared her intention of increasing her merchant fleets and regular navy, Japan was as alarmed as Britain, for Germany possessed many groups of islands in the mid-Pacific. Equal suspicion of Germany led Japan and Britain to conclude a defensive alliance in 1902.

Meanwhile, a conflict was developing between Russia and Japan as a direct result of China's weakness. Antagonism to new reforms and to foreign influence in China had stirred a secret society, the Boxers ('patriotic harmonious fists'), to murder Europeans and Chinese converts to Christianity. The German minister, Baron von Ketteler, was killed in the street in Peking, and foreign legations were besieged. The government supported the Boxers and an international relief force marched to Peking to rescue the legations. While the nations were thus engaged Russia took the opportunity of invading Manchuria under pretext of protecting the railway and preserving order. Russia later agreed to restore Manchuria to China and the evacuation was to be completed by October 1903. But far from withdrawing, it soon became evident that Russia was preparing to stay and was building fortifications, even in Korea. This enraged the Japanese, who proposed that the two countries should guarantee the territorial integrity of China and Korea, and should recognize the policy of 'open door' to trade. Japan was willing to acknowledge that Russia held the dominant interest in Manchuria if Russia would reciprocate by recognizing Japan's interest in Korea. Russia ignored the main issues raised, and in retaliation proposed a set of restrictions on Japanese activities in Korea. Negotiations soon broke down. In 1904 the Japanese under Kuroki occupied Korea, defeated the Russians at the Yalu River, and besieged Port Arthur, which eventually surrendered with the loss of 41,000 Russians and much equipment. A petition by hungry, wounded and disillusioned strikers, outside the Winter Palace in St. Petersburg demonstrated the feelings of the Russian people against the war. It ended in catastrophe when the crowd was fired upon. Worse was yet to come. In October 1904 the Russian fleet under Rozhestvensky was despatched from the Baltic to Japanese waters. A few days later they mistook an innocent British fishing fleet in the North Seas for a section of the Japanese Navy, and promptly opened fire, killing two British fishermen. The Russian fleet was detained at Vigo, the incident investigated by an international commission, and a fine imposed. In May 1905 the Russian fleet of thirty-two vessels steamed into the straits of Tsushima, only to be annihilated by the Japanese under Admiral Togo. The world awoke to the realization that Japan was unquestionably a country to be reckoned with, and in Russia a wave of riots, mutinies and assassinations swept the land. With the United States acting as mediator the Russians accepted the terms of the Treaty of Portsmouth (the American naval dockyard) whereby Russia acknowledged Japan's paramount interest in Korea, transferred to Japan the lease of Port Arthur, ceded the southern half of Sakhalin, and granted valuable railway rights on the mainland. Manchuria was to be evacuated by both powers and restored to

China. But even these generous terms failed to satisfy the Japanese who resented the failure to exact a heavy indemnity from Russia. Resentment persisted, and suspicions deepened between the two countries. In 1907 Japan obtained by treaty a protectorate over Korea, and in 1910 annexed it.

At the outbreak of the First World War in 1914 when Russia was attacked by Germany her attention and energy were diverted from the East. Japan was relatively free for the moment from Russian threats. She herself declared war on Germany within three weeks of the outbreak, and spent the new few months capturing German possessions in the Far East—Kiaochow, Tsingtau, and a number of islands—most of which she held from 1914 to 1922. Distress and turmoil in Europe served her expansionist aspirations well. But the war also gave Japan an admirable chance to stake claims against China, for China had overthrown her ancient dynasty in 1911, had established herself uneasily as a republic, and lacked political stability after this constitutional change.

So in January 1915 with military forces already in Shantung province, Japan presented China with her famous Twenty-one Demands. China was asked to consult Japan in certain political, financial and military matters; to use the services of Japanese advisers; to give Japan permission to engage in railway construction; to open further ports; and not to cede or lease any harbour or bay along the coast of China to any third power. China demurred for as long as possible but eventually concluded two separate treaties, one dealing with Shantung, and the other with South Manchuria and Eastern Inner Mongolia. Western Powers suspected that these were the first stages in the establishment of a Japanese protectorate, but the Chinese later disregarded the Demands as having been imposed under duress.

Once German possessions in the Pacific had been occupied and the nuisance-value of German marauding warships nullified, the Japanese came to the assistance of the Allies by using their navy to protect trade routes, escort convoys, and counter the U-boat campaign. These operations were mostly in the China Seas and the Indian Ocean, but also in the Mediterranean. The Allies, though cautious of Japan's new power, had good reason to be grateful for her wartime co-operation.

3. EXPANSION OF EMPIRE

At the end of the war, Japan was treated generously at the Peace Conference at Versailles. The more progressive of her statesmen felt that the time had come to work out some synthesis between East and West, some compromise or reconciliation between the forces of reaction and the momentum of material progress. A few idealists hoped that a sense of justice would obviate the need for rivalry. Japan was now recognized as a leading power, and was granted a permanent seat both at the conference and in the newly-formed League of Nations. She acquired territorial concessions in the province of Shantung and was given all the former German islands in the Pacific north of the Equator. These islands included the Marshalls, Carolines, the Marianas and the islands of Pellew and Yap. These islands brought the Japanese within range of the Dutch East Indies and the Philippines and also brought them more than half-way south from Japan towards Australia. Australia took fright; her one wish was to exclude all Asians from her sub-continent. Even more alarmed were the Americans because the American cable system was carried across some of the islands now to be held by the Japanese, Yap in particular.

In many ways these tremendous gains might have been thought to satisfy Japan's ambitions. There were more outlets for her increasing population, more markets for her expanding production. Japanese industry began to boom and her exports of cotton goods began to affect the cotton industry in Lancashire. But in spite of all this Japan suffered four serious setbacks.

The first came in 1919, when Japan tried to obtain the recognition of the principle of racial equality at the Versailles Conference. She was not wholly successful and this reluctance to admit the principle unanimously was interpreted by the coloured races as an insult and a further token of the assumption of superiority on the part of the white races. Secondly, in 1922 a Conference was held in Washington to work out an agreed relative strength between the great Navies of the United States, Britain and Japan. Japan expected that she would be given equality with the other two countries, but this was a forlorn hope. The naval ratios ultimately agreed were 5 : 5 : 3, to the United States, Great Britain and Japan respectively. This limitation imposed upon Japan only made the Japanese more than ever resentful and hostile and the Japanese Prime Minister was promptly assassinated. It was not until 1934 that this arrangement was ultimately terminated. Thirdly, in 1923, parts of Japan were devastated by a shattering earthquake and Tokio and Yokohama in particular suffered tragic devastation and loss of life. This appalling experience unnerved the country for a time. Fourthly, in May 1924 an American Immigration law was passed forbidding Asians any longer to enter the United States. The marvel is that the Japanese accepted this racial slight with calm and restraint. Nevertheless, it was yet another rebuff that could not be forgotten or forgiven. The only immediate answer was to develop the country and make it strong enough to be able to hit back one day. If the outside world needed any proof that Japan was at pains to understand the Western way of life and the trends of modern democracy, ample evidence was provided by a six-months' tour by the Crown Prince. Prince Hirohito travelled through many lands, in South Asia and Europe, and his tour was a matter of daily interest in the Japanese newspapers.

When Japan set about building up her industry she proved her capacity to manufacture cheaply and efficiently, but unfortunately was short of raw materials and markets for her products. Here were others reasons why she needed to expand, especially into areas where she would find coal and iron and the raw materials needed for production.

The wealth that came from all this industrial development was largely organized by two enormous financial combines. These commercial consolidations tended in time to represent the interests of particular parts of the national life and, therefore, became intertwined with the power politics of the day. For example, the Mitsui and Mitsubishi concerns represented an amalgamation of wealth founded upon commerce, which was bound to take note of political views and national aims. Generally speaking the commercial combines allied themselves with the Liberal politicians, Minseito, and these were the strong supporters of the Navy. On the other hand, the great landowners of the country, together with the old nobility and aristocrats tended to be members of the more Conservative wing, Seiyukai, who in turn were the main political support of the Army. In between both Parties came the military

Chiefs of Staff, who dictated policy to Army and Navy and derived their authority from the Emperor.

So long as Japan was forging ahead militarily and commercially there was inevitably a large degree of unity; everyone concerned was caught up in the spirit of progress. But behind this apparently prosperous advance there were new democratic forces also at work. In 1925 universal manhood suffrage was introduced and for the first time many workers had an opportunity of expressing their views. Sweated labour in the factories and slums in the big cities, as well as hardship in country districts, were the material out of which a Labour Party and a Peasant Party began to grow. It even looked as though the dreaded doctrine of Marx might take root in the country—and the Marxist doctrine of state ownership ran entirely contrary to the way of the financial combines.

In this setting of social change and unrest one great reformer stands out among the Japanese, a Christian named Kagawa. He lived among the poor and worked for their welfare, and his efforts helped to introduce legislation to deal with some of the economic problems of the time.

4. MILITARY AGGRESSION AND COLLAPSE

Between 1922 and 1930 Japan enhanced her reputation as a nation by her concentration on internal reform and her success in the world of commerce and trade. But she was beginning to react to Western customs and habits, and the trusting atmosphere that had grown up was to be dramatically and disastrously shattered. The reasons were complicated.

The Chinese in Manchuria resented the concessions allowed to Japan in 1915 to develop the railway system and the mines. The Japanese needed the iron and coal, and wasted no time in exploiting them. The Chinese Inspector-General, Chang Tso-Lin, was partly in league with the Japanese, who subsidized him and supplied him with arms. Enormous profits flowed to Japan from the slavish labour of the Chinese in Manchuria, who were aggravated against the controlling Japanese minority. This led to a Chinese boycott of Japanese goods, touching Japan's pride as well as her prosperity. The Japanese also complained that China was failing to pay interest on loans already advanced, and this inflamed the militarist front in

Japan to urge on the Liberal government to a stronger policy of threats and reprisals; the Liberals did not want to go to war.

The world economic crisis of 1929 and 1930 hit Japan seriously. Her shipping, exports, and industries all suffered a severe slump. Blame was attached to the Western powers, who were accused of conspiring against Japanese prosperity. Explanations of the world-wide nature of the crisis failed to convince the Japanese. The spectre of mass unemployment in America and Europe merely added to the alarm. The fact that Russia was transforming the Trans-Siberian Railway eastwards into a double-track system reinforced Japan's worst fears. The League of Nations was talking vigorously in Geneva of disarmament, a theme which found no sympathy among the militarists of Japan. Eventually the rising tide of political friction and suspicion could no longer be contained, and broke through in Manchuria.

On 18 September 1931 a bomb exploded on the South Manchurian railway; it was the signal for a lightning campaign. Mukden was seized by the Japanese. The Chinese were taken by surprise. Manchuria was overrun, and the speed with which vital cities were invested left no room for doubt that the operation was meticulously planned, and that the Army had forced the hands of the government. The League of Nations, faced with its first major war crisis, ordered that the Japanese troops were to be withdrawn from Manchuria by 16 November. The Japanese replied by capturing the city of Tsitsihar, an important railway junction, on 18 November. This was a direct challenge to the authority of the League and to world opinion. The League appointed a Commission headed by Lord Lytton to investigate the situation on the spot. The report of the Commission recommended that the League should not recognize the new puppet-government in Manchuria, but hinted that there were legitimate reasons on the Japanese side to justify a policy of expansion. Nevertheless, Japan was to evacuate the country except the railway zone.

The Japanese, meanwhile, landed a force in Shanghai, first bombarding the International Settlement and then disembarking there, and gave the Chinese a violent demonstration of what they might expect if the Japanese ever really dominated them. They then withdrew. Japan was so incensed with the findings of the Lytton Report that she withdrew from the League. The failure of the League to enforce its authority and uphold the rule of law opened the door to a decade of catastrophe and tyranny. If the writ of the League did not run in Manchuria it could be ignored, infringed, or violated elsewhere, as the new dictators were soon to prove in Europe.

Meanwhile, the Japanese had settled Pu Yi, the former child-Emperor of China, on the throne of Manchuria, which was re-named Manchukuo. In 1933 the northern Chinese province of Jehol was added to the new state of Manchukuo, and in spite of the Lytton recommendation Japanese control of Manchukuo was soon complete. In 1935 the Japanese bought the Russian shares in the section of the Trans-Siberian Railway which ran through Manchukuo; henceforward Russian influence in the area was negligible.

Japanese fear of Communism was always acute and sensitive and it is not surprising that in the next year, 1936, Japan signed an anti-Comintern pact with Germany. But her quarrel with China was not yet settled. Japan needed still more room for her growing population, and she needed more markets for her manufactures. In 1937 she once again attacked the mainland of China, knowing the weakness of the League and its preoccupation with crises in Europe. Japanese troops succeeded in taking many hundreds of miles of the coastline and also began to penetrate along the railways and lines of communication, but throughout the war, euphemistically known as the China Incident, they never fully conquered any part of rural China, nor the mountainous regions.

In 1938 an American patrol ship, the *Panay*, was attacked on the Yangtse River, but mercifully for the Japanese this act of provoca-tion did not at the time lead to an extension of the war. By 1940 Japan had become so closely linked with her ally Germany that she had adopted many of Hitler's own propaganda phrases. Japan began to speak of 'living space', 'encirclement', 'liberation'. When France and Holland fell to the Nazis in the early summer of 1940, the position of their colonial empires in the Far East was seriously weakened. For Japan this seemed the moment for aggression. Britain and Russia were preoccupied in Europe and their posses-sions in the Far East were poorly defended. In 1940 the old Minseito and Seiyukai, representing in effect the Liberal and the

Conservative Parties, were dissolved and a war machine was put into full operation to conduct the war more efficiently.

Prince Konoye was superseded as Prime Minister by General Tojo. Talks took place in Washington to clarify differences between Japan and the United States, but these were merely a decoy. On 7 December 1941, Japan struck. Pearl Harbour in the Hawaiian islands, more than half-way across the Pacific, was heavily bombarded and Japanese forces at the same time attacked Hong Kong. Though fully occupied in China, Japan felt herself strong enough to take on Great Britain and the United States, and later the French and the Dutch, in spite of the overwhelming resources which these combined countries could command.

The bombing of Pearl Harbour brought America into the Second World War, for hostilities could not be carried on with Japan without involving her allies, Germany and Italy. The Japanese took Hong Kong after fifteen days of ferocious fighting, and then launched other attacks in Indo-China, Malaya, Singapore, and Burma. Their pilots dive-bombed the Western navies and the British suffered the loss of H.M.S. *Repulse* and H.M.S. *Prince of Wales*, warships which at that moment they could ill afford to lose in the Far East. China was soon isolated from the rest of the world by the cutting of the main communication route between Burma and 'free' China.

Within six months of the attacks on Hong Kong and Pearl Harbour in December 1941, the Japanese had engulfed most of the coastal areas of East Asia, and the possessions in the Far East of Britain, France, Holland and the United States. The dream of a Greater East Asia under Japanese domination which the Japanese had been encouraged to expect was suddenly within grasp. The military techniques which Japan had learnt from the West, and tried out in the East, were bringing in rich territorial prizes at the expense of Europe and America. Japan was making the most of Europe's civil war. Her political scheme, put out in the form of clever propaganda, was to induce the inhabitants of Indo-China, Malaya, Burma, the Philippines, and Indonesia to resign their allegiance to Europe, and to work instead with the Japanese authorities in the creation of a new East Asia—a Co-Prosperity Sphere, in which Japan would be the senior partner. For a brief spell of nearly two years Tokio held sway from Siberia to the

Indian Ocean. But the political structure depended solely upon the armed forces of Japan. Hurriedly erected, it was basically unsound and when put to the test soon fell.

It was not until 1943 that the full weight of the American war-machine began to tell against the Japanese. By the end of 1944 the certainty of Allied victory in Europe made possible a switch of manpower, leaders and equipment to the war in the Pacific. British, Indian, Australian, New Zealand, and American forces co-operated on a gigantic scale to drive the Japanese out of the lands they had invaded. By August 1944 the Japanese Prime Minister had to admit that Japan was on the defensive, and the country began to prepare for the bombing raids which Germany and Italy had experienced in the West.

In 1944 Russia's military successes against Germany so impressed Japan that she tried to improve her relations with Russia while time allowed. She signed two agreements, one surrendering oil and coal concessions in the Russian half of Sakhalin, made in 1925, and the other settling the vexed question of fishing rights.

In 1945 the Americans were within striking distance of Japan itself. The end was only a matter of time, yet the Japanese resistance was unyielding. Though the loss of life was beyond count suicide squads volunteered to steer live missiles—aircraft, submarines and even bombs—on to enemy targets in order to protect their country. But the end came with suddenness and horror. On 26 July 1945, an Allied declaration issued from Potsdam on behalf of Britain, the United States, and China, set forth conditions of peace for Japan. The militarist clique was to be deposed from power, strategic points in Japan were to be occupied by the Allies, the Japanese to be disarmed and their war potential destroyed. The declaration added a warning that failure to accept the terms would involve 'utter destruction', a term which the Japanese interpreted as meaning nothing more than what had already been experienced in 'total war'. The declaration and warning were ignored.

On 6 August, for the first time in human history, a nuclear bomb was exploded over the city of Hiroshima, almost totally destroying it. The whole nation was stunned. Three days later a second bomb was dropped on Nagasaki, and the same day Russia, which had not until this moment declared war on Japan, suddenly attacked Manchuria. On 10 August the Emperor himself broadcast an appeal for terms of surrender. The war came to an end on 15 August.

Having for a time held Formosa, Korea, Manchuria, and vast areas of Eastern Asia, victorious over Russia, China, and many Western Powers, Japan was now back in her island kingdom—temporarily subdued.

V

CHINA

I. EXIT THE MANCHUS—ENTER THE REPUBLIC

MODERN China has had a more complicated background than any of the countries so far mentioned. First, she had to overthrow a foreign dynasty, the Manchus, who had come from north of the China wall. Secondly, she had to eliminate or reduce the influence of the Europeans and Americans who had so firmly attached themselves to the life and soil of China. Finally, she had to expel the Japanese. These successive operations took approximately fifty years, from 1900 to 1950, and until these foreign influences had been removed China was not really in a position to re-create herself. In the process she suffered years of civil war, including countless small local wars carried out by self-seeking war lords. Political control was often negligible unless reinforced by one or other of the rival armies. During this period of widespread unsettlement China had to make her choice of a pattern of constitution and government which would suit her needs, and bring fresh life to the country. Her first instinct was to try the way of Western democracy, to proclaim herself a republic, and to inaugurate a new system of party rule. For ideas and support she turned to Washington, Paris and London. For nearly forty years, from 1911 to 1949, she experimented in the main with the democratic ideas she had imbibed from Western Europe and the United States, but the experiment failed.

Even as early as 1924, China had taken serious note of the success of Marxism in Russia. Some of her young leaders saw in it a more operative political creed than the various versions of Western democracy. In the end, as we shall see in a later chapter, true to her past and guided by her realism, China accepted an authoritarian régime which was keenly nationalistic and highly centralized; her own adaptation of Marxism.

China

Our starting-point is 1900, the year of the Boxer rising. This began as an anti-Manchu demonstration, but the Manchus very cleverly deflected the movement into an anti-Western and anti-Christian revolt. Many foreigners were killed and much of their property destroyed. Apart from rousing the hostility of the West, China was forced to pay an enormous indemnity to those countries whose subjects had been molested. Five years earlier, in 1895, China had suffered military disaster at the hands of the Japanese; now the Boxer setback brought further humiliation. Taken together, the Japanese victory and the Boxer indemnities indicated an internal weakness in China which no political manoeuvre could explain away. Furthermore, the Boxer failure now proved conclusively how entrenched Europeans and Americans were within the economy of the nation. Extra-territorial rights and privileges granted by treaty in preceding decades had enabled foreigners to establish international zones in the main commercial centres, such as Canton and Shanghai. Immense sums of foreign capital lay behind much of the nation's trade, and the customs organization, salt concessions, transport systems, and other public utilities were largely under foreign control. The Chinese were well aware of the extent of this economic penetration and many did not resent it, for they stood to gain and learn from it. Nevertheless some deeper pride was hurt when sovereignty was infringed by extra-territorial concessions, and the Government seemed powerless or unwilling to act. There were murmurings of revolution and a leader was already prepared.

Sun Yat-sen had been born near Canton, and after leaving school he entered the hospital in Canton to train as a medical student, later moving to Hong Kong. He became in fact the first practitioner of modern medicine in China, so it is not surprising that he felt the urge to introduce into his own country all the advantages of scientific knowledge which the West was in a position to give. He first tried to set up in practice in the Portuguese colony of Macao, not far from Hong Kong and Canton, but was very soon squeezed out by the rival Portuguese practitioners. This convinced Dr. Sun that he would have to fight not only against a natural reluctance on the part of his own countrymen to accept modern ideas and methods but also against strong foreign competition.

The End of 'Europe in Asia'

At the age of twenty-seven Dr. Sun travelled north to Tientsin and asked for an interview with the Viceroy, China's most powerful statesman, Li Hung-chang. His request was granted and with fantastic courage Sun Yat-sen appeared before the Viceroy and asked for a complete reform of the Chinese Empire from top to bottom. It is said that Li Hung-chang bowed in mock humility to the brazen youth and begged to be excused.

But the interview was more than impudence or drama. It was symbolic of a rising generation in China, dissatisfied with a dynasty in decay, and discontented with an outworn system of government which was often incompetent and backward looking. Sun Yat-sen represented a generation eager to work out a new way of life for China. The interview with the Viceroy took place in 1894; the first attempt at an insurrection was in 1896. It failed, but Dr. Sun was ready to learn by the mistakes he made. At Canton he now organized an innocent-looking trading company, but astute customs officials suspected its purpose and raided it, discovering 600 pistols in a load of ham. The plot collapsed, and seventy of his followers were executed, but like St. Paul at Damascus, Dr. Sun was lowered over the city wall in a basket at dead of night and managed to escape.

For a time Sun Yat-sen lived in Japan, disclaiming loyalty to the Manchu régime by cutting off his pigtail. Meanwhile, he had become a member of three of the great Secret Societies of China —The White Lilies, The Triads, and The Elder Brothers— because he thought that through them he might be able to spread his ideas of national rejuvenation. Now that he was exiled from his own country with a price on his head he had to be content to travel wherever there were colonies of Chinese who might be willing to take his vision seriously. He travelled to America, stimulating rebellion among Chinese there, and eventually reached England, where he was kidnapped in London in 1896. He was held prisoner in the Chinese Legation until, mercifully for him, a note was smuggled out by a charwoman to one of his friends, who promptly wrote a letter to *The Times* demanding his release. Sun was set free just before he was due to be shipped back to an unknown fate in his own country. 'The Manchu government has lost its reputation over this', he wrote.

For the next fifteen years Dr. Sun travelled from country to country spreading his revolutionary propaganda, building up his organization and collecting vast sums of money. Those who knew him have always agreed that he was a man of the utmost integrity who never feathered his own nest as have so many other revolutionary leaders and dictators. Whatever his faults may have been, dishonesty was never one.

In 1905 he established his National People's Party, the Kuomintang, which was to become the machinery of government. At this time the Civil Service organization of China depended largely on a unique feature of Chinese life—an aristocracy of learning. So high was the prestige of scholarship in China that the tradition was that only those steeped in the Confucian classics were competent enough to govern the country. But this mandarin class was essentially traditionalist and generally out of touch with modern change and development. Their administration was too much by rule-of-thumb and, therefore, inflexible.

China had had no industrial revolution. Untold mineral wealth was as yet untapped. Superstition prevented any attempt at modern mining, for to touch the soil to any depth below the surface was thought to be an invasion of the domain of the spirit world. Furthermore, pride prevented the average Chinese from thinking that he could learn anything from the 'foreign devils', and for many politicians and administrators the very magnitude of each problem, whether it concerned disease or education or famine or tax collecting, filled them with a sense of despair. China was simply too great in extent and population to be able to be administered efficiently. Such despair led to lethargy and inaction and gave great scope for Sun Yat-sen's agitation for new methods and new leadership.

In 1908 the Dowager Empress died and was succeeded by the child-Emperor Pu Yi. The real personal and autocratic power which she had wielded throughout the country was removed. At this time the central government was distressed over a matter of railway contracts. The Provinces protested against the decisions of the central government which they considered had not taken provincial feeling sufficiently into account. Active rebellion started in the remoter provinces. The revolution swept down the valley of the Yangtse and province after province joined in; Nanking was quickly captured by rebel troops. Dr. Sun Yat-sen, who first read the news in a newspaper while travelling by train in the United States, was hurriedly recalled from his lecture tour. One might have expected Sun Yat-sen to go straight back to China, for after fifteen years of frustration in attempting to bring about a Revolution, it had now come in his absence and without his knowledge. However, he took ship for England, where he tried to gather financial help for the Revolution from a financial group, a Consortium, who were in a position to advance funds.

This Consortium, representing five Western powers who were interested in economic progress in China, especially the development of railways and commerce, insisted that certain rights over the salt tax and its collection should be under their control and that no help would be forthcoming until he had set up a stable government capable of gaining the recognition of other nations.

With this slight hope of support in the future, Sun Yat-sen set off for China. He arrived in Shanghai on Christmas Day, 1911, and was formally elected President on 29 December. He took the oath of office on 1 January 1912 in Nanking, former capital of China in the great days of the Ming dynasty, the last truly Chinese dynasty.

Fifteen provinces offered their allegiance to Sun Yat-sen in these early weeks. A brilliant American military adviser, Homer Lea, attached himself to the President and offered to train for him a properly disciplined modern army which would give China a new unity and stability. Homer Lea was an invalid hunchback, with an imaginative mind and dynamic energy, but he died before he was able to put his dreams into practice. In some ways Sun Yat-sen had lost one of his most valuable assistants. He needed a first-rate organizer, for though he might be called the architect of the republic and advocated the principle of democracy, he lacked the power of application and organization necessary to bring his ideas to fruition.

The Kuomintang was not yet a strong enough political organization for his needs. His only immediate support came from the thousands of Chinese students who had been educated in Christian mission schools and modern universities. Most of these organizations had been established and financed by foreign funds, particularly British and American. To them he looked for officers in the Army, members of the Civil Service and general support in positions of responsibility. Sun Yat-sen had already laid down a programme of progress for the development of railways and trade and contact with the Western world, all of which arose out of his own experience and travel.

But there were grave weaknesses from the outset. First, the three northern provinces had failed to join the republican movement; secondly, Yuan Shih-kai, the Premier of the Manchu government, had not been displaced; and thirdly, Peking was still the official capital of China and the only one recognized by the rest of the world. It is not surprising that Yuan Shih-kai, an astute statesman who was well known to the outside world, should have been the person whom foreign governments continued to regard as the effective head of a stable government, in spite of the success of the Revolution in central and southern China. There was no guarantee that the government of Sun Yat-sen would survive. He was known to be short of money and his many previous attempts at engineering a revolution had conspicuously failed. Yuan Shih-kai alone was in a position to bargain with the Consortium.

He was clever enough to realize that he would not be able to maintain his authority in the new situation unless he first disassociated himself from the moribund Manchu regime. He persuaded the new Empress to abdicate and renounce the right of her son to be considered the Emperor of China, at the same time promising them safety and substantial pensions. With the Empire at an end the struggle lay between Yuan Shih-kai and Sun Yat-sen. Besides his international prestige and accredited position as an elder statesman, Yuan Shih-kai also had full control of an efficient army. Sun Yat-sen was politically a doubtful factor, with only a nominal title and an untrained company of supporters.

It became clear almost at once that if the republic was to remain Sun Yat-sen would have to surrender the Presidency to his rival, Yuan Shih-kai, who was now giving every indication of sympathy with the new ideal. This he did in the Spring of 1912, and China was momentarily united as a republic. To mark the triumph the old Imperial flag of China, with its symbol of a yellow dragon, was replaced by the new flag of the Chinese republic. This consisted of five colours: red, yellow, blue, white, black—red, for all the people in the previous Empire; yellow, for the people of Manchuria; blue, for the people of Mongolia; white, for the people of Tibet and black for all who professed Mohammedanism. Chinese everywhere cut off their pigtails as a token of their break with the Manchus.

In taking over the reins of Government from Sun Yat-sen, Yuan Shih-kai could claim to have avoided the indignity and distress of civil war; Sun Yat-sen could claim that previous to this he had driven out a foreign dynasty. The day after he gave up the Presidency Dr. Sun made a pilgrimage to the tomb of Ming Tai-tsu, the founder of the last pure Chinese dynasty, and announced to the spirit of the departed Mings that he had restored sovereignty to the Chinese people and freed them from the alien rule of the Manchus. It was not long before Sun Yat-sen began to regret his trust of Yuan Shih-kai.

He gravitated back to his native Canton and set up a rival republican government. The story of China for many years after this was one of divided loyalties, continuous factions and civil war. Dr. Sun's marriage with Ching Ling Soong, who had been educated in a Methodist university in the United States, brought a powerful influence into his life, and more and more he tended to look for sympathetic support from Christian leaders in China, who were rapidly increasing in numbers, and also from America.

In 1914 when the First World War broke out, Japan laid claim to German territory in China, and to certain German railways in Shantung, mentioned earlier, which she proceeded to take over. In January 1915 came the Twenty-one Demands, almost in the form of an ultimatum, to the Peking Government. Japan threatened to strangle the economic life of China. For the time being China was powerless, although resisting many of the demands, and 9 May 1915 became for China a day of humiliation as certain concessions were made to the Japanese.

Meanwhile Yuan Shih-kai became personally ambitious and made a bid for the title of Emperor. His ambitions became an open secret and his proclamation as Emperor only lasted a few days. He died in June 1916, covered with shame and personal humiliation. Many Provinces on the outer fringe of China which had regarded themselves as tributary to China proper took the opportunity of breaking away from the new republic soon after its establishment. Mongolia, Tibet, and Turkestan explained that their loyalty had been to the Emperor in person, and that their allegiance no longer held from the time the Manchu dynasty fell.

China

On the death of Yuan Shih-kai continuous civil war set in and rival war lords fought for political control in Provinces all over the country. China had no stability. A succession of comparatively short-lived Governments took over in Peking and Sun Yat-sen was unable to persuade the Chinese to entrust themselves again to him. China officially remained outside the First World War until August 1917, when she eventually declared war against the Central Powers, Germany, and Austria-Hungary.

Meanwhile China was becoming indignant at some of the effects of her occupation by foreigners, which were a direct affront to her national pride; for instance, fixed customs tariffs which were determined by other countries; and also the system of extra-territorial jurisdiction by which foreign citizens were granted immunity from Chinese law, and were always to be tried by the legal system and the legal authorities of their own countries. This practice ensured considerable protection for foreigners and imposed a severe limitation upon any methods of restraint or punishment which China might wish to inflict. Furthermore, Chinese residents in international settlements and those employed by the foreign powers were often covered by this immunity and could escape Chinese justice.

The territories granted to foreigners had quickly become centres of commerce and trade, where consulates, big business houses, and expensive residences became established in the very midst of a Chinese population—such were the international settlements in Shanghai, the island of Shameen in Canton, and many other quarters. China was not to be satisfied until all these matters were put to rights. The process was to take another thirty years.

At the end of the war it soon became evident that Japan was going to be the main beneficiary in the Pacific. She was granted the German colonial possessions in the Far East, including the German islands north of the equator, and certain territorial rights on the mainland. In view of this China had no inclination to be a party to the Versailles Treaty, even though she had declared war against the Central Powers; she showed her indignation by a series of anti-Japanese demonstrations throughout the big cities and towns of China.

2. WESTERN DEMOCRACY OR ASIATIC COMMUNISM

What political pattern was China to follow? The traditional pattern based on Confucianism, with its strong family life and clannishness and its civil service led by an intellectual aristocracy, was rapidly losing its hold over the people. In its place Sun Yat-sen had envisaged a political pattern closely following those he had observed during his travels in the West, that is to say a combination of strong national pride with a system of democracy expressed through Parliamentary government by debate and discussion.

He was realistic enough to know that a period of military rule might first be necessary to bring order and control to the country, and he then hoped that villages and districts would learn to rule themselves satisfactorily and gradually evolve a democratic system of central government to which the whole nation would give its allegiance. But this was to be a slow process. It required political recognition by other countries as well as their financial support, and it was precisely these two factors which were lacking. In 1923, Sun Yat-sen, failing to find support from the West, began to look towards Moscow. The Communist Party in China dated from 1921, but it had begun independently of Sun Yat-sen. By 1923 the experiment of a Marxist state in Russia was already showing sufficient signs of control and stability to impress Sun Yat-sen, and in that year he sent an officer, Chiang Kai-shek, whom he had first met in Japan in 1906, to Moscow to study the Soviet system.

The outcome of this visit was the arrival of an ardent Marxist, M. Borodin, in China as political adviser to Sun Yat-sen. Borodin introduced a new programme of social, economic, and political reform, and set about a reorganization of the Kuomintang. Indeed it may be said that he was the 'organizer of victory' in China from 1924 to 1927. So unsettled was the state of affairs in the country that a firm lead in almost every department was acceptable. Borodin gave it. One particularly significant institution was the establishment of a new military academy at Whampao for the training of the future officers of the Chinese Army. Chiang Kai-shek was appointed its first director. Seventy Soviet officers went to China to help in the training, and the Director of Propaganda, whose purpose was to indoctrinate the new officer class with the principles of Karl Marx, was none other than Chou En-lai. These two men, one of whom was later to become Generalissimo of the Nationalist Forces, and the other the Communist Prime Minister of China, were for the moment working in double harness, under the direction of Borodin. Later they were to become deadly rivals.

It was an open question whether Communism was going to be allowed to dominate the Kuomintang, or whether Sun Yat-sen would try to evolve a nationalist state with or without a strong socialist element, and without the link with Moscow, and this split in policy kept China divided, in spite of the external and internal dangers which might have unified the country. The dilemma was eventually settled by the Communist government of Mao Tse-tung and Chou En-lai which prevailed from 1949.

For a moment in 1925 it looked as though Sun Yat-sen and the Peking government might be reconciled. Sun Yat-sen was invited to visit the ancient capital for discussion. Almost on arrival he realized that he had stepped into a trap, for he was not given the welcome he expected, and he knew that he would be required to concede more than he would ever gain. This acute disappointment coincided with a severe illness, from which he died in March 1925.

The situation that immediately followed Sun Yat-sen's death was almost farcical. Moscow announced at once that it would provide a coffin 'just like Lenin's'. When the coffin arrived in a special carriage from Moscow, the measurements were wrong. It was too short. Furthermore, as soon as it became known that the Russian Ambassador intended to be present at the funeral, all the other Ambassadors decided to stay away; the Western powers preferred not to be identified in any way with the representative of revolutionary Russia. Sun Yat-sen's body was laid in a temple outside Peking for the time being, and four years later, in 1929, was moved with solemn and spectacular ceremony to a majestic mausoleum on Purple Mountain outside Nanking approached by a broad flight of hundreds of steps.

A few days before he died he drafted his will, which enshrined the three main principles for which he fought. This will became tantamount to a National Charter. It was read each Monday in every school and Government office throughout the country for many years to remind officials and the rising generation of the fundamentals for which the revolution had been fought and the republic established.

The will reads as follows:

MY WILL

For forty years I have devoted myself to the cause of the People's Revolution with but one end in view, the elevation of China to a position of freedom and equality among the nations. My experiences during these forty years have convinced me that to attain this goal we must bring about a thorough awakening of our own people and ally ourselves in a common struggle with those peoples of the world who treat us on the basis of equality.

The work of the Revolution is not yet done. Let all our comrades follow my Plans for National Reconstruction, Fundamentals of National Reconstruction, Three Principles of the People, and the Manifesto issued by the First National Convention of our Party, and strive on earnestly for their consummation. Above all our recent declarations in favour of the convocation of a National Convention and the abolition of unequal treaties should be carried into effect with the least possible delay. This is my heartfelt Charge to you.

As already stated Dr. Sun Yat-sen was honest to a degree and beyond corruption—a somewhat new feature in oriental politics. He died a poor man, as indeed a crumpled note found under his pillow when he died demonstrates. 'I beg Ching Ling, my wife and comrade, to accept my books, my old clothes and the house in Shanghai, not as a bequest—because my few accumulations cannot be called an estate—but as a souvenir.'

Sun Yat-sen's natural successor was Chiang Kai-shek, his trusted friend, his military adviser and an ardent nationalist. Chiang Kai-shek doubted the wisdom of the link with Moscow. His policy was to unify China by military means as quickly as possible and then bring about a true republican government. This clashed with the policy of Borodin, and the tension within the Kuomintang bedevilled the whole country from the moment Chiang Kai-shek came to the fore in 1925 until he was exiled to Formosa in 1949. In 1926 Chiang Kai-shek was appointed Commander-in-Chief; he led an army of 50,000 to conquer the northern areas and rid them of local war lords, thus unifying the country. Unfortunately 1926 and 1927 were also the years in which national feeling was so stimulated that it over-reached itself by attacking foreigners and foreign property. In September 1926, for example, the British concession in Hankow was seized; in March 1927 both the British and American consulates in Nanking were looted and Europeans were murdered. By the following August it is estimated that there were no less than 44,000 foreign troops on garrison duty in China. Their presence naturally aggravated the situation, but they were necessary for the protection of life, as well as treaty and trading rights.

Chiang Kai-shek established a government at Nanking only to find that a Communist faction had established a rival government at Hankow. By June 1928, Chiang Kai-shek had captured Peking, and by the following October had set up a National Government. The turning point, both in his own life and in his declared policy, came in 1927. In this year he married May Ling Soong, the sister of Ching Ling, Sun Yat-sen's widow, and was also converted to Christianity. From this year we may date his final break with Soviet Russia, and at the same time a break with the old Confucian tradition in favour of a Western and Christian rejuvenation for China.

In this policy he could depend upon the support of no less than thirteen Christian universities in China and their output of thousands of graduates, in addition to the thousands of Chinese students who at this time were being educated in universities in Europe, the United States and elsewhere, many of them being educated on endowments provided by the Boxer rising indemnities. On 15 December 1927 diplomatic relations with Russia were broken off. Borodin fled from Hankow. Nevertheless, he left behind him a legacy of propaganda and training in Marxism which was to bear fruit in years to come. There were pockets of Communism in several provinces and a Soviet was set up in Kiangsi, in South China, which Chiang Kai-shek proceeded to blockade from 1927 to 1934 in order to prevent Marxist ideas spreading. Eventually the supporters of this Soviet decided to march through Southern and Western China to set up a new Soviet control nearer the Russian border. This fantastic trek to North-west China, covering a distance of several thousand miles, culminated in the establishment of a Marxist regime in the Yenan district of Shensi. In November 1931, Mao Tse-tung declared the Communist area in Kiangsi to be a Chinese Soviet republic.

The government of Chiang Kai-shek undertook two measures to restore national sovereignty and pride. On 1 January 1929, after

China had concluded tariff autonomy treaties with foreign countries, China was in a position to introduce her own customs schedules and fix her own tariffs. This was the first significant step. Exactly a year later, on 1 January 1930, the National Government announced that all extra-territorial rights must come to an end. This was a broad hint to the Great Powers, especially Britain, France, and the United States, that they must begin to give way on the subject of legal protection for their citizens and their employees. To put pressure upon them by precedent China had already concluded treaties with the smaller nations, Belgium, Italy, Denmark, Spain, and Portugal, into which clauses were inserted by which they expressed their willingness to renounce extra-territorial rights.

Meanwhile, in an attempt to remould the character of the nation, Chiang Kai-shek launched the New Life Movement in February 1934, in which public-spiritedness, courtesy, honour, cleanliness, and hatred of all wrong were held up before the Chinese as virtues to be followed and inculcated. The New Life Movement appealed to all that was highest in the Confucian ethic and also dovetailed in with the spirit of Christianity in China at this time.

In July 1929 the civil war in China came officially to an end. Chiang Kai-shek had reached Peking and the rival military overlords had either capitulated or been defeated. The main rival in the north, Chang Tso-lin, had abandoned the struggle and retreated to Manchuria, but was killed when the train on which he was travelling was blown up near Mukden in Manchuria. His son, Chang Hsueh-liang, for a time agreed to throw in his lot with Chiang Kai-shek, and together they went to the tomb of Sun Yat-sen to announce to his departed spirit the successful end of the war. China was unified militarily; the first of the three stages which Sun Yat-sen had envisaged was completed.

The next was the period of tutelage. Some wits began to say that the Soong dynasty was now established. One Soong daughter had married Sun Yat-sen. Another was the wife of Chiang Kai-shek. A third was the wife of H. H. Kung, who claimed to be a descendant of Confucius, and was to become one of the chief Ministers in the new-born republic. Last and not least, these three sisters had a brilliant brother, T. V. Soong, who was in time to become Minister of Finance and later Prime Minister. Here indeed were

the makings of a single family control, but it was not to be. Madame
Sun Yat-sen had given her sympathy and support to the Marxist
ideal and insisted that the other members of her family had
betrayed the direction which her late husband had set them by his
alliance with the Communists. When China later became a Communist Republic she became one of the six Vice-Chairmen of the
Central People's Government Council, one of the eminent figure-
heads of the nation.

3. THE STRUGGLE AGAINST JAPAN

The period of tutelage was rudely shattered by another impending
threat from Japan. As early as May 1927, a Japanese defence force
in the province of Shantung occupied Tsinanfu, a railway junction
which was Chinese property. This led to immediate Chinese protests and an anti-Japanese boycott. A further incident took place
in May 1928, when a body of Chinese troops were repulsed after a
similar occurrence. Such events, trivial in themselves, indicated
that trouble was brewing, and the reasons were not far to see. First,
the increase in Japanese population demanded space for expansion
and encouraged the idea of emigration from the Japanese islands
to the mainland of Asia. The very fact that Japan had succeeded
in defeating China in 1895 and Russia in 1905 had given her ideas
of Imperial expansion, and these ideas were easily harnessed to the
new growth of imperialism in Japan in 1930. Political power was
increasingly in the hands of the military High Command.

Secondly, Japan, fervently nationalistic, recently feudal, and
increasingly industrialist, dreaded the advance of Communism.
Ever since the revolution of 1917 Japan had thought that it was
only a matter of time before the tentacles of Marxism would
indoctrinate province after province right up to the Pacific coast
of northern Asia. She felt it, therefore, in her interests to occupy
whatever areas she could before this encroachment happened and
it was too late.

Japan already had interests in the railway system in Manchuria
and used her rights there to increase the numbers legitimately
present in the country. It was doubtful whether Chiang Kai-shek's
writ ran for Manchuria, and Japan realized that there was an

opportunity of penetrating the country before the National Government of China became too powerful in those parts.

Most foreign governments regarded Manchuria as part of China and in December 1928 the Kuomintang flag had been hoisted there, but in 1931 Manchuria was virtually a condominium. Legally the country was the property of China and most of the population was Chinese; on the other hand in 1915 the Japanese had persuaded China, in the day of her weakness, to extend their leases from twenty-five years to ninety-nine years, and in this way Japan was rapidly developing all the industrial resources of the country to her own advantage. Any effort which the National Government of China made to re-establish control in Manchuria affronted both Japan and her near neighbour Russia.

A particular point at issue was whether China or Japan had the right to levy taxes on the South Manchuria Railway. Japan had the right to maintain soldiers to safeguard the railway system, an arrangement which heightened the possibility of any minor incident flaring up into a full-scale war. Ever since 1910 the Japanese had been settling in Korea in numbers and the Chinese expressed their resentment by a series of anti-Japanese boycotts.

Suddenly, on 18 September 1931, Mukden was seized by the Japanese. It is obvious that the move was carefully premeditated. The Liberal Government in Japan, Minseito, fell. The Chinese national army offered little effective resistance. Whether this was because Chiang Kai-shek felt that he was not strong enough to carry on war on the scale necessary to defeat Japan, whether he was still too preoccupied with the problems of internal government south of the Great Wall, or whether, as is sometimes claimed, he preferred the idea of Japanese occupation of Manchuria to that of Communist Russia, it is difficult to say. It was probably for all three reasons.

In December 1931 he actually resigned, as if to disclaim responsibility for the loss of Manchuria and the failure to retaliate in any way beyond a protest. However, by January 1932, he was back in power. Fighting also took place in Shanghai in January 1932, and this was most serious because it endangered vital trade centres and the coastline. A truce was concluded in March and an armistice signed in May. Meanwhile, in February, the Japanese had occupied Harbin, which was the headquarters of the Chinese

Eastern Railway. Before the spring was over Manchuria was declared a republic under a new name, Manchukuo. As if to justify their occupation of the country and endear themselves to the people the Japanese offered the headship of the state to the deposed Manchu Emperor of China, Pu Yi. He who had lost the throne of China became now head of his own country, Manchuria, and that at the hands of China's enemy, Japan.

China implored the League of Nations to denounce the aggression of Japan and the commission headed by Lord Lytton sailed for the Far East in February 1932. This was a test of whether or not the League of Nations would have the courage to arbitrate, whether it had the moral power to enforce a resolution. The report declared that for the time being Manchuria should have an autonomous Government which would respect the rights of all the countries concerned, China, Japan, and Russia, with the probability of return to Chinese sovereignty. The League declared that it would not recognize Manchukuo as such, and the report was adopted by 42 to 1 (Japan). Japan, not surprisingly, resigned from the League of Nations and this was a direct challenge to the international authority of the League. An aggressor nation had been able to embark on military occupation without suffering severe economic sanctions or deprivation of her conquests. Apart from the stigma attaching to aggression, Japan had escaped lightly. Her success in Manchuria in 1932 encouraged the dictators who were soon to perpetrate far greater horrors in Central Europe.

Meanwhile, in December 1932, Russia, disturbed by Japanese advances, re-established diplomatic relations with China.

On 12 January 1933, the War Office in Tokio laid claim to the province of Jehol, north of the China Wall, and on 4 March the capital itself was captured. On 3 May the Tangku truce was signed and China agreed under pressure to carry out demilitarization of a zone south of the Great Wall.

In April 1934 Japan warned the nations of the world to keep their hands off Eastern Asia, a warning made possible by the reluctance or failure of the League of Nations to act firmly. One of the most thorny and immediate problems that had to be resolved following the Japanese occupation of Manchuria was the question of ownership of the Chinese Eastern Railway. Besides the rival claims of Russia, Japan, and China, France had also sunk capital in the railway system, and it was not until March 1935 that it was ultimately decided to sell the railway intact to Manchukuo.

Meanwhile, as we have mentioned above, Chiang Kai-shek was busy with the Communist enclave in Kiangsi, and in 1934 the Red Army began their retreat to the province of Shensi. Russian fear of Japan increased throughout the 1930's, especially when Japan tried to create another autonomous state in north China, a state which incorporated the provinces of Chahar and Hopei. Chiang Kai-shek was determined if possible to come to terms with the Communist forces within China, and twice visited his rival, Chang Hsueh-liang in the lost capital of Sianfu. It was on his second visit to Chang Hsueh-liang that he was suddenly kidnapped and held for some days. For a moment it looked as though the National Government would crumble, but on Christmas Day, 1935, Chiang Kai-shek was released and flown back to freedom. He admonished Chang Hsueh-liang severely and the latter asked forgiveness. This release from kidnapping raised Chiang Kai-shek's prestige enormously, especially after the setback in Manchuria. It was just in time. On 26 November 1936, Japan and Germany signed an anti-Comintern Pact. Japan was drifting further than ever from her alliance with Britain, and China had good cause to resolve her differences so far as possible with Communist forces inside the country.

In July 1937, a clash known as the Lukouchiao incident occurred at a rail junction eight miles south-west of Peking. This touched off a war which lasted for eight years and merged into the Second World War. Japanese troops in the neighbourhood of the railway junction were said to have been on manœuvre, but all the indications are that the move was backed by full-scale preparation, for by the end of July Peking and Tientsin were in the hands of the Japanese. There was no official declaration of war, nor was there ever to be throughout the next eight years. No sooner had the Japanese taken Peking than they set about the occupation of Shanghai and the territory inland. By the end of the year all territory north of the Yellow River was in their hands and most of the railway system north of the Yangtse Kiang.

Once again it was a crucial test for the League of Nations, and once again the League proved that it could do nothing but pass resolutions. The League possessed 'no teeth'. The success of Japan in the Far East so raised her prestige in the eyes of Germany that in November 1937, while the powers were actually discussing the problems of China in Brussels, an alliance was formed between Japan, Germany and Italy, making the Axis into a triangle. The forces of military aggression and totalitarianism were aligned against the freedom-loving nations.

In December 1937, two British gun-boats were fired on in the Yangtse and the United States gun-boat *Panay* was sunk. The Japanese offered an apology and compensation for loss and damage, but did little to prevent any future recurrence of such episodes. Meanwhile Japan began to threaten other European commercial interests along the Chinese coastline and along the main lines of communication. Mr. Anthony Eden in England threatened to oppose the Japanese advance by calling upon other nations to help Britain resist, and went so far as to say that he would enlist support 'from Melbourne to Alaska', but in the event it proved to be only a threat. Probably the fear of Hitler prevented other countries committing themselves to any engagement in the Far East when clearly the severest threat lay in Europe.

In October 1938, Hankow and Canton were captured by the Japanese, who were encouraged by the fate of Czechoslovakia. If the European Powers could not prevent Hitler from taking over the Sudeten territories, what chance had they of preventing Japanese expansion at the expense of China? Meanwhile, Chiang Kai-shek moved his capital up the Yangtse to the city of Chungking in Szechwan. This was his capital for the rest of the war. Although Japan was to hold all the vital ports for the duration of the war and also the bulk of the Eastern Railway system, yet her hold on the country continued to be tenuous. Behind the lines of communication and in the rural areas Chinese forces continued to resist and molest the Japanese. Nevertheless, the life blood of China in her greatest centres of population and fertile agricultural areas was being sapped, and hundreds of thousands of Chinese, taking with them what little they could in the way of possessions and equipment, began to trek westwards into the areas not held by Japan. This vast migration of Chinese into 'free' China was a remarkable feature of the war. Even colleges and universities moved and accommodated themselves to a minimum of comfort and poor equipment. Meanwhile hitherto remote areas of China were made more accessible for the supply of materials to 'free' China. A route was opened up from Burma to Yunnan, known as the Burma Road, and Chiang Kai-shek derived much of his equipment and war potential from this supply-line, until it was eventually cut by the Japanese when they overran Burma. Aircraft later flew in supplies over a range of mountains nicknamed 'The Hump'. In the previous chapter it was shown how Japan's drive southwards and westwards continued until Japanese forces were in control of countless Pacific islands and the bulk of South-East Asia. For the first half of the Second World War all the advantage was on the side of the Japanese. The fall of Hong Kong, the command of Indo-China, and the capture of Singapore gave Japan control of territory thousands of miles from her island kingdom, and reinforced the blockade of China.

By the autumn of 1943 Chiang Kai-shek's success in holding out for six-and-a-half years had raised his international prestige, and he and his wife flew out of China to meet the Prime Minister of Great Britain and the President of the United States for a conference in Cairo. It was in 1943 that Britain and the United States voluntarily surrendered their extra-territorial jurisdictions in China, a source of considerable gratification to the National government, even though these extra-territorial rights were at that time in Japanese-held areas.

But China's most acute peril was internal. Japan's blockade was taking effect. Scarcity and hardship, defeat and disillusion, resulted in violent inflation. Prices of food and goods rocketed upwards until currency denominations bore no relation to true values. When food cost three hundred times what had been customary the impulse to survive was the only law. The economic breakdown was more deadly than any military setback. In this emergency it was imperative to restore confidence in the power of the government. American advisers were willing to help, but the chief obstacle to recovery was the attitude of Generalissimo Chiang Kai-shek. He resented and resisted the initiative and advice of certain Americans specially sent to help him, and withstood any suggestion of working with the rival Communist government in North China. In October 1944 General Stilwell, leading a Chinese army against the Japanese in North Burma, fell foul of Chiang Kai-shek and had to be recalled to America just at a time when it was essential to re-open the Burma road, and when the Japanese grip of Southern China was tightening rather than loosening.

As for the Chinese Communists, they had continued to maintain a separate government in Yenan, separate armies in the north, and a campaign of their own against the Japanese. They protested that they were at one with the Nationalist Kuomintang government of Chiang Kai-shek in their extreme dislike of Japanese imperialism, and that their first wish was to expel the enemy. This overture from the chairman of the Chinese Communist party had little effect on the Generalissimo, who sensed danger in co-operation and dreaded the possibility of a revolt. But he was prevailed upon to negotiate with the Communists by Mr. Henry Wallace, Vice-President of the United States, who paid a flying visit to Chungking and put the case for co-operation. Negotiations began. At first Chiang Kai-shek rejected the idea of a Coalition government and a unified High Command. But in the spring of 1945 the Generalissimo announced that he would be ready to convene a National Assembly to work out a new constitution, and would be willing to recognize the Communist party in an all-party assembly on condition that the Chinese Red Army and all Communist organs of government were integrated with the Chungking government. These terms were unacceptable, and any hope of reconciling the differences was gone. The Kuomintang, at its sixth National Congress in Chungking in May 1945, made a bid for national unity, with all manner of promises, and allowed the formation of a new political party, the Democratic League, as a bridge between the Kuomintang and the Communists, but it was a futile compromise.

In 1945 T. V. Soong, the President of the Executive Yuan, the office equivalent to Prime Minister, and Wang Shih-chieh, the Foreign Minister, visited Moscow, and eased the strained relations which had existed for so many years between the Kremlin and the Kuomintang. The revered memory of Sun Yat-sen served as an ideological meeting point. Russia's denunciation in April 1945 of her pact with Japan opened the way for a treaty of friendship and alliance. Several matters of dispute were clarified. Molotov, the Russian Foreign Minister, declared that the Soviet government 'had no intention of interfering with Chinese internal affairs', while Wang Shih-chieh undertook to recognize the independence of Outer Mongolia if a plebiscite so decreed. The Manchurian railway was to be operated jointly for thirty years before reverting to China; similarly with Dairen, but Port Arthur was to be open to Russia and China alone, with Russia responsible for its defence.

In August 1945 when the war in the Far East came to an end, China was still politically and militarily divided. The Communists held the northern provinces of China—Shantung, Shensi, and Suiyuan—and withdrew their forces from south of the Yangtse. Against the policy and wishes of Chiang Kai-shek, Communist forces were in a position to accept the surrender of many Japanese and to appropriate their weapons and ammunition. The Generalissimo was unable to prevent it—to his subsequent cost.

The Communist leader, Mao Tse-tung, negotiated for some weeks in Chungking with Chiang Kai-shek after the defeat of Japan, and promised not to permit the outbreak of civil war. On his return to Yenan he gave a very different account of his discussions with Chiang Kai-shek to a Communist party congress, and warned them of the civil war that was about to break. The die was cast. Fighting broke out in Shantung and spread quickly. The Kuomintang even asked the Russians to remain in Mukden until they could take it over so that it would not fall into the hands of the Chinese Communists. The threat of military upheaval throughout China induced President Truman in December 1945 to plead with both sides for a cease-fire. He recognized the government of Chiang Kai-shek as the *de jure* authority, and the deadlock was unresolved. Japan's defeat brought no peace: China merely reverted to civil war.

VI

SOUTH-EAST ASIA

INTRODUCTION

SOUTH-EAST Asia is the term generally used to describe the vast area that lies east of India, south of China, and north of Australasia, largely consisting of mainland but including the Malay archipelago and innumerable other islands, large and small. This part of Asia, relatively backward and undeveloped, fell a prey to the European powers, and by the end of the nineteenth century was shared between them, with the exception of one country. Only Siam escaped annexation by the expanding empires of Europe.

Spain and Portugal had been the first on the scene as early as the sixteenth century. Then the Dutch occupied the Moluccas in 1615, the Celebes in 1667, and later on Java, Sumatra, and Borneo, building up an extensive Dutch Eastern Empire. Britain took Bencoolen on the south-west coast of Sumatra in 1684 and held it until 1828, but it was no more than an isolated base and not the front-door to a colony. In 1786 the British gained possession of the island of Penang, and during the French Revolutionary and Napoleonic Wars took over Malacca from the Dutch, who had been overrun by the French in Europe. In 1800 the British established a colony, Wellesley province, on the mainland opposite Penang, and these possessions—Malacca, Penang, and Wellesley province—were collectively known as the Straits Settlements. Singapore became British in 1819, and rapidly developed from an island of little consequence into a great commercial centre and naval base. Gradually British influence extended over the Malay peninsula. Hong Kong, Sarawak, and North Borneo became incorporated within the British Empire, and by 1900 British interests in that part of the equatorial Pacific were deep-rooted and vigorous. Typical of the British, this extension of empire had been curiously

79

haphazard and unplanned, brought about far more by the individual initiative of merchants, pioneers, and men of vision like Sir Stamford Raffles and Rajah Brooke than by any concerted action or official encouragement from Britain.

France's penetration into the East largely coincided with the British advance into South-East Asia. By the beginning of the twentieth century she had consolidated herself in the various territories now grouped together under the name of Indo-China, lying east of Siam and south of China proper. The United States, born of revolt and contemptuous of empire, joined in the rush for colonies in 1898 and captured the Philippines from Spain, with initial enthusiasm but subsequent misgivings. The Asian countries had not the means of resisting the intruders, and in fact they profited immensely by the many developments which the Western nations introduced, for they had not previously been able to develop and market their own resources. Generally speaking, South-East Asia has so far produced no one comparable to Sun Yat-sen or Mahatma Gandhi, no one whose idealism, stubbornness, or magnetism could rally a people to overthrow foreign domination. Not that these countries were without their ardent nationalists, political reformers and visionaries, but the time had not yet come for the emergence of great leaders.

For the first forty years of this century Holland, Britain, and France were left comparatively free to develop their colonial territories as they wished, with varying concern for the welfare of the individual and the increasing prosperity of the territories. The turning-point came in 1941 when Japan swept over much of South-East Asia, subjecting it to military domination. This was the first serious threat to the political supremacy of the West in these lands; the Japanese régime demanded co-operation from the vanquished and yet at the same time intimidated and cowed by its ruthlessness. Countries that had long been parts of great empires breathed an air of rebellion.

Our concern here will be to trace briefly the extension of European influence and colonization in South-East Asia. What happened after the defeat of Japan in 1945 will be left to a subsequent chapter.

South-East Asia

Britain's empire in the East was acquired gradually, beginning with the occupation of Penang in 1786, Malacca in 1795, and Singapore in 1819. Then Sir James Brooke acquired Sarawak in 1841 by concession from the Sultan of Brunei, and next year by the Treaty of Nanking, Hong Kong became British. In 1874 British protection was extended over various Malay States, including Perak, Selangor, Negri-Sembilan, and Pahang. Johore was similarly protected in 1885, and in 1909 four more states were transferred to British protection by Siam. The Straits Settlements and Singapore formed a single Crown Colony from 1867 to 1946. Sarawak, Labuan, Brunei, and North Borneo were open to trade with Britain from 1841 onwards, and in due course the various Sultans either ceded the areas to Britain, or invited protection. Thus the British Empire grew in the Far East, trade rather than possession being the driving impulse.

Burma

In 1821 Burma conquered Assam, threatening the British in Bengal, and two years later, an attack was launched on Bengal and the British retaliated. By the Treaty of Yandabo (1826), the Burmese gave up Assam and ceded the two long coastal strips of Arakan and Tenasserim to Britain. These now constituted a buffer area lest there should be any future threat to India, and at the same time the British acquired trading rights in Burma itself. Such obstacles were put in the way of trade, however, that Dalhousie, the Governor-General in Calcutta, demanded assurances of respect for the treaty of 1826. These were ignored, and in 1852 an expedition, sent to obtain redress of grievances, captured Rangoon, and annexed the rich delta of Lower Burma. The conquest of the rest of Burma was merely a matter of time and was prompted largely by fear of French aggression into the area. Burma was now cut off from the coast. The whole country was subjugated in three stages between 1826 and 1886, sometimes against fierce resistance in guerilla and jungle warfare. Burma became known for a time as Further India, though racially and geographically the Burmese were quite distinct and separate. Its pattern of administration was modelled on the Indian Civil Service. The British now found themselves neighbours of Malay, Siam, and China.

The British began by making villages entirely responsible for their own internal organization. Bit by bit these villages were encouraged to amalgamate, developing their own general supervision. Ultimately this would lead to the need for central direction of affairs. This pattern of indirect control was foreign to tradition, and however gradually introduced, stirred up a wave of resentment.

Even more did the Burmese resent the way in which large numbers of Indians were beginning to migrate into Burma in the wake of the British.

Hundreds of thousands of Indians began to pour into the Delta regions of the country, and it was not long before trade and industry were in the hands of British, Indians, and Chinese rather than the Burmese. As in other parts of the East, acute problems of land ownership and land cultivation existed, and at the time of this immigration many an owner or tenant was deep in debt if not already bankrupt. Indians, who came from South India in particular, rapidly became money-lenders (*chettiars*) or agricultural bankers, and whenever their clients became bankrupt took over their properties as part payment of debt.

In this way Indians soon owned one quarter of the agricultural land in thirteen of the richest rice-growing areas, although they were often reluctant to take over these agricultural holdings with the responsibility of letting or farming them; but the risk of ownership was inherent in the business of money-lending. An atmosphere of mistrust and dislike prevailed between the Burmese and the Indians, and the continued immigration led inevitably to communal disorders. These were both racial and economic in origin.

The many different native peoples of Burma faced the British administration with several problems. In Central and South Burma lived the Karens, fairly numerous but widely scattered. In the north were the Shan states, inhabited mostly by tribesmen. Also in the north were the Chins and the Kachins, and in the west the Arakanese. Finally, in the south, and especially in the Tenassarim Peninsula, were the Mons.

With such a variety of peoples it was obviously no light task to hit upon a satisfactory form of government. First, the Monarchy was abolished and a system of indirect rule was initiated. As a result ecclesiastical authority, which had always counted for much in so religious a country as Burma, was implicitly challenged, for there had been a close link between it and the Monarchy. The question arose as to whether the Buddhist authorities would be recognized or not by the new rulers. Fortunately the British were able to point out that in the India Act of 1858 the principle had already been laid down that there was to be no interference with religion, and the same principle would hold in Burma. This strengthened Burmese trust in British justice.

Meanwhile the British Government set to work to develop organizations for dealing with forests, agriculture, sanitation, public health, and communications. These necessitated the growth of a unifying Secretariat; its first actions were understood in the cities, but were regarded as interference in the more backward and rural areas. Very careful administration was needed to develop the country and generate a sense of unity.

In 1909 the Minto-Morley recommendations led to an increase in the Burma Legislative Council. Ten years later the Montagu-Chelmsford Reforms claimed to have given special consideration to Burma, but fell so short of what the Burmese had hoped for that there was an immediate outcry. In view of this reaction the British Government saw fit to accelerate the process towards the ultimate ideal of self-government by offering a promise of diarchy in 1921 as in India. From this year on there was a definite demand on the part of the Burmese for self-government and a newly-formed General Council of Buddhist Associations became the mouthpiece for it.

A Government of Burma Act was passed in 1921, promising to review the constitution ten years later. The principle of diarchy was put into operation. In 1923 Burma became a 'Governor's State'. The Legislative Council was increased to 103, of whom 79 were elected members, 22 were nominated and 2 were ex-officio. In the Executive Council two members were made responsible for transferred subjects—education, forests, excise, and public health —and two members were responsible for the reserve subjects— finance, defence, and internal security.

Perhaps the most significant advance was in the extent of

franchise. The vote was given to all men and women over the age of eighteen, a remarkably bold step. The policy had two obvious advantages:it was simple to operate, and it was undoubted evidence of good faith in the judgement of the people. Curiously enough two quite opposing viewpoints began to emerge. There were those who agitated for complete self-government, and on the other hand there were those who claimed that a link with India might continue to be valuable, provided Burma always had the option of seceding from any connexion with India if and when this was required.

In 1930 Burma was hit by the world economic crisis. It is estimated that 1,300,000 acres of delta were lost to the Indian money-lenders through debt. Nations for a time could ill afford to import rice, and this hit the peasants who produced it between 1916 and 1930. It was indeed a critical day for the economy of Burma. Little wonder that there was a nationalist rebellion; it was inspired chiefly by the Pongyi, the Buddhist monks of the country.

As the country gradually recovered its economic balance the British were planning its ultimate independence. By the Government of India Act of 1935 a new constitution was promulgated, which provided for separation from India on 1 April 1937. A separate Burma Office was to be set up in London which would deal with Burmese matters alone. But this idea of a separate Burma office tended to strengthen the feeling in some quarters that if Burma was separated from India at a time when India was heading rapidly towards self-government it might only delay self-rule for Burma, by placing Burmese affairs more than ever in the control of the British Government.

In 1938 there were a series of anti-Indian riots, chiefly stirred up by resentment against the *chettiars*, who it was felt were strangling the Burmese rice trade. On the outbreak of war in 1939 the Burmese made a very generous gesture in offering to support the war effort against the Axis Powers (Japan was not involved at the outset) in return for a promise of independence. Most unfortunately this offer, generous in sentiment and symptomatic of resurgent nationalism, was declined.

In 1942 Burma was overrun by Japanese armies, and some Burmese put more faith in Japanese promises of independence than in previous British pledges. Their confidence was misplaced. The military crisis came in 1944 when the Japanese, strongly supported by Burmese revolutionary forces, all but seized the Manipur plain in Assam and isolated the capital, Imphal. The Allied Fourteenth Army, largely made up of Indian troops under the brilliant strategy of General (later Field Marshal Sir William) Slim turned the tide of battle, drove the Japanese out of Assam, eliminated the danger to India, and set about the liberation of Burma. The main Japanese surrender came in September 1945, and only a few pockets of resistance remained. During the war the rice trade had suffered disastrously, and the general dislocation of life and livelihood left the country in urgent need of material aid and political direction. The British government promised Dominion status as soon as possible, but Burmese nationalists, now emerging as a strong political party, demanded self-government without delay.

Malaya

The group of separate states which gradually became incorporated in what we now know as Malaya, became an extraordinarily valuable territory within the British Empire, largely as a result of farsighted and energetic development. It is well known how rich are the resources of the country in tin and rubber and timber, and it is too easily assumed that the British merely stepped into the country ahead of their possible rivals and exploited it, to Britain's great advantage and at the relative expense of the inhabitants. Such a theory bears little or no relation whatever to facts. To take but one example—rubber. It is astonishing to think that there was no rubber industry in Malaya until the rubber plant was introduced by British planters. Rubber was not indigenous, no rubber existed in Malaya until rubber seeds, which had been taken from the Amazon region, were cultivated at Kew Gardens in London and then, as an experiment, introduced into Malaya. So rubber was not exploited in the sense that it was already there and had merely to be tapped.

For two or three years their growth was not encouraging, but suddenly the saplings caught on and prospered at such a pace that rubber soon became the foremost source of wealth in the country. The boom began in 1907, and by 1920 over half of the world's processed rubber came from Malaya. This was rapid development indeed.

The End of 'Europe in Asia'

Meanwhile the tin was mined, owing to a British capital outlay in engineering, and by 1938 nearly 30 per cent. of the world's output of tin came from Malaya. It is not surprising that between 1900 and 1925 Malaya's population more than doubled, including thousands of Chinese and Indian immigrants. Here as elsewhere, there was the problem of debt on the land. The easy-going Malays were content to grow far less rice than they were able and were quite used to being in debt. They preferred to let the debts increase and remain in possession of the land, rather than run any risk of being dispossessed by trying to pay them off. As much as two-thirds of the rice consumed each year had to be imported either from Burma or Siam, though the country could have grown much more.

Economically Malaya went through all the ups and downs of production cycles. The main task of the British administration was gradually to bring about a sense of unity and co-operation within the area, for hitherto there was little semblance of cohesion. Nationalism, as a political force, was only generated in the course of Japanese occupation.

Meanwhile Malaya owed its economic development, as well as its international importance, to several other factors. Sir Stamford Raffles had predicted that Singapore would one day become the Malta of the East. To this end the island and naval base were developed apace (£20,000,000 had been spent on the development of the naval base by 1938) until shortly before the Japanese arrived in 1942. Secondly, Britain did not monopolize the commercial control or development of Malaya. Any country which could afford to provide capital or engineers was at liberty to work alongside the British if they so chose; there was no restriction on foreign investment in Malaya. Many facts support this statement.

All the iron mines in Malaya before the Second World War were controlled by Japan. The world at large never realized that the island kingdom of Japan, long before her thrust into the South China seas, had already staked commercial and industrial claims in the southernmost tip of the continent of Asia. Another significant fact is that China had a total foreign capital investment in South-East Asia of no less than 640 million dollars, which was not really very much short of the British total investment of 860 million dollars. The United States, in spite of their possession of the Philippines, had invested approximately half (330 million dollars) what China held. In the matter of population and migration it is interesting to note that whereas in 1911 the Malays numbered 1,437,000, the Chinese 916,000 and the Indians 267,000, in 1941 the Malays had increased to 2,278,000 (considerably less than 1,000,000 increase), but the Chinese had increased to 2,379,000 (far more than double and now outnumbering the Malays) and the Indian population had grown to 744,000. These factors provided Britain with some of the problems associated with any multi-racial grouping. The capture of Singapore in 1942 came as one of the most sudden shocks of the war. Military strength was of little use without adequate naval and air support, both of which were lamentably weak. Not until the defeat of Japan in 1945 could the future of Malaya and Singapore again be seriously considered.

Hong Kong and Concessions in China

Britain's acquisition of Hong Kong in 1842 gave her a base from which to develop a commercial Empire in the East. She transformed this mosquito and pirate-ridden island into a prosperous trading centre. In various Chinese cities, chiefly up the great rivers, she obtained territorial concessions where merchants could feel secure and pursue their trades. The lease to Britain of Weihaiwei in the north of China gave her a coastal position in the Far East, which it was optimistically hoped would be developed into a naval base, but which in fact only enabled a watchful eye to be kept on Japan, Russia, Germany, and other countries which had designs on China in the north. Weihaiwei became a holiday resort with a well-known school.

The British were trusted by the Chinese even in the days of the Manchus, as is clearly shown by the fact that from 1863 to 1906 Sir Robert Hart was entrusted with the organization and control of the Chinese customs service. Great firms like Butterfield and Swire, Jardine Matheson, and others rapidly built up a trade with China, and it is doubtful whether China herself could have made all the commercial progress she did had it not been for the stimulus of capital investments and competition by countless European and American firms. Inevitably, trading rights carried with them the need for consular protection, and this led to extensive

Western infiltration into China. The drive towards commercial development was gradually pumped into the arteries of that vast country. For the first time China was brought closely in touch with Western ways of life and Western ideas.

Borneo

British North Borneo was governed by a Company under royal charter from 1881 until 1946, in which year it became a Crown Colony. Together with the states of Brunei and Sarawak, and the island of Labuan, North Borneo represented a commercial foothold in the South China Seas, in an area dominated first by the Dutch and Spanish, and later by the United States and France. In 1841 the Sultan of Brunei granted Sir James Brooke authority to govern part of Sarawak, and in 1888 this came under British protection. All these territories were engulfed by the Japanese in December 1941, until their defeat in 1945.

2. FRENCH INDO-CHINA

By 1900 the five countries of Cochin-China, Annam, Tongking, Laos, and Cambodia had been united by conquest into what was called French Indo-China. Cochin-China had previously been a separate colony and the other four had been protectorates, but the work of the distinguished politician Monsieur Paul Doumer, who was Governor-General from 1897 to 1902, transformed the whole area from a French protectorate to a directly administered colony. For some time the local kings and mandarins were permitted to carry on side by side with the French administration, but as time went on a new Consultative Assembly was brought into being, to give effect to closer co-operation. In reality the Assembly was so carefully chosen that French influence predominated. In three respects especially was this so. The Civil Service followed the French pattern and was sympathetic to France; locally enlisted Civil Servants were most carefully trained and encouraged to emulate the French system; and in educational policy the whole emphasis was to inculcate and encourage French culture—language, literature, and habits of thought. The tariff system was so arranged that France derived enormous benefit from the raw materials and other trade which she obtained from these possessions. On the other hand France contributed greatly to the well-being of Indo-China by engineering works in agriculture, irrigation, and communications. It is probably true to say that France never seriously contemplated giving these Colonies any measure of self-government. She appears to have been anxious that they should be assimilated within the French civilization and her policy was, therefore, aimed in this direction. So long as the inhabitants of French Indo-China looked to France for leadership, ideas and inspiration there existed a period of comparatively peaceful development, but the moment French policy began to challenge or stifle local traditions there were the beginnings of trouble.

French Indo-China was so close to Canton that the country was bound to feel some of the repercussions of the Chinese revolt against the Manchus. Indeed, Annam had been the centre of one of Sun Yat-sen's attempted insurrections. Furthermore, the Vietnamese, who were a naturally industrious and skilled people, had a long history of struggle behind them, and were only too ready to become the leaders in any national movement, whether it sprang from their attachment to property and the old family system, or from a nationalist impulse.

The liberal policy of the Governor-General, General Albert Sarraut, from 1911 (November) to 1914 (January) and again from 1917 (January) to 1919 (May) helped to keep Indo-China relatively quiet and peaceful at a time of great commotion throughout the world. But proud as France was of her possessions, she also expected much of her citizens. No less than 100,000 Vietnamese fought in the French forces in Europe during the course of the First World War.

The French seemed to have no wish to entrust genuine responsibility to the people of Indo-China, even by the most gradual stages, and it is not to be wondered that in 1925 a Nationalist Party appeared in Annam, which in course of time was recognized as a local manifestation of Communism.

The first outbreak of revolutionary Communism was in 1930; it was severely repressed. The leader was Nguyen-Ai-Quoc, far better known to the world as Ho Chi Minh. Ho Chi Minh had joined the Communist Party in France even before the First World War. He had studied in Moscow and had lived and worked for a time in Canton. The success of the revolution in China had given him hopes of overthrowing French domination in Indo-China. The success of the October revolution of 1917 in Russia only strengthened that hope. As a leader he was strict and relentless, and when his own revolt failed in 1931 he fled to Hong Kong, where he was arrested and imprisoned for two years. It was in 1939 that he formed the League for the Independence of Vietnam, which he has so successfully led ever since.

When France fell to Germany in June 1940 there was little hope that her colonies in the Far East would be able to hold out against Japan. The Japanese presented an ultimatum to the Governor-General of Indo-China, General Catroux, but he refused to accept the terms of the ultimatum and left the country. In September 1940 the Japanese conditions were eventually accepted, and they were given permission to set up three aerodromes in Tongking. Control of the air sealed the fate of Indo-China. The country was occupied by the Japanese in July 1941 and the 'Vichy' French authorities were persuaded to carry on the administration of the country. The Japanese held Indo-China with only 35,000 troops, while the 'Vichy' French kept the people subservient to Japanese domination, until the latter's defeat in 1945.

3. THE DUTCH EAST INDIES

Of all the Empires in South-East Asia the Dutch was by far the most extensive. It included Java, Sumatra, a large part of Borneo, the Celebes and hundreds of islands. From this area the Dutch derived oil, rubber, and a wide category of other goods and raw materials. The bulk of the population was Moslem, and the total figure is estimated to have been in the region of sixty-five million at the beginning of the century, but totalled something like seventy-seven million by the Second World War. There had been Governors-General of the Netherlands East Indies (Insulinde, or Island-India as it had been called) ever since 1609, and it is, therefore, understandable that the Dutch hoped to remain in possession of territories in which they had such long-standing vested interests.

In 1903 a Decentralization law was passed and schemes for social, political and constitutional improvement were put forward. This raised in some Indonesians the hope that they would one day have a greater part to play in the affairs of their own country, but a series of postponements prevented most of these schemes from ever reaching fulfilment.

In 1906 de Graaff's Village Regulation increased the volume of village administration, and naturally led to increasing intervention and control. A few nationalists felt the need for an Association to advance their cause. This first nationalist body, composed mainly of intellectuals who derived their inspiration from Tagore, was founded in 1908. Meanwhile, a revival of Mohammedan influence helped to increase the sense of nationalism, for Islamic culture was a much earlier importation and acceptable, whereas Dutch authority, not always sympathetic, was regarded as alien.

However, in some ways Dutch government was rather more compromising than French administration in Indo-China, and less of an artificial imposition, partly because the Dutch showed willingness to inter-marry with local inhabitants, and partly because their very long settlement had brought appreciation of local customs and traditions.

Although in many respects the Dutch East Indies were among the least advanced of the countries of South-East Asia, the first attempts by Socialists and revolutionary Communists to gain a footing there were feeble and failures. In 1916 a People's Parliament (Volks Raad) was suggested as a suitable political organ, and this met for the first time in 1918, but as the majority of the members of this Parliament were European it could not be said to be in any way a representative assembly.

In 1925 yet another constitution was brought into being whereby the Dutch granted the Indonesians a total thirty-eight seats out of the sixty-one in the Council. Far-sighted and generous as this may have seemed at the time, it did not keep pace with the increasing agitation. The Dutch East Indies were fully aware of the success of nationalist leaders in other parts of Asia and watched the struggles of Sun Yat-sen, Gandhi, and others with calculated interest. Generally speaking, the Dutch gave little opportunity for Indonesians to acquire experience in the art of self-government, and this policy continued right up to the Second World War.

In 1940, when Holland, the parent country, was overrun by the Germans, the effective link with the East Indies was broken. In 1941 the Japanese conquered the islands with extraordinary rapidity and were quick to set up an Indonesian National Government under Ahmed Sukarno. The story from this point will be taken up in a later chapter.

4. THE PHILIPPINES

The group of countless islands which is known as the Philippines (named after Philip II of Spain—consort of Queen Mary I of England) belonged to the Spanish for three-and-a-half troubled centuries, from 1569 to 1898. Then came the Spanish-American war, during which the United States took the Philippines from Spain. This was indeed a reversal of American policy, for the United States had hitherto condemned imperialism, and had been born in reaction to it. Nevertheless, several of her leading politicians at the turn of the century adopted the very principles of expansion which the United States had loudly condemned, but this was a short-lived phase.

In May 1898 the Spanish fleet was destroyed at the Battle of Manila, and in the following December the Philippines were ceded to the United States by the Treaty of Paris. For the first three years a period of guerrilla warfare ensued. In October 1907 the first move to give the Philippines an assembly which would prepare the people for self-government was initiated by Mr. Taft, Secretary for War. In 1909 the Philippines were incorporated in the United States tariff system and were, therefore, given such benefits as arose from free trade with the U.S.A.

In the course of the First World War the Jones Act (1916) granted the Philippines local autonomy, and two years later a Council of State was created somewhat along the lines of the American constitution. There was to be a Senate of 24 members and a House of Representatives of 92 members. In 1934 the American Congress declared that in the following year the Philippines would become independent and created a Philippines Commonwealth with a single chamber government and an elected President. The first President to be elected in 1935 was Manuel Luis Quezon, who had been something of an agitator for freedom, but became thoroughly co-operative once he realized that the Americans were willing to grant self-government. The new constitution of 1934, ratified by a Filipino plebiscite in 1935, provided for a ten-year interim period, at the end of which independence was assured. But war in the Pacific postponed this realization until the Philippines were free of Japan.

5. THE KINGDOM OF SIAM (THAILAND)

Siam holds a unique position in the heart of South-East Asia. Throughout the cut and thrust of imperial conquest and commercial infiltration, Siam alone managed to maintain her independence and never capitulated to European advances. The ancient name of Siam had been Muang Thai, 'Land of the Free', and to this she remained true. In some ways it was to the advantage of the European powers that one country at least should remain neutral and a buffer state, as indeed Siam was to become between Burma, Indo-China, and Malaya.

The Anglo-French Convention of 1896 recognized that Siam should remain independent. Only the French had made any serious attempt to intrude, from the East, and had succeeded in separating certain districts from the old kingdom of Siam.

The reign of Rama V (Chulalongkorn) which extended from 1868 to 1910, was a period of great development. Treaties were signed with other powers, railways established and there were advances in education and in modern technical knowledge. In most cases the advisers chosen by the King for Government departments were Europeans, and the King insisted that many of his children (he was credited with seventy-seven) were given a European education and gained experience in various European armies.

His successor, Rama VI (Maha Vajiravudh), who reigned from 1910 to 1925, was educated at Cambridge and served in the British Army. He turned out to be incurably shy and extravagant, pathetically histrionic and with a love of pomp and pageantry—a strange mixture. He adapted the Boy Scout movement to his own country, calling it the 'Wild Tiger Scout Corps' and encouraged its growth in schools. Compulsory elementary education was introduced in 1921.

In July 1917 Siam declared war against Germany and came in on the side of Britain and the United States. She became a member of the League of Nations and had accepted Western advice to such an extent and had acquired such an international outlook that in 1922 the United States abandoned her extra-territorial rights in the country.

In early times Siam had been governed by the collective authority of many Princes, but in the twentieth century this system became increasingly archaic and out of touch with the general trend towards democratic responsibility. In 1925 the new King, Prajadhipok, introduced Cabinet rule with a Privy Council, and reduced the authority of the Princes to a Supreme Council of five Princes only. He also ordered drastic reduction in the national expenditure, wherever economies could be made.

The economic slump of 1930 hit Siam rather more lightly than many other countries because she had virtually no industries, with a result that she suffered almost no mass unemployment. However, her trade suffered for the time being because of her link with the Gold Standard, and her troubles came to a head in 1931 as a result of discontent with salary cuts in the Army. On 24 June 1932 there was a bloodless revolution and a new constitution was proclaimed. Princes were dismissed from Ministerial and Army posts. Royal powers were reduced and absolutism abolished. The People's Party assumed control for the time being, but such was their dearth of administrative and executive experience that they reappointed a number of trusted politicians to continue in office.

From 1932 onwards a political rivalry began between two natural leaders. On the one hand was Nai Pridi Panomyong, the leader of the radical or extreme left-wing group. Educated in Paris, where he had read law, he advocated reforms in agriculture, education and in government. It was thought at one time that he was probably a Communist, though this was by no means certain.

His rival was Luang Pibul Songgram, the right-wing nationalist leader. Luang Pibul Songgram was brought up in the Army. He was educated in Denmark and Germany and was a contemporary of Herman Goering at the same Cadet School (an interesting parallel with Napoleon, who was at school with Robespierre's brother). It may not be too fanciful to suppose that Luang Pibul Songgram's acquaintance with Germany and Goering may account for the spate of propaganda that poured into Siam during the 1930's through the medium of the radio and press.

The next ruler of Siam was Ananda, whose reign began in 1935 and ended when he was found dead on 9 June 1946. At the outbreak of the Second World War Siam became the ally of Japan, and her trade suffered as a result. It might be said that she was too small to be able to resist such an alliance but one must remember that her close cultural and military links with Germany may have helped to persuade her to accede to Japanese pressure for the time being. Be that as it may, Siam alone of all the Asian lands managed to retain her monarchy under the limitations of Japanese supervision.

VII

CENTRAL ASIA

1. RUSSIA'S COLONIAL EXPANSION EASTWARD ACROSS ASIA

THE vast area of Asia that extends east from the Caspian Sea as far as the Pacific Ocean, north of Sinkiang and Mongolia, is relatively unknown to the European, though increasingly important in world politics. This enormous territory, which includes Siberia, is to Russia what Canada has been to the British Commonwealth —a land of boundless possibilities and largely untapped wealth, an open space for expansion and extensive development. It is to Russia what all the territory west of the Mississippi became to the United States throughout the nineteenth century and later. Its value for Russia cannot be exaggerated, being not merely a matter of size and space, but of wealth ready to hand in raw materials and population; apart from its incalculable productivity it has strategic importance. The territory is so vast that it can be for Russia at one and the same time a granary, an arsenal and a workshop for the Russian nation and her satellites.

Unlike the old British Empire Russia does not have the problem of seas to traverse and ocean lanes to protect. Her lines of communication are all internal and, therefore, in some ways easier to supply. On the other hand Russia has the disadvantage of an extremely lengthy frontier, little of which provides any access to the open sea, or at least to harbours which are open all the year round. On the occasions when she has endeavoured to penetrate to warm-water coastlines she has roused suspicions of other nations and met with immediate opposition. This has happened in the Baltic, on the Black Sea and Mediterranean and on the Pacific coast. Russia has been baulked time after time and is conscious that a watchful eye is always being kept on her territorial advances. Valid as these suspicions may be they have induced in Russia a feeling that she is in danger of perpetual encirclement and blockade, and this in turn has made her defensively wary and retaliatory.

Blame attached to both sides—or neither. It is the old story of the clash of Empires, but now of Empires more highly organized and terrifyingly strong than perhaps ever before, and it is also a clash between fundamental ideas and policies which are utterly opposed to one another and which underlie the political struggle of this generation.

Russia's path to the Mediterranean through the Balkans was blocked by her defeat in the Crimean war, by the frequent buttressing of the Ottoman régime, by Austro-German infiltration into that area, and then by the rise of modern Turkey. The only alternative for Russia was to find a way south between the Black Sea and the Caspian in the hope of one day reaching the Persian Gulf. Britain was alive to this intention and was determined to maintain the sovereignty of Persia and the friendship, or at least co-operation, of Afghanistan, so that they might be buffer states against Russian advance. At the time, India had to be safeguarded.

Hampered once again in her southward drive through Persia and Afghanistan, Russia realized that the only other hope of success was to push even further east and consolidate her possessions the whole way across Siberia to the Pacific coast. The Himalaya, the Gobi Desert and the size and population of China, offset any temptation to infiltrate south before reaching the Pacific.

In 1858, therefore, Russia and China concluded a treaty demarcating uncertain frontiers: territory north of the Amur River was to belong to Russia; territory east of the Ussuri River was to be jointly controlled. But this proved so unsatisfactory that from 1860 Russia took over this eastern territory. Oddly enough Russia was willing to sell Alaska to the United States in 1867, and doubtless regrets it now. If Russia had maintained her foothold on the North American continent the balance of power politics might have become very different from what it is today. She would also have reaped the full benefit of Klondike gold. The United States and Russia now stand to each other across the Bering Straits in much the same relationship as France and Britain stood to each other for centuries across the Straits of Dover—near neighbours but very wary.

In 1870 the weakness of Manchu rule on the fringes of the

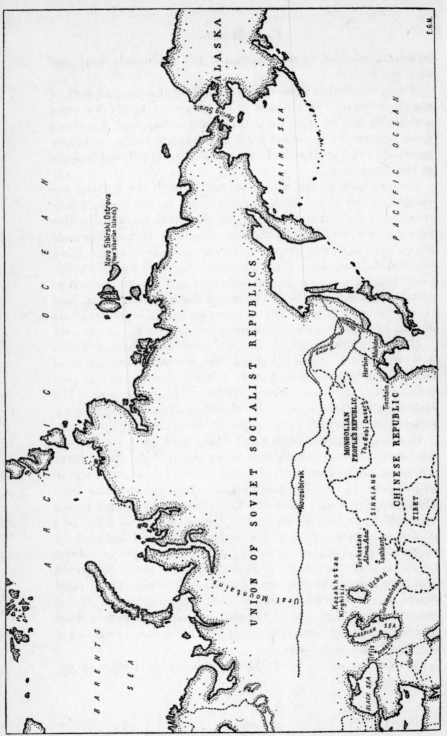

CENTRAL ASIA

Chinese Empire failed to deal with unrest in the province of Sinkiang, an excuse for Russia to move in troops to maintain order and control. An attractive inducement was held out to troops serving great distances from home in the granting of tracts of territory in various parts of Russian-held territory to different Cossack regiments in return for garrison duty. Generally speaking these tracts of land were fertile strips along rivers. This tactful and sensible encouragement to military duty during a period of territorial expansion was inevitably carried out at the expense of the more backward local inhabitants.

In 1899 the civil code which had been initiated in the reign of Tsar Alexander II was extended to the central Asian territories, and an attempt was made after the war with Japan to carry out the land reforms initiated by Stolypin. But in the main this policy of Russification was too optimistic. Policies that could be put into operation with a comparatively static community west of the Urals could not be applied to peoples and tribes in Siberia and elsewhere, many of whom were still enjoying the freedom of nomads. A multiplicity of languages and dialects, racial differences and widely divergent traditions complicated the policy of Russianizing Northern Asia. Not until the advent of the arterial railways—Trans-Siberian and lateral branches, chiefly between 1886 and 1905—did the population begin to shift and settle and increase.

The moment these trends set in habits of life began to change and nomadic tribes and peasants began to stay put. In the southern territories impinging on Persia and the Arabic-speaking world Russia came up against the full force of Islam (Mohammedan culture and rule) with its wholly different atmosphere of itinerant Mullahs, Koran schools, Shariat courts, child marriages, and slave raids. Any policy of Russification in these areas was scarcely likely to succeed unless new economic and social influences came into play. A religious outlook was no seed-bed for an essentially materialist political creed. Communism had a difficult start in these areas.

In Northern Asia even taxation presented a problem. It was difficult to levy—it was equally difficult to collect. A start was made with a simple tent tax, the proceeds of which were generally consigned to local needs. But even the unlettered nomad could sense the policy of encroachment, and feared the prospect of slavery.

After the defeat of Russia by Japan in 1905 and especially after the Revolution of the same year, Russian policy was at pains to strengthen the links between the peoples of Asia and the central Government in St. Petersburg, the capital. It is noteworthy that in the first two Dumas there were 36 and 43 Muslim representatives at St. Petersburg, and 21 Central Asians, out of a total of 524 members. On any reckoning this may be said to have been a fair or even generous allocation, but the reaction soon set in, and in the 3rd and 4th Dumas there were only 10 Muslim representatives and no Central Asians whatsoever.

During the course of the First World War, between 1914 and 1916, outer Mongolia was drawn more and more within the Russian sphere of influence. In 1915 China, hard pressed with her own internal problems, agreed to autonomy for outer Mongolia, although suzerainty remained with China. However, in November 1919 China withdrew her assent to autonomy and endeavoured to win outer Mongolia back to full allegiance to the Chinese republic.

2. RUSSIA IN ASIA 'UNDER NEW MANAGEMENT'

After the Communist revolution of October and November 1917, the new Soviet Government made an immediate effort to carry with it the sympathy and support of the peoples of Asia by issuing a 'Declaration of the Rights of the Labouring and Exploited Peoples' and also a proclamation 'to all the toiling Moslems of Russia and the East'. The declaration enunciated the right of self-determination, the equality of all peoples, the abolition of all privileges and private property, together with the abolition of all religious and national restrictions. This was calculated to appeal to those who had been suppressed by the Tsarist army, the Secret Police, and the dictates of the Russian Orthodox Church.

The next most important task of Soviet foreign policy was to undertake Russia's withdrawal from 'the Imperialist war'. This strategic retreat was brought about by the Treaty of Brest Litovsk in March 1918. It meant the surrender of the Baltic provinces and the loss of much territory in Eastern Europe, but the temporary withdrawal from war-stricken Europe gave the new Russian

Government the chance to consolidate its rise to power and establish its hold over the people.

A Soviet-Chinese agreement re-established some form of diplomatic relationship and in 1918 Dr. Sun Yat-sen sent a telegram of greetings to Lenin—one revolutionary congratulating another —on the successful overthrow of an outmoded dynasty. So complete and triumphant was the Communist Revolution that Lenin had great hopes that similar Soviet governments might be established in other parts of the world. For a brief moment it even looked as though Communism might find a footing in Hungary and Bavaria, but Lenin's hopes were soon to be disappointed. A civil war on Russian soil and a war of intervention in which the Western allies tried to smother the infant Soviet state were troubles enough for the Communists to deal with for the time being.

The province of Georgia, the very state in which Stalin was born and bred, broke away from Russia after the Revolution and set itself up as an independent state. It only survived until 1921, when the withdrawal of British troops from Russian territory made it possible for the Red Army to subordinate Georgia to the new Communist régime. In 1924 Georgia made one further bid for independence, but by now the Communist régime was far too strongly established and the small state of Georgia had no hope of success against the might of the new Russian Government.

Meanwhile Soviet Russia was beginning in her foreign policy to shut herself off from the company of other nations, and some attempt must be made to try to understand her attitude. In the first place it was natural enough for a struggling embryonic pattern of Government, essentially untried and experimental, to be rather suspicious of other countries, which had already given every evidence of resistance and distaste. There were good reasons why Soviet Russia should be suspicious of most of the great powers in the world. She had overthrown an ancient dynasty, closely related to the British Royal Family, and King George V was horrified at the brutal murder of his cousin the Tsar. France had intervened against Russia and was anxious to dismember her as far as possible, encouraging the suppression of the infant Soviet republic in Hungary.

On the Pacific Japan stood to gain enormously in the Far East from her alliance with the victorious powers, and there seemed every indication that Britain, the United States and Japan between them, with their enormous military, naval and commercial strength, would make every attempt to offset and hamper Soviet Russia's climb to power. In 1922 the new economic policy for Russia (N.E.P.) was put into operation, with the main object of recovering from the dislocation and setbacks of the period of civil war.

At this early stage it was impossible to pursue a fully Marxist policy and the period of N.E.P. was, therefore, a compromise between a measure of planned economy and private enterprise, in which both systems were allowed to work together to give Soviet Russia some degree of economic stability.

In 1924 Lenin died and Stalin eventually took his place—soon to become one of the greatest dictators the world has ever known, shrewd, ruthless, brilliant, far-seeing. The Foreign Secretary (Commissar) of Soviet Russia from 1918 to 1929 was Georgi Chicherin, whose aim was to extend Soviet influence as far as possible into all the countries which bordered on Russia, concentrating his attention on Persia, Afghanistan, Turkey, and notably China, where Borodin was sent to advise Sun Yat-sen on matters of political strategy and party organization. Thus within eight years of the Communist revolution the new Russian Government had adjusted itself to the business of ruling an extensive Empire which she had taken over, and had already set herself up as a model Socialist state born in revolution. She hoped other nations would be quick to follow her example.

3. THE PLANNED SOCIETY IN CENTRAL ASIA

The first of the famous five-year plans which were intended to bring about the creation of a full Marxist state was promulgated in 1928. The two main objectives were to develop industries in towns and to undertake the collectivizing of agriculture. These were tremendous aims, for personal liberty and possessions were seriously threatened and in fact affected by the obligation to do as the Central Government decreed. It did not happen in a twinkling, but the objective was so clear, so categorical, and so thoroughly pursued that there was ultimately no room left for objection or resistance. It was all just a matter of time.

So far as Central Asia in particular was concerned the aims of this first five-year plan were fourfold. The first necessity was to build and complete the Turksib Railway, which was an extension from the Trans-Siberian Railway, beginning at Novosibirsk and running to Alma Ata and to Kirghizia. Secondly, an enormous agricultural machinery plant was established at Tashkent. Thirdly, Karaganda was developed as a coal base and fourthly, a new impetus was put into the development of copper, lead, and textiles.

Such aims were laudable, but their achievement cannot obscure the ruthlessness with which they were implemented from 1930 to 1933. An example is the enforced elimination of the Kulaks, the relatively well-to-do Russian peasants and land proprietors. They had hitherto been the backbone of Russian agriculture, and they suffered most from the new Communist doctrine, which demanded that all the means of production must be taken out of the hands of owners and put into the hands of the state, as representing the working community. In some districts the process was so expeditious and the Kulaks were so hurriedly eliminated that the Central Government even had to warn ardent supporters of the new policy not to be in quite so much of a hurry to dispossess others.

No matter how remote districts and provinces were from the seat of government in Moscow, the object of Communist Russia was to build up an enormous unitary superstructure which would bring every aspect of life into one vast, closely knit organization. All local Soviets (Committees) were responsible to provincial Soviets, which were in turn responsible to the Supreme Soviet. This was calculated in a relatively short time to bring about a centralization which was administratively in touch with the whole territory under Soviet control. It was a process of assimilation and engulfment within which radical differences of opinion were to be regarded as not merely unpatriotic but treasonable. This process of incorporation began with the Treaty of Union adopted in December 1922. Turkmen and Uzbek, the vast areas east of the Caspian Sea and north of Iran and Afghanistan, became Soviet Socialist republics in 1925 within the Union. In 1929 Tajik (Tadzhik) reached the same status, and in 1936 Kazakh, Georgia, Azerbaijan, Armenia, and Kirghiz were proclaimed constituent republics of the massive Soviet Union.

Many of the outstanding Communist leaders, such as Stalin (who was Commissar for nationalities), Kaganovitch, Kuibishev,

Kalinin, Lenin, and Frunze (who led the Red Army on the Turkestan front) played some vital part in one way or another in the gradual subjugation of Central Asia to the Communist theory of life. In the 1924 and 1936 Constitutions special provision was made for the safeguarding of the rights and interests of the 'nationalities', who were not strictly Russians in race, culture and allegiance, and this protection was a subtle way of encouraging the humble folk to feel that they were being supported by the state against the interests of those who had hitherto been their repressive rulers or social superiors, or were in one way or another culturally privileged.

This certainly appealed to people who had long been brought up to believe that the Tsar was their protector or 'Little Father'. How any committee of revolutionaries could quite fill this bill it is difficult to see, but it was not long before an efficient and thorough propaganda machine mesmerized the Russian nation into believing that Stalin was to be regarded as a benevolent and patriarchal 'Little Father'. He now ruled where Tsars had reigned.

One pressing need was to develop a consciousness of allegiance to the new state and this was the responsibility of political education. It was no easy matter where so many different nationalities were concerned. Millions of copies of a booklet entitled *Building with Stalin* were disseminated all over Russian-held territory and Summer schools were held in which adults and young people could be trained in Communist doctrines.

In 1928 the Latin alphabet replaced the Arabic in Arabic-speaking parts of the Union, and as if that was not enough of a change, in 1939 the Russian alphabet replaced the Latin. The process of Russianization which had failed in the nineteenth century was beginning to be successful under the efficiency and unquestioned authority of the Soviet state.

In agriculture the Soviet procedure was to establish machine tractor stations all over the country to serve as centres for technical advice, and from which to borrow modern machinery. Each M.T.S. (Machine Tractor Station) became a hub from which Soviet authority radiated. All taxes were paid into them, and the technicians, engineers, and agriculturalists who gave the advice required in the collective farms also sowed the seed of Communist politics.

Central Asia

In the great areas of Central Asia, where corn, wheat, rice, and fruit were grown, and cattle were bred, these stations served to knit together the whole agricultural economy into the Soviet centralized system. It is said that by 1935 Kazakhstan alone had no less than 206 of them. On the other hand collective farming was not established without considerable opposition. Farmers who had depended for their livelihood on cattle breeding suddenly found their herds confiscated and had no alternative but to trek eastwards in the hope of finding new land and even new occupations. In most cases this was a forlorn hope.

It is easy to see that an efficient state could not tolerate the possibility of a minority of disaffected persons wandering about at large and it was in order to put a stop to any possibility of organized resistance that the Soviet Government took upon itself the responsibility, where need be, of moving whole sections of the population, or whole communities. For example, it is said that no less than 200,000 Koreans were removed to Central Asia 'as likely to prove untrustworthy in the event of a war with Japan'. When it came to the Second World War the need to move people was naturally more pressing and justifiable in face of German military advance. It is estimated that during the war years $12\frac{1}{2}$ million people were moved east along the Turksib railway into the neighbourhood of Tashkent, into West and Central Siberia and right down into Central Asia. On the other hand it is said that there was a heavy return flow when the danger of German occupation receded.

The scale of such movements, however alarming to the European, is nothing to the Chinese or Indians, who tragically are all too familiar with the catastrophes of famine, flood, and warfare and their attendant compulsory evacuation.

To give a few examples of the rate of growth of cities in Russian-held territory, the following may be cited. Sverdlovsk (formerly the town of Ekaterinburg), where Tsar Nicholas II and his family were so cruelly put to death in 1918, and which later became a great centre of heavy industry, developed from a town of 40,000 people in 1915 to approximately half a million in 1938. Novosibirsk (the former Nevorikolaievsk) grew from a medium-sized village in 1915 to a city of over 300,000 in 1938. Alma Ata, the capital of Kazakhstan, had a population of 30,000 in 1915; in 1929, before the Turksib railway connected it with Siberia, this had only grown to 50,000; but after the railway had reached it its population jumped to 230,000 within the next six years. Communications, the establishment of industry, agricultural development and Government encouragement, all added to the rapid growth in population caused by the move eastwards from Russia proper. It has been said that 'by 1939 the Central Asian republics had the largest ratio of European to indigenous population (varying from 1 : 2 to 1 : 3) of any territories inhabited by plural societies in the world'.

It is also estimated that by 1939 the combined populations of the five provinces, Kazakh, Kirghiz, Tadzhik, Turkmen, and Uzbek, reached a total of 16½ million. By now, Soviet Russia had every right to be proud of its progress and achievement. It had set out to accomplish an ambitious programme and on the whole it had succeeded. To give but one example of achievement: the Ferghana canal, stretching for 350 kilometres, was built in 1939 with such single-minded drive that it was completed in six months by a labour force of 160,000 former peasants.

The time had now come for the Communists to try to prove that internally all was now well in Russia and that the outside world had nothing to fear; a model Marxist state being now well established, no one was in a position to challenge its existence. So in 1929 a new Foreign Commissar was appointed, who guided the foreign policy of Russia for the next ten years. This was Maxim Litvinov. In his affable and amiable way he set out to disarm the rest of the world of any suspicion, prejudice or fear. He knew the West and his wife was English. When Russia grew alarmed at the gathering momentum of Nazism and Fascism in Central Europe, from 1933 onwards, and decided that her own interests were best served by identifying herself with collective security, Litvinov became the Soviet representative at the League of Nations from 1934 to 1938.

It was soon a matter of pride that Russia was recognized once again in the community of nations—a token of social and international respectability once again. But in the middle of this period of reassurance came one of the blackest moments in Communist history. In 1937 the Communist government set out to rid itself of all the individual leaders whom it could by accusing them of high

Central Asia

treason, sabotage, or espionage. A series of purges struck terror into the outside world and probably intimidated the Russian Empire as well.

Among those who were tried and punished were many of the most eminent Communist leaders. They included Bukharin, one-time Secretary-General of the Communist International, and an intimate friend of Lenin's; Rykov, Lenin's successor, and Molotov's predecessor as President of the Council of the People's Commissars; Yagoda, who had been the supreme head of the Ogpu—N.K.V.D.—and also People's Commissar for internal affairs; and Faisullah Khojayev, who was one of the quite outstanding figures in Central Asia and had been President of Uzbekistan.

The trials were held in a ballroom of the former Nobles' Club, and the Public Prosecutor was none other than Vyshinski, who was later to become one of the outstanding Foreign Commissars of Russia after the Second World War. Russian documents claimed that 'the Soviet government punished these degenerates with an iron hand, dealing ruthlessly with these enemies of the people and traitors to the country'. This is all very surprising when we remember how much each of these people had done to establish the Soviet republics. The theory is often advanced that some of them had become too powerful and knew too much and were the political rivals of those who were now in power. To eliminate rivals was to strengthen one's own position, and from the time of these trials in the mid-thirties Stalin had virtually no rivals for the last twenty years of his dictatorship.

It was at about this time that certain Western countries who had lent engineers, technicians, and advisers to Russia thought it wise to bring them home; the sense of fear and apprehension induced by these purges was more than the outside world could accept. Unquestionably Soviet Russia seemed to be becoming riddled with secret agents and a thoroughly efficient secret police. It was in fact rapidly becoming a police state, and a closed country—closed to visitors, who feared to travel there for fear of not coming home; and shut off from the outside world, because Russians did not travel abroad. If they did emerge they came as agents, or propagandists or remained strangely silent.

One of the greatest tragedies of world history began to occur when this large area of humanity was forcibly cut off from the rest, and all interchange of people and ideas was brought to a halt. Two rival systems of life had begun to oppose each other.

In foreign affairs Russia's membership of the League of Nations did little to ease her anxieties in the West. Germany under Hitler had obvious designs on the Ukraine, and militant Nazism was as likely to come eastwards as go westwards. On 24 August 1939, Russia signed a non-Aggression Treaty with Germany, which served its purpose as a blind or bluff for precisely one week. On 1 September Poland was attacked from both sides, and before the month was out was partitioned between Germany and Russia. Hitler's duplicity had benefited Russia, but he was not to be trusted. Russia began to strengthen her new western frontiers by the creation of a succession of new Soviet republics —part of Finland, all of Latvia, Estonia, Lithuania, and Moldavia —from the Baltic to the Black Sea vast territories were incorporated.

In 1940 Hitler and his Foreign Minister Ribbentrop tried to persuade Stalin and Molotov that the Second World War was practically at an end, and that the time had come to work out in advance the partitioning of the British Empire. It was assumed that Russia would be interested in all territory south of Soviet Asia. But Molotov preferred to deal with realities, and made it abundantly clear that although Russia was interested in all regions bordering on the Persian Gulf, she was even more concerned with territory that lay nearer home. Hitler's worst fears were confirmed: Russia was not to be deflected into Asia. He awoke to the realization that Russia stood in the way of his plans to subjugate Eastern Europe. On 22 June 1941, Hitler launched a full-scale attack against his (technical) ally, and drove Russia and the Western Powers into each other's arms as partners against a common foe. German thrusts into Russia forced the Soviet authorities rapidly to develop industries east of the Urals, and this brought an entirely new significance to Siberia and Soviet Central Asia. It was a hard struggle to stem the German tide, but it was halted and turned at Stalingrad. By the end of the war in 1945 Soviet Russia, controlling member of the Union of Soviet Socialist Republics, stood out as one of the most colossal nations in history. Stalin's writ ran from the Elbe to Kamchatka, from the Arctic to the Southern Balkans. The U.S.S.R., stung to battle by Hitler's treacherous attack in 1941, had recovered sufficient vitality not only to vanquish her enemies but to enlarge her borders beyond all expectation.

4. IRAN (PERSIA)

At the beginning of this century Persia was in danger of partition at the hands of either Russia, Germany, Britain, or Turkey, on account of her lack of stability, so clearly shown by the constitutional revolution which lasted from 1905 until 1909. Russia had long cast her eyes on Persia and hoped that the day would come when that backward country would become a Russian province, and Britain had equally feared such a prospect. In 1907 Britain and Russia agreed to resolve their differences, and Edward VII met the Tsar at Reval. An agreement was reached in which the northern sector of Persia was to be considered a Russian sphere of influence, and the southern part of the country was to become a British sphere of influence, with a neutral zone in between.

With this encouragement Russia did not hesitate to do everything possible to infiltrate into Azerbaijan and Asterabad. Four years later, in 1911, unbeknown to the British, Russia concluded the Potsdam Agreement with Germany, by which she recognized German interests in the railway which was to run from Berlin, through Constantinople, all the way to Baghdad, and possibly beyond. It was planned that a network of railways in Persia would be linked with this Berlin–Baghdad railway system. In return Germany undertook to recognize that Russia had territorial interests in the northern part of Persia and gathered that Russia intended perhaps to carry out some policy of piecemeal occupation. By the Treaty of Brest Litovsk in 1918 Russia granted Germany permission to have access to Caucasian oil, causing immediate alarm in Britain at the possibility of German influence on the Persian border. Therefore Sir Percy Cox was instructed to do his utmost to bring about a treaty between Britain and Persia guaranteeing Persian sovereignty, and offering technical advice and financial loans in return for firm resistance to Communist and German influence. But there was a delay in the ratification of the agreement.

Meanwhile the Russian (Red) Army was being so successfully

reorganized that its successes in the field encouraged the Persians to take a more sympathetic view of the new Russian régime. In April 1920 the anti-Communist republic which had been established in Azerbaijan collapsed and Russian troops entered Persia. For a short time a Soviet Government was even set up in the Persian province of Gilan on the Caspian. At this very moment the unexpected happened. Riza Khan, a born and forceful leader, took command of a Cossack brigade and swept on the Persian capital, Teheran, performing a *coup d'état*. Once in charge he came to an agreement with Soviet Russia which was advantageous to both sides. Russia agreed to give up all her claims upon Persian debts, and also promised to recognize Persian sovereignty, on condition that if any third party arrived in Persia and threatened to become a menace to Russia, then Russian troops were to be given permission to enter the country forthwith. Thus Persia became closely linked in a military and diplomatic alliance with Soviet Russia. In 1932 great difficulty arose between the Anglo-Iranian Oil Company and the Persian Government, and once again Russia saw her opportunity to step in. Russian advisers and technicians began to appear all over Persia.

In March 1940, at a time when Russia and Germany lived under a promise of mutual non-aggression, a commercial treaty was made with Persia by which Persia might supply Germany with duty-free goods via Russia, and vice versa. Riza Khan's policy was intensely nationalist and certainly unfriendly to Britain, but when Germany made her great mistake of attacking Russia in 1941 Britain and Russia quickly concluded an alliance in June of that year, and within a few weeks Russian troops were occupying northern Persia and British troops the south. It was through Persia that valuable 'Lease-Lend' equipment was subsequently passed from the United States into Russia to help her to sustain her war effort against Nazi Germany. Russia's failure to withdraw her troops from Persia in 1945 was one of the first causes of friction in the war-time alliance between Russian and the Allied powers. The last British and American forces left Persia in October 1945, well within the stipulated six months following the end of the war. It was not until April 1946 that Russia, under heavy moral and diplomatic pressure from the United Nations members, agreed to withdraw.

PART TWO

Asia Speaks for Herself

INTRODUCTION

THE re-birth of Asia may be said to have taken place in the short span of a single human generation. As we have seen, for a century before the First World War Europe dominated Asia; then, between the two World Wars, many parts of Asia were busy asserting their right to govern their own destiny; and since the end of the Second World War Asia is for the most part free once again from external governance.

If some readers protest that one cannot justly speak of Asia as if the continent as a whole had any collective consciousness it may be just as well to quote Nehru, one of the greatest Asians of our day. At a conference held in Lucknow in October 1950, the eleventh conference of the Institute of Pacific Relations, the Prime Minister of India declared in his address of welcome:

> Great countries like China, Japan, India, Indonesia, Burma, or the countries of the Middle East, have ancient traditions and cultures, with a tremendous background of history and past experience. It is difficult to jumble them together and call it Asia because geographically they happen to be in that area. Yet I think it is true that in the present context there is such a thing as an Asian sentiment, although there may be large differences between these countries. Possibly it is merely a reaction to the past 200 or 300 years of Europe in Asia.

The period of Europe in Asia is now past, so far as political control is concerned. An entirely new era has begun, and the whole continent of Asia is passing through a stage somewhat parallel to the Renaissance period in Europe, which marked the transition from feudal and medieval society to 'Modern Times'.

The first part of this book described the period of Sun Yat-sen, Mahatma Gandhi, Kemal Ataturk, Ibn Saud, and many other creative minds of that age—some spectacular, none without verve, all pioneers. The second part will discuss leaders such as U Nu,

Syngman Rhee, Menderes, Sukarno, Ho Chi Minh, Bandaranaike, Nasser, and countless others, with Nehru and Mao Tse-tung as relative giants in the task of forging a pattern of life for the new Asia.

And what were they creating? Can any estimate of their place in history yet be made? The chapters following trace the essentials of this recent renaissance, which is indeed still at its peak. Some of the main outlines are becoming more defined.

During the last fifty years Asia has revolted as much against her own past as against her link with Europe. Both ties have now been almost completely severed, leaving the way open to new conditions of life. Therein lies the embryonic situation which seers and Asian political leaders of all sorts have created for themselves and their millions of dependants. A few years ago nations could be inflamed and united by common antipathy to the foreigner. Much of the rise of nationalism throughout the continent took the form of re-action to European ways and attitudes, but also resulted in a sense of injured pride, due to an awareness of scientific and economic backwardness and an apparent Western attitude of superiority. But this unity of purpose began to break down as independence developed in Asia, and Asiatic countries became responsible for the management of their own affairs.

Then came the political test. Which of the various competing systems of government was each nation to adopt? The answer was bound to be different in different places. Dynasties had vanished, and change was everywhere evident. Republics appeared. The classical scholars of China, the aristocratic and intellectual civil service, have been replaced by a new type of party propagandist and organizer. The autocratic rule of certain Indian Princes has been replaced by representative government. Former nomadic sheiks are now oil magnates, the fabulous beneficiaries of petroleum combines. But although the civilization veneer has rapidly changed, the basic problems of poverty, illiteracy, disease and low production are almost as acute as ever they were.

One system offers the solution of government by discussion and debate, the 'open' system of parliamentary democracy, with freedom to differ and the possible time-lag of gradual evolution. Another system offers one-party rule, the dictatorship of a party and the committee that directs it, a 'closed' system with the prospect

Introduction

of quicker results and an inevitable constriction of liberty amounting in places to political tyranny. Some nations hope for a compromise between the two, and for that very reason keep closely in touch with the advocates of both, and are scornfully labelled 'neutralist' for their pains. Each of the three alternatives offers itself as a genuine, tested pattern of government capable of dealing with the problems of the day, and any reconciliation between the three is as likely in Asia as anywhere else—perhaps more.

Industrially and economically, Asia wants to 'catch up' with other parts of the world, especially with Europe, North America and other progressive areas of the world. The first major economic effort in Asia in which a whole group of nations worked to a clear-cut policy in this direction was the COLOMBO PLAN for 'Co-operative Economic Development in South and South-East Asia'.

The principle of multilateral co-operation had already been well-established by the Marshall Plan of 1947, which aimed at restoring European economic stability following the distress and dislocation of war. Sixteen nations had joined this organization for European economic co-operation which was prompted by the American desire to help Europe. Asia followed the example already set.

After a series of preliminary meetings in Colombo (January 1950), Sydney (May 1950) and London (September 1950), the Colombo Plan was set in train as from 1 July 1951. The immediate aim was to disburse a sum of nearly £2,000 million in the course of six years, 1951 to 1957, in order to increase productivity, to alleviate hardship, and provide equipment, technicians and capital for the undeveloped parts of South and South-East Asia. The scheme was impelled by the highest motives—the desire to help other human beings. The first necessity was to train as speedily as possible hundreds of experts, agricultural, engineering, medical, scientific, and a sum of £8,000,000 was allocated to this task alone in the first three years.

Before the scheme was even contemplated, India, Pakistan, and Ceylon, between 1946 and 1949, had drawn no less than £340,000,000 from sterling fund reserves piled up in Britain during the war to pay for extra imports to meet emergencies. This was a critical drain on Britain, a crisis which was promptly met by the most generous gifts and loans from the United States, Canada,

Australia, and New Zealand. The New World helped the Old World to help the newest nations. Could there be sounder proof of interdependence between nations?

The Colombo Plan was not narrowly conceived. All the countries within the Commonwealth—India, Pakistan, Ceylon, Malaya, Singapore, North Borneo, Sarawak, and Brunei—were members from the outset. But Burma, Thailand, Indonesia, and the Associated States of Laos, Cambodia, and Vietnam also joined the Plan and now share the benefits of this concerted economic development. It is estimated that in an area with a population of some 600 million people the Colombo Plan will bring approximately thirteen million more acres under cultivation, produce at least six million tons more food a year, and increase the electricity generating capacity of the area by an extra 1·1 million kilowatts. Vast new dams, new housing and education projects, better transport and communications, expenditure on mines, and improvements in agriculture generally are among the main targets, all steps in the right direction so far as food, welfare, and material well-being are concerned.

Four years later, in 1955, Soviet Russia, in the course of the visit to India, Burma and Afghanistan by Marshal Bulganin and Mr. Khruschev, entered the same field of economic development in parts of the same area by offering a technical college here, technical advice elsewhere, and exchange of commerce generally. The outcome of a series of 'high-level' visits to the Middle East by Mr. Shepilov, together with the Bulganin-Khruschev tour, was the creation of a chain of trade centres between Communist and non-Communist countries. The tension between East and West which had developed in 1946, become acute in 1948, and increased once more in 1950, now suddenly altered in character.

The military threat which had always existed in the post-war lifetime of Stalin became much more an economic issue in the hands of his successors. The ideological battle remained the same, but the impulsion behind it was less and less a matter of force than a resort to the more subtle advances through personal overtures, to governmental concord and commercial penetration. 'Peaceful coexistence' was a mild way of describing a period of intense competition from all sides. With the United States boycotting Communist China while Britain tried to keep the door open no-one could be sure what hope of compromise remained. Meanwhile, Soviet Russia accomplished the unexpected by 'jumping' the so-called 'Northern Tier' and drawing closely alongside the new Republic of Egypt, thus planting herself right in the midst of Middle Eastern affairs, and on the circumference of Africa.

But Asia is never likely to be satisfied with the bare fruits of political independence, now attained, nor even with the fruits of material improvement, which are everywhere planned or conjectured. These can never be the heart of the matter. Asia, after all, is a continent of deep religious faith. Faith and belief are the very breath of Asia, probably more so than any other continent. It is no accident that the Old Testament patriarchs, the Hebrew Prophets, and finally, the self-revelation of God Himself in the person of Christ, should have given new life and hope to the world through the Jews in Palestine. Christianity is essentially Asian in origin. It is no accident that the great religious leaders in the history of the world—the Buddha, Confucius, Zoroaster and Mohammed—should have sprung from Asia. This is the greatest legacy that Asia has given the world—faith in a supernatural power and purpose which is something far greater than trust in 'man' himself, apart from his Creator. No other continent has ever had, nor can ever have, such a comparable treasure to offer. The rest of the world stands already in deepest debt to Asia for all the divine teachings and holy Scriptures that holy men have handed down from the depths of their experience and insight and knowledge of God. How, then, have these deep-rooted religious forces survived the upheavals of the last fifty years or so?

A secular wave of thought has struck right through Asia. It is as if the ghost of Voltaire has accompanied European rule, challenging Asian foundations of faith, ridiculing, deriding, and destroying. What are some of the consequences? The Caliphate, a pillar of Islamic unity, has gone. Republic after republic has declared itself to be a lay or secular state, declining to tie itself to any one religious allegiance. The anti-God movement of the Communist states did its best to discredit the Orthodox Church, decry the need for faith, and bedevil the minds of many. But the religions of the world have withstood, and survived their sternest test.

Judaism has been strong enough not merely to survive the most barbarous assault ever made on one race and religion, but has even effected the improbable—crystallized itself in nationhood, religion and politics working together, the one drawing strength, nay, more, its very *raison d' être*, from the other. Zionism has many facets—traditional, reactionary and backward-looking as well as progressive, liberal and Utopian—but viewed from one aspect it is proof of the power of religion to hold a nation together in hope, through adversity, to the day of fulfilment.

Mohammedanism likewise has been a powerful motive force behind the world of politics and in the evolution of states. The Koran, the mullahs and imams, the Islamic culture have together served as rallying-points for political parties, have been the spearhead of spiritual revival, and have also provided resistance to the encroachments of secularism in countries as widely separated as Indonesia, Persia and the Arab League countries. Pakistan, in particular, may be singled out as a nation founded essentially on the basis of its religious faith. The force of Mohammedanism cannot be discounted when it can give birth to a new and sturdy nation.

Buddhism has also proved a consolidating influence, especially in South-East Asia. Monks and politicians have at times been indistinguishable, and monasteries have been strongholds of resistance and influence. The decision to revise the Buddhist scriptures, and the 2,500th anniversary celebrations in 1956, gave a new impetus to the religious vitality of many a Buddhist.

In 1951 the Burmese Parliament passed a resolution designed to remind the world that social problems can never be solved by material betterment alone. Burma, Thailand, Ceylon, Cambodia, Laos, Tibet, India, and other Asian countries sent representatives to the Sixth Buddhist Council, which was in session from May 1954 till December 1956, when it dispersed after solemn celebrations in Katmandu (Nepal) and New Delhi. The Dalai Lama of Tibet visited India for the occasion. In Ceylon the election to power of the government of S. W. R. D. Bandaranaike in 1956 probably owed more to the support of Buddhist leaders and influence (especially priests, doctors, and teachers) than to any other single factor. Buddhism was largely synonymous with nationalism, at least for election purposes.

Christianity also has been severely put to the test in Asia, partly because it has been so closely associated with European and American missions. Christians are still very much a minority, numbering perhaps no more than some thirty million or so in the whole continent of Asia. This total is almost entirely the result of missionary work in the last century and a half. The most devastating attack on Christianity came, incongruously enough, from Russia, where the anti-God movement drove the Church underground. But in 1942 the authorities were induced to allow the Russian Orthodox Church to come to life again, and to elect a Patriarch as a symbol of its revival and a slender pledge of state recognition. In other parts of Asia, especially in Japan, China and India the Christian churches had meanwhile established National Christian Councils, in which most churches, except the Roman Catholic, worked together, and in the last few decades they were busy training Asians for positions of leadership and authority.

Christian churches were rapidly becoming indigenous against the day of the foreigners' ejection. In this way, Christianity may even be said to have led the way in the transfer of power—from European and American leadership back to Asian. In 1951 Communist China expelled many hundreds of Christian missionaries, confiscated their property, schools, universities, and hospitals, and began a systematic persecution of Christians in the country. In India attempts were made to turn out the missionaries, but Nehru himself explained that so long as Christians were the only people willing to tend lepers and carry out similar works of mercy and sacrifice, Christians must be allowed to remain. The future of Christianity in Asia now depends, humanly speaking, on local witness and local leadership.

In a sense the people of Asia will continue to derive far more comfort and encouragement from their religion and way of life than from any other modern palliatives, though that is not to say that all the other struggles towards political freedom and material development have not been part and parcel of the same process of re-birth.

We must now turn to the post-war events in Asia, and the starting point must be the decisions taken at the Yalta conference which have a bearing on these events.

VIII

THE CLASH OF EMPIRES AND
IDEAS

1. FROM THE YALTA CONFERENCE ONWARDS

A BATTLE of wits began when Stalin, Roosevelt, and Churchill met at Yalta in the Crimea in February 1945. As they looked ahead into the immediate future and laid their plans for the defeat of Japan, the settlement of Europe, and continued international collaboration, self-interest and fear inevitably poisoned the results. What these three men had in mind has had an enormous effect on the events of the post-war era and still influences the world for better or worse. The Yalta Conference was decisive in countless respects.

Stalin promised that Russia would become a founder member of the new world organization. This was a matter of much gratification to Roosevelt in particular, who had set his heart on the establishment of an international peace organization, somewhat as his predecessor, President Wilson, had bent his energies towards the formation of the League of Nations.

At first Russia insisted that all the sixteen Soviet republics should be members of the United Nations Organization, a request which took the British and Americans completely by surprise. They had little idea that Stalin would claim that some of his fledgling republics now counted as adult nations. Eventually it was agreed that Ukraine and White Russia (Byelorussia) should at any rate be allotted seats in the General Assembly on a par with India and the four British dominions of Canada, South Africa, Australia, and New Zealand.

With Russia and the United States included, and neither of them standing aloof any longer, there was every hope that the United Nations would become a genuinely world-wide forum in which matters of common concern might be raised and sound decisions reached. One danger that presented itself was that the Big Three —Britain, the United States, and Russia—might assume the right to govern the world without due regard to the voices of the multitude of smaller nations. Stalin's argument was that the three Great Powers which had borne the brunt of the war should be the ones to preserve the peace, and not submit themselves to the criticism of the small nations.

It fell to Churchill to champion the rights of all sovereign powers, however small, by saying the eagle should permit the small birds to sing and care not wherefore they sang. Was the post-war world to become dominated by the Big Powers, or was it to grow into the family of free nations envisaged in the Atlantic Charter of 1942? Much depended, therefore, on the rules of the United Nations Charter which would govern procedure and debate. Thus arose the problem of the veto. All three Powers were agreed that the veto was justified as a safeguard against unwarrantable interference in domestic matters. Not to have some means of nullifying decisions or of warding off interference by outside powers was to surrender sovereignty itself, and this was obviously out of the question, except in the widest possible international interest.

It was fondly hoped that any Power which was a party to a dispute would refrain from using its power of veto in order to enable some peaceful settlement to be reached by the processes of discussion. This was optimistic. It was also hoped that the veto would never be used in any question of procedure or in the course of actual discussion, but only when it came to a matter of decision. This also proved to be wishful thinking, for the veto came to be used to block certain questions from even coming on to the agenda. Time was to prove how serious a deadlock this power of veto could cause.

But the Yalta Conference was not only concerned with the broader issues of post-war organization. It was as urgently concerned with the business of finishing the war both in Europe and in Asia, and the two were inter-related. At Yalta, with the war in Europe coming nearer and nearer to a close, Stalin put forward his plan to partition Germany; to divest her of 80 per cent. of her heavy industry; to impose harsh treatment in reparations; and to create a strong Poland with a frontier as far west as the

Oder-Neisse line. Churchill insisted that France be given a share in the post-war control of Germany; that no foolish step be taken to destroy out of hand the recovery of Germany's economy; that reparations be not utterly crippling; and that the Lublin Committee, which Stalin recognized, was in fact unrepresentative of Poland and Polish interests. In the face of such divergent viewpoints, with Churchill and Stalin so often in disagreement, Roosevelt was pushed more and more into the role of conciliator, trying by compromise to fashion agreement. This unexpected role served his purposes well in another regard.

Roosevelt was of the opinion that the war in the Pacific might drag on for very many months after the conclusion of the war in Europe. The brunt of this vast campaign, especially the attack on Japan itself, fell squarely on the American forces, with, of course, the help of Australians, New Zealanders, British, and others; but the Americans stood to suffer most. It was estimated that over three million Americans would be required in the Pacific theatre of war. There was no telling what the toll in American lives might be and this weighed heavily on Roosevelt's mind. He was, therefore, more than ever determined to make sure that Russia would come into the war against Japan and thus hasten the end of hostilities. Roosevelt himself was physically near exhaustion. His health had been failing rapidly and it has been suggested that this made him, perhaps sub-consciously, all the more anxious to draw Russia into the Pacific arena. The more he indicated his need of Russia the more Stalin realized he could strike a hard bargain. Stalin pressed for territorial concessions and guarantees in the Far East, to which Roosevelt gave his concurrence. Some of these were to be at the expense of China and were likely to alarm Chiang Kai-shek, but Roosevelt undertook to smooth the way and offset any difficulty from that quarter.

The province of Outer Mongolia, which was virtually a Russian satellite, was to be preserved intact for Russia. The southern part of Sakhalin was to become Russian (it had been leased to Japan in 1905 after Russia's defeat by Japan). Russia was to gain the valuable harbour of Port Arthur and special interests in Dairen, the civil port. The Chinese Eastern Railway and the South Manchuria Railway were to be managed by a joint Chinese-Russian company and the Kurile Islands, stretching from the main

Japanese islands towards Kamchatka, were to become Russian possessions.

Roosevelt felt sure that Chiang Kai-shek could be induced to ratify these provisions in return for a Russian promise to conclude a treaty of friendship with Chiang Kai-shek's Nationalist government. It was thought that this would lay the bogey of Communist resurgence in China which had been a continuous threat to the life and existence of the Nationalist government. Thus Stalin stood to gain by extending the Russian sphere of influence more securely than ever before along the Pacific coastline, with the moral and political support of the President of the United States, and with little fear of serious opposition. Roosevelt on the other hand had the assurance of Russia's military support against Japan.

The agreement generated goodwill between the United States and the U.S.S.R. and was signed on 11 February 1945. The two ascendant powers had reached what looked like solid agreement and friendship—but it was only at the Stalin-Roosevelt level, arrived at in camera, and known to a select company only some time later. Another implication underlay this Russo-American rapprochement. It is said that Roosevelt and several of his advisers had come to the conclusion that Britain and France ought not to be allowed to recover, or go back to, their colonial territories in the Far East. Such anti-Imperialist policy, alleged to have had Roosevelt's support, naturally appealed to Stalin's expansionist ambitions, and helped to cement the friendship between the two statesmen. It may also explain why Roosevelt was so careful to conduct private negotiations with Stalin in regard to the Pacific campaign, and why he was so careful to exclude Churchill from these conversations.

Roosevelt's attitude to the Dutch was different. He fully expected the Dutch East Indies to be granted self-government in accordance with an earlier promise from the Dutch Government to give this, but in the event his trust proved to be misplaced. It was the British who led the way in granting self rule in country after country in rapid succession in the post-war years—India, Pakistan, Ceylon, Burma, and Malaya. France was reluctant to make any such concession. It destroyed her conception of the French Union. Holland proved to be at least as obstinate and inflexible as France.

Such was the situation at Yalta. The provisional settlement of occupation rights, frontiers and arbitration claims left the door open for further adjustment and diplomatic jockeying in the years to come, but policies proceed from personalities, and the personalities were about to change. Roosevelt lived just long enough to know that the war would end in victory for the Western Powers. Roosevelt died within sight of his objective, whereupon Truman reigned in his stead. Within a matter of weeks a transfer of political responsibility occurred also in Britain. When the war in Europe came to an end Party politics succeeded national coalition and the Labour Party was swept into power in Great Britain at the expense of the Conservatives. Clement Attlee became Prime Minister in place of Winston Churchill.

Thus, in the latter stages of the Potsdam Conference in July 1945, when crucial matters came up for consideration among the Big Three, Stalin alone maintained the continuity of the war-time alliance. Neither Truman nor Attlee had the flamboyance, statecraft or imaginative genius of Roosevelt or Churchill, but both turned out to be men of relentless courage and hard-headed realism; both had a certain insight and were prepared to be patient without compromise. Stalin may have expected to meet a couple of cubs, but they were grizzly enough to take on the Russian bear a few years later.

Two new leaders, therefore, appeared on the world scene, but there had been enormous changes in the balance of power as well during the course of the war. In 1939 three nations were holding the world to ransom: Hitlerite Germany, Mussolini's Italy, and Japan. At the time there seemed to be no stopping the advance of these three militant nations, and yet in 1945 all three were broken. Naturally, an entirely new situation was created by their total collapse.

Secondly, Soviet Russia had proved herself to be an outstandingly great power, clever in strategy, resilient in warfare and capable of producing great leadership. Her success in stemming the advance of Hitler's armies on the eastern front won the sympathy and admiration of the world. The fact that she was able to hold the German forces at Stalingrad and prevent Hitler's armies from marching through Georgia and the Caucasus into the Middle East helped to prevent one arm of a gigantic pincer movement from closing in on Iraq, Syria, the Suez Canal zone and Egypt. The other arm of this gigantic pincer was, of course, Rommel's thrust eastward along the North African coastline. Had Stalingrad and El Alamein not held, there is no possible telling how far the German armies might have moved or what might have been the outcome of the war. But the prestige of Russia did not only depend on the success of her armies.

Her ability to hold Hitler proved once and for all that the Russian power was nothing ephemeral. Russia more than ever before had come into her own and was on an equal from the point of view of unity and strength with the greatest nations throughout the world.

Furthermore her example and fortitude encouraged the growth of Communist parties in many parts of Asia and Europe. Russia, therefore, assumes an entirely new international significance from 1945. This does not mean to say that all sense of suspicion and antipathy had been dispelled by her opposition to Nazi tyranny. The public memory was still aghast at many of the atrocities which accompanied the establishment of the Communist régime and the restrictions, intimidations, blackmail, brutality, and purges which followed its development in Russia. No amount of material progress could excuse the methods which impelled this advance. But the very fact that contact had at last been re-established with the power that reigned in the Kremlin gave hope that some measure of accommodation and goodwill might be the order of the future.

Marshal Stalin, around whom such enigmatic legends had accrued, was gradually becoming a known quantity to countless statesmen, politicians, military leaders and foreign officials. At last it was possible to gauge the tremendous strides taken by his country against the character of the man responsible. The almost mythical giant, the boy from Tiflis, who had held the world in terror, had come out of his lair. Churchill was getting to know him intimately and was in a position to size up his combination of astute duplicity and somewhat Asiatic blandness. Sir Stafford Cripps, Lord Beaverbrook, several of the Astor family and many others had already come face to face in conversation with the very person who had made them most suspicious of everything emanating from Russia.

Not least important perhaps is the fact that in 1942 Stalin had allowed the Russian Orthodox Church to come once again to life. The Church was allowed to elect a Patriarch and to re-establish its organization of worship and instruction after years of terrible persecution. Hundreds of priests who had been driven into hiding were allowed to return to their proper vocation and it really seemed at last as though Stalin, who had himself revolted from the intellectual discipline of two years at a theological seminary in Georgia, had recognized that the religious life of any nation ultimately refuses to be smothered or suffocated.

Gradually the Patriarch Sergius and his fellow bishops were allowed to begin once again the difficult business of reviving the theological colleges in which the future Orthodox priests were to be trained, and to reorganize the diocesan and parish life by means of which the Russian nation might be brought back to faith in God. This insight and encouragement gave hope to Christian people outside Russia. Not only did the Archbishop of York (Dr. Garbett) pay a courtesy visit to Moscow to mark this revival of the Russian church, but the Patriarch's successor, Alexis, was in 1945 allowed to leave Soviet territory and visit his brother patriarchs of Antioch, Jerusalem, and Alexandria. It was indeed remarkable that the head of the Church in Russia should have been allowed to visit several countries right outside Soviet authority and outside his own ecclesiastical jurisdiction and come into contact with free-thinking people in the outside world.

It is perfectly true that his tour was more than justified by his visiting many colonies of exiled Russians who adhered to the Orthodox Church, and it was right and proper that one patriarch should come into personal touch with his brother patriarchs. Nevertheless as a gesture of goodwill and of new-born confidence it was a journey which was welcomed and much noticed by people everywhere.

Thirdly, a new orientation of policy was bound to arise from the vitally important part played by the United States in the war. In spite of the Monroe Doctrine and the strong feeling of isolationism in parts of America, the United States had for the second time in a generation been forced to participate in resisting aggression and the violation of treaties in Europe. It was increasingly obvious that from this position of responsibility there could be no retreat. The time was past when the United States could take shelter behind the shield of the Monroe Doctrine. The Atlantic and the Pacific were no longer a moat surrounding the citadel of America. American troops and equipment had traversed the world in the allied cause and the conscience of international obligation was now beginning to be felt deeply in America.

Whether or not the relationship between the United States and Soviet Russia would continue at the level of war-time alliance was the crucial issue. The leaders were in touch with one another and had experienced the compromise resulting from give-and-take in discussion, but the people of the two countries had seen practically nothing of each other, so that the prospect of continuing goodwill was by no means certain.

Fourthly, new forces were making themselves felt in eastern Europe and Asia. In the Far East in particular as we have seen, the spread of nationalism, immeasurably encouraged by the war, was well on the way to eliminating European control of former territories and colonies. But there was similar restlessness in the Balkans and Eastern Europe. As fast as the German forces were pushed back from these occupied areas the Russian armies marched in and rapidly took over all authority in administration and control.

The question began to arise as to whether or not the Russian-dominated areas would ever revert to such forms of independent sovereignty and non-Communist government as most of them had known before 1939. The whole area from Finland to Albania and eastward to the Russian frontier was suddenly caught up within the Russian sphere of influence, and statesmen in the west began to wonder if the Russian armies would ever be called back into Soviet Russia and leave the occupied areas to work out their own salvation. Their doubts were justified in the event. Politically, Soviet Russia engulfed nearly one-third of the continent of Europe.

2. HOW SUSPICION AND ILL-WILL CREATED THE COLD WAR

As the American armies closed in on Japan and consolidated their advance across the Pacific, Russia tended to become suspicious of American intentions. It was all very well for the United States to become a victor in war, but would she be willing to withdraw once peace was restored? In other words the very suspicion which the West felt about Russia in Eastern Europe found its parallel in

Russian suspicions of the United States in the Far East. Furthermore, American aid had been going to the rescue of Chiang Kaishek in Western China and American military advisers were so close to the Generalissimo that the Russians appeared to think that the Kuomintang was virtually dependent on American support. To a certain extent their fears were well-grounded, and it had been so ever since the Cairo Conference, at which Chiang Kai-shek conferred with Roosevelt and Churchill. Russia well knew that thousands of Chinese Nationalist officials had received their education in the United States, as indeed had Madame Chiang Kai-shek. China turned hopefully to America for moral as well as material reinforcement. However, the policy of ensuring victory by offering equipment and supplies from America applied also, of course, to Russia herself. In Russia's moment of her extreme peril Roosevelt, with tremendous generosity, had offered to send all possible means of support in the way of war equipment. As we have noted earlier, the only means by which this material aid could reach the country safely was across Persia, and a corridor across that country was created, Russia providing troops to guarantee the safe conduct of supplies across Northern Persia, and Britain and the United States doing likewise in the south.

The United States sometimes had reason to think that the Russian government was grateful for the tanks and other military equipment which were sent her, but felt that the Russian government was less than grateful in withholding from her general public the fact that this equipment was American built. For instance, on one occasion when fourteen British Members of Parliament visited Russia as a delegation they were astonished to discover that Russian soldiers and officers hotly denied that any equipment they had seen or used was other than Russian manufactured. It was all the M.P.s could do to persuade the Russian troops to have a look at the trade-marks on certain parts of the vehicles and be persuaded that they had been imported for their use from the United States, largely at the expense of American citizens. The same reluctance to admit any indebtedness to any outsider Power revealed itself even in works of mercy.

As soon as the United Nations Relief and Rehabilitation Administration had been established, money, officials, food, and clothing were promptly sent to stricken areas where famine or destruction had created urgent problems. One would have thought that no honest person could fail to applaud such a humanitarian effort, but even this came to be misconstrued. Just because so many of the officials who administered the relief were citizens of countries in the west the work itself came under suspicion, and just because so much of the money which supported the work of U.N.R.R.A. came from the United States Russia began to think that it was a settled form of economic penetration into countries where the West had no footing or justification for helping.

Since the United States had not suffered wholesale destruction of property and industry at home she was in a position to help others to recover, while Russia on the other hand, like so many other countries in Europe and Asia, was busily engaged in rebuilding her own smashed cities.

Then we come to the more fundamental question of the basic principles on which East and West established their political structures. Churchill and Roosevelt together had made it clear in their statement, known as the Atlantic Charter, on what principles they intended to bring about world peace and world recovery after the end of the war. The document is shot through and through with the doctrine that people of every country, race, and group must be allowed to be free to possess the particular government of their choice. The essence of the Atlantic Charter is freedom—personal, religious, economic, and social freedom. But this, of course, did not in the least square with the basic assumptions of Russia. Russia being an expanding nation with a new-found unity and strength and representing an entirely different political and economic doctrine was out to impress this structure upon all territories that came within her grasp. Russia was on the march. It has been said 'a Communist bloc is a missionary society which expects to inherit the estates both of its allies and of the vanquished'. This was true of Russia immediately after the war in 1945 and is, of course, an undeniable pre-supposition of all future Communist penetration or advance.

There is no possible shadow of doubt whatsoever that all who profess to follow the teachings of Communism have set their face towards the conquest of the world in order to overthrow capitalism and replace it with Marxism. The Atlantic Charter, therefore, was a direct challenge to all that Russia stood for.

The suspicions of the West as to Russian intentions continued to mount. A whole series of claims and counter-claims began to diminish the store of goodwill that had been collected through the war-time alliance. One of the most astonishing incidents was a claim coming from Mr. Molotov. As a complete surprise and to the immediate bewilderment of the Western statesmen, Molotov suddenly laid claim to the ex-Italian colony of Tripoli in North Africa. To Western ears this was unbelievable. Had not England and France and the Ottoman Empire spent generations preventing Russia from pushing through into the Mediterranean? Had not wars been fought in the Balkans and in the Crimea precisely for this purpose? Yet here was Russia daring to claim as part of her war-time spoils not merely a city and harbour on the Mediterranean, but indeed on the far side of the Mediterranean, and on a continent upon which she had at this time no foothold. This was indeed putting the cat among the pigeons.

The claim came to nothing, but the fact that it was lodged was never forgotten and was taken as a warning that the Russian victors were liable to make unexpected claims in any sphere that appealed to them. In Germany, as in Austria, the three Western powers and Russia agreed to set up zones for military administration in occupied territory. Russia went so far as to suggest that there should be a similar system of zones in Japan, but this was resisted by the West and the entire occupational responsibility for looking after Japan was handed over to the United States. Nevertheless, Russia was allowed to send an enormous military mission to Japan, which it later proved very difficult to diminish or dislodge. When Persia was persuaded to allow lease-lend equipment to be taken through their country it was understood clearly by Russia, Britain, and the United States that protecting troops should be withdrawn within six months of the end of hostilities. To this promise the Western Allies were true, all British and American troops being withdrawn by October 1945, but the Russians made little or no attempt to reduce their garrison force or give any indication of willingness to withdraw. This only served to increase the suspicions of the West that given half a chance Russia might elect to stay put on foreign territory and gradually create a new Soviet republic on Persian soil. Persia, therefore, protested through the United Nations.

But perhaps the most devastating act of ill will which the

Russians perpetrated, and which is inadequately realized at present, is the treatment of Japan by Russia in the last few days of the war. The Potsdam Declaration of 26 July 1945 had made it clear that the Allies demanded complete unconditional surrender on the part of Japan. Japan did in fact make overtures to Russia to mediate on her behalf with the Western Powers, and Russia was in a position to do so, for no state of war yet existed between Russia and Japan. Although it is true that they viewed each other with grave suspicion they were nevertheless still technically at peace, even though their armies were poised ready for battle. It must go down to history as an incontestable fact that Russia chose to ignore Japan's plea for Russian mediation. There can be no reason for the delay, except that Russia herself intended to make the utmost of a state of impending collapse in Japan, and to rush in at the very last possible moment in order to be on the side of the victors.

The first atom bomb was dropped on Hiroshima on 6 August 1945. After this it was obviously only a matter of days, if not hours, before Japan would throw in her hand. Russia, therefore, quickly came in. She declared war officially on 8 August exactly one day before the second atom bomb, dropped on Nagasaki, brought Japan to her knees and an end to the war in the Pacific. Russia had come into the war just in the nick of time.

Meanwhile a state of great confusion existed in Greece. Civil war had broken out in which it seemed that Greek Communist forces were quite likely to overwhelm the rest of the nation, which desired a return to constitutional monarchy. A similar state of unrest existed in Palestine and in Syria, and even in Turkey. In face of this state of political instability, which lent itself to Communist penetration, President Truman quickly took a decision to send military and technical aid to both Greece and Turkey in order to help to put them on their feet again politically and economically. This came to be known as the Truman Doctrine—the principle that a strong nation might go to the rescue of a weaker nation in the hour of need, especially when the threatened danger was ideological.

All these factors contributed to what became known as 'the cold war'.

3. THE NEW SCALE OF STRATEGY AND THE NEW ALLIANCES

In the spring of 1946 Mr. Winston Churchill broke his silence when he addressed a public meeting at Fulton in the United States. He took this opportunity of issuing a solemn warning to the nations of the world by pointedly asking whether it was realized what Russia was trying to do. What evidence was there of Russian demobilization? Why was it that Britain and the United States and all the other allies had been only too eager to cut down their armed services as rapidly as possible, while at the same time Russian armies were sitting down firmly on countries now occupied by them?

This apprehension was confirmed in the course of the next two or three years by a whole sequence of events. Britain was busy withdrawing from countries which she had dominated, and independence was being given successfully to India and Pakistan, Burma and Ceylon. It is true that these countries had struggled hard for the principle of self-rule, and true that tremendous pressure and agitation and suffering lay behind their demands, yet it is equally true that Britain had genuinely tried step by step to pave the way towards this ultimate objective of self-government. It may be said in retrospect that the steps may have been too slow, too feeble or too ineffective, and that they were often out of step with the degree of agitation, but in spite of everything that may be said by ill-wishers, the British government always did intend that home rule for each of these countries would one day be put into operation. When the day of fulfilment arrived friendship for Britain soon followed.

In complete contrast with this willingness to entrust full responsibility for self-government to these nations was Russia's attitude. All the territories within the sphere of Russian occupation accepted or were forced to accept Communist control and were swept within the fold of Russian domination. Between the end of the war and the end of 1948 a whole succession of pacts were ratified between all the states in Eastern Europe over which Russia had influence, that is to say, between Russia, Poland, Czechoslovakia, Bulgaria, Roumania, Hungary, and Albania. Treaty agreements bound them together into a solid phalanx subservient to Moscow. The monolithic structure was formidable.

Furthermore instead of these pacts being valid for a limited period, say of ten, twenty or even thirty years, as so many treaties were, almost all these pacts were to hold for an indefinite period. Thus military occupation turned into political domination. Such a development ran counter to all the hopes upon which both the League of Nations and the United Nations, as well as the Atlantic Charter were founded. The principle of self-determination was completely distorted by the Communists into a new process of single-party rule. Criticism and opposition was stifled by intimidation and fear, and the western world soon came to know these countries as a further addition to the so-called police states. This political suffocation, in which the freedom to think and say or write as one believed was denied, affected the lives of millions. How different it all was from what some of the people had once known, especially the freedom-loving Czechs. How different also from the situation in Southern Asia, where the people in India and Pakistan and Ceylon could take pride in the fact that nationalism had been vindicated, a sense of fulfilment reached and their countries were at liberty to evolve as they saw fit. A paradox was becoming more and more apparent. One great nation, Britain, which had been the centre of an Empire, was prepared to give full recognition to the new adult status of its component parts, and accept the idea of change from Empire to Commonwealth, a voluntary association of free nations. At the same time another nation, Russia, while condemning the old conception of imperialism, was in fact becoming one of the greatest Empires in history. Behind an unscrupulous use of slogans like 'peace', 'democracy', and 'freedom', Russia concealed a totally different intention.

The critical year was 1948, and we may say that in that year the cold war became a reality. In February 1948 a *coup d'état* took place in Czechoslovakia, and the country was successfully swallowed by the Russian-dominated bloc. The great statesmen Benes and Jan Masaryk, who were among the staunchest supporters of the idea of government by discussion and personal freedom, were among those who fell. Masaryk is said to have committed suicide, but evidence is lacking. Benes was already at the end of his tether. Both had realized that the end was near and that political freedom was to disappear from Czechoslovakia. This coup came as a shattering blow to the outside world, although they had not been altogether unaware of the possibility of its happening. Masaryk had warned Trygve Lie in Moscow earlier the same year. Within a few weeks Marshal Tito, the dictator of Yugoslavia, doubtless sensing that he might be next on the list for Soviet attention, disclaimed all allegiance to the Cominform. Brought up politically as a protégé of the Kremlin he knew the motives and techniques of the Communist authorities and judged that the moment was ripe for revolt or give the slip if he intended to keep any show of independence for his country.

He did not disavow his faith in Communist doctrines, nor did he promptly desire any alliance with the Western powers, but he did make clear that his break in relations with all Russian dominated states was complete (at least for the time being) and that he intended to hold an independent position between the Western powers and Russia. Almost before the world had had time to recover from these two shocks in Czechoslovakia and Yugoslavia, a third conflict awoke the world to the seriousness of the situation. The Russians made an attempt to cut off Berlin from the western occupation zones by imposing impossible restrictions on travel by road, rail, or water. It was hoped in this way to squeeze out the British, American and French forces from their zones within the city. Millions of Berliners were faced with the possibility of starvation, lack of fuel and bankruptcy, and the Russians expected that they would soon be forced to yield by the need for food from the eastern zone. That this did not happen was due to the remarkable efficiency of an air-lift, which operated for more than ten months and kept life and commerce going in Berlin throughout that period. Providentially, the three big aerodromes of Berlin were in the British, French, and American zones respectively. To these aerodromes aeroplanes flew continuously 'like beads on a string', carrying stupendous quantities of food and fuel. It was not till the early summer of 1949 that the Russian authorities were forced to admit to themselves that the attempt to squeeze Berlin from the west had been an utter failure. The prestige of the West was enhanced and the confidence of Germans in the West redoubled.

It may seem strange to dwell so much on events in Central Europe which, on the face of it, can have little connection with the story of the rise of nations in Asia. But only in this way can we see clearly how diametrically opposed in principle and objective

were East and West, and only in this way can we also see how an
event in one part of the world was inextricably bound up with
things that were happening many thousands of miles away elsewhere. At a time when British, French, and American forces were
being pinned down in Germany on guard and in readiness, great
Communist moves were taking place in eastern Asia. At a time
when political attention was deliberately being concentrated in
Central Europe, moves were being planned to take place in remote
parts of the East and statesmen were beginning to realize how
completely world-wide was the new strategy of the Communist
front. It will be well at this stage to try to see what evidence there
is for this statement.

4. THE NEW TECHNIQUES AND THE IDEOLOGICAL BATTLE

It is difficult to discover whether between 1945 and 1947 there
was much official or concerted Communist support from Russia
for many of the local Communist movements which were stirring
throughout Eastern and South-East Asia. On the whole there is
little evidence of any such support. The impression is gathered
that Russia, being occupied with her own recovery at home and
the situation in Eastern Europe, and in the light of increasing international tension at the United Nations level, was really waiting to
see what internal life and energy each of the separate Communist
movements possessed, and how far they might be able to make
headway against the European empires which they were struggling
to dispossess.

But a change came in the autumn of 1947. A speech by Zhdanov
at the opening conference of the Cominform made it clear that
Russia was deeply interested in the National Liberation movements throughout Asia. By the middle of 1948 insurrections had
broken out in Burma and Malaya. In the former a 'liberated area'
was established and survived for the time, but the rising in Malaya
failed, although it left a legacy of terrorism which ran the length
of the country. Indonesia also felt the full impact of Communist
agitation, though this failed to come to a head in the way it wished.

In June 1949 Zhukov issued a statement which quite definitely
encouraged these revolutions and civil wars and hinted at Soviet
support. He gave three reasons. First, the threat of increasing

aggressiveness on the part of the United States. This shows clearly that Russia was alarmed at the way in which the United States maintained her vigilance throughout the Western Pacific. Secondly, Zhukov drew attention to the success of the People's Democracies both in China and North Korea, hinting that similar democracies might soon be established throughout the Far East. And thirdly, he gave a warning to the liberation movements not to trust the kind of bourgeois nationalism on show in India. This was a measure of Russian distrust at that time of Nehru, whose gratitude for independence was thought to have rendered him the tool of Britain.

In November 1949 a conference of the World Federation of Trade Unions took place in Peking, and there are many signs that this conference set up an organization which was to become responsible for the co-ordination of Communist movements in Eastern Asia. One thing is certain. Russia was brilliantly successful in inducing other Asian countries to fight for the cause of Communism in district after district, while all the time giving the impression that Russia herself was quite outside the conflict and even disinterested.

On 1 October 1949 China proper became a People's Republic. It is not in the least surprising that Russia gave her full political recognition immediately. Nor is it altogether surprising that the very next month Peking was chosen as a centre from which the co-ordination of the liberation movements might be controlled. Chiang Kai-shek had by now moved his headquarters from Chungking to Formosa, and the so-called bamboo curtain had fallen between the two parts of China. Mao Tse-tung visited Moscow in 1950, and on 14 February 1950 the Soviet-Chinese pact was signed to run for thirty years. Together these two countries were formidable. Populations of something approaching 800 million people were now linked by treaty and friendship. Russia's interests in the South Manchuria Railway and the naval base at Port Arthur were to be transferred from Russian control to China, and it is not without significance that Russia insisted on compensation being paid to her for all the money that she had expended on this base in the five years since the end of the war. Meanwhile Mao Tse-tung persuaded Russia to increase the grant-in-aid of 300 million dollars which had already been promised to China.

The Clash of Empires and Ideas

In the face of all that had happened in Central Europe twelve countries decided, on the strength of Article 51 of the United Nations Charter, which allows for collective self-defence, to form a regional pact by which they undertook to come to each other's assistance in the event of aggression. This North Atlantic Pact was signed on 4 April 1949 by Belgium, Canada, Denmark, France, Iceland, Italy, Luxemburg, the Netherlands, Norway, Portugal, the United Kingdom and the United States. It was to run for a period of twenty years and to be reviewed after the first ten years. If any of the twelve countries was attacked that attack was to be regarded as a threat to all the signatory countries. Greece, Turkey, and Western Germany later joined the North Atlantic Treaty Organization.

Just when the Western Powers were thinking that they had built up some political and military strength in the West to deter Russia from further intimidation or advance in Europe, war broke out in Korea between the North and the South on 25 June 1950. All attention now switched hurriedly to the East. Russia had recognized the sovereignty of Northern Korea as early as 12 October 1948, and had effectively sealed it off as a Communist state. It held a population of approximately eight million, was a very rich agricultural area and was more industrialized than the south. Russian military officers and advisers had trained its army and given it equipment. Northern Korea, therefore, was unquestionably within the Russian sphere of influence and Communist dominated. Such responsible Russian representatives as Malik and Gromyko later declared that the conflict in Korea was nothing more than a civil war and proceeded to blame the Americans for interfering in it and dragging in others. But the forces of Northern Korea, which swept over the 38th parallel, were so well prepared and successful that they very nearly smothered all resistance and pushed all opposition into the most southerly corner of the peninsula. They nearly won the war in a matter of weeks, having taken Southern Korea almost by surprise. The war in Korea was obviously another instance of the complete deadlock that existed between East and West. An ideological battle was involved in the purely military. Was it to be another Manchuria, as in 1931, the first of a succession of wars? Could it be quickly concluded or satisfactorily contained, or would it be the means whereby North

Korea, subsequently helped by Communist China, and undoubtedly encouraged by Russia, might be in a position to lock up in this corner of the Far East a vast military potential of American and Western European forces? It certainly did that.

Russia constantly denied any participation in the war, or support of it, and on the face of it seemed to be keeping clear, but there is ample evidence that she well knew when it was to happen and had indeed supported its preparation.

In September 1951, the United States, Australia and New Zealand concluded the Pacific Pact, sometimes known as the ANZUS Pact, and on 9 September 1951 the United States concluded a security treaty with Japan. But in spite of these regional defence organizations the Liberation movements in South-East Asia indicated that Communism was on the way to establishing itself elsewhere unless immediate steps were taken to meet the situation. Two steps were, therefore, taken—one economic and one military.

By the Colombo Plan economic aid was to be given at once to undeveloped areas in order to strengthen their economic life and raise the standard of living, in the hope that it would ward off the spread of Communism. Then in September 1954 the South-East Asia Defence Organization was created, which was designed to do for Asia what the North Atlantic Treaty Organization was doing for Europe. Inevitably the Russians interpreted this as the next stage in an act of encirclement, but the countries concerned were simply committed to help each other in the event of any attack on one of the parties involved. The membership was composed of the United States, Australia, New Zealand, Siam, the United Kingdom, France, Pakistan, the Philippines and a protocol which covered South Vietnam, Laos, and Cambodia. In this way the Western powers continued the process of hedging themselves round with military alliances designed for self-defence.

Meanwhile in August 1954 Yugoslavia, Greece, and Turkey had signed a Balkan Pact by which the two European countries were linked for self-defence with one Asian country, and this was soon followed by the Baghdad Pact (February 1955) by which Iraq and Turkey were joined in mutual defence and co-operation. Pakistan joined the Baghdad Pact in September 1955 and Persia in November. Pakistan became the link that connected the South-

East Asia Defence System with the Baghdad Powers, and through Turkey the Baghdad Pact found alliance with N.A.T.O. To Russia this was a gigantic encirclement. Meanwhile the Communist countries replied with the Warsaw Pact, a defence consolidation of Eastern Europe.

In many ways these military and diplomatic alignments achieved little in solving any basic problems. They merely served as a means of deterring threats of war in the first instance, though in fact they tended only to provoke more aggravation and hostility than allay apprehension. It was a reversion to old time Power politics and diplomacy with little acceptance of the view that the world is now so completely inter-related and interlocked economically and geographically that the days of even regional organization and self-interest are well-nigh over.

We must now turn to the post-war developments in Asia, dealing with them area by area. We begin with the Middle East.

IX

THE STRUGGLE IN THE MIDDLE EAST

In one way and another the Middle East is a concern to everyone—Jew, Christian, Moslem, traders, travellers, and industrialists, of whatever political creed or fancy, and all the interests involved are constantly in the melting-pot. The same area that has been in turn the cradle of civilization, the home of prophets, the lure of crusaders, and the cockpit of nations, is again fashioning a new social, political, and economic pattern. For the outsider the Middle East must always be an international cross-roads, and the chief concern is to maintain the simple right of transit, either as pilgrims to the Holy places, as passengers through the Suez Canal, or as travellers by air.

For many who live in the Middle East the main problem has been to build up some adequate political strength which can take the place of the authority that once reigned from Constantinople, but which has been silent ever since the abolition of the Sultanate and Caliphate. For others the Middle East today signifies the fulfilment of a time-honoured hope—the return of the Jews to Palestine. For countless multitudes the Middle East is significant for its oil; and this results in a fabulous financial boom for the Middle East countries lucky enough to produce it, and a vital dependence of all countries that required it for everyday life.

The first stage in the recent progress of reconstruction was the overthrow of the Ottomans and the interim period of subdivision, mandate rule and tutelage. The second stage began to take shape during the Second World War as nationalisms became more and more articulate and the need for a new regional grouping began to challenge the old. A more involved and complicated situation it is difficult to imagine.

The Struggle in the Middle East

The influx of foreign troops throughout the Middle East during the Second World War gave rise to an increasingly acute sense of nationalism in country after country. While the war was in operation it served the Middle East states best on the whole to accept the obligations that were demanded and to suffer patiently all temporary limitation of sovereign independence. Minor campaigns in Iraq and Syria in 1941 were a token of Western control, in the endeavour to maintain a condition of stability, without which the Middle East could not serve its purpose as a barrier to Nazi and Fascist designs in the East. But once the immediate dangers of German and Italian victory were removed the Arab states drew together in a great alliance—the Arab League.

Following a preliminary meeting in Alexandria this League was established in March 1945 at Bludan in Syria and was composed of the five kingdoms of Egypt, Saudi Arabia, Iraq, Trans-Jordan, and the Yemen and the two republics of Syria and the Lebanon. Eight years later, in March 1953, they were joined by the new kingdom of Libya. The Sudan was admitted to membership in January 1956.

The Arab League arose out of the natural aspirations of millions of people who share a common language and a common religion. Certainly, political idealists hoped that a new Mohammedan state or empire might arise which would dominate the situation in the Middle East and in Western Asia and which would justly claim the place vacated by the defunct Ottoman Empire. The Peace Conference at Versailles in 1919 had decreed that Britain and France should share between them the major political influence in the Levant and Middle East. France's authority had survived for about twenty years; Britain's lasted nearer thirty, but both reaped local resentment and served in the end to stimulate the wave of Arab nationalism upon which the Arab League was launched.

The other main stimulus to Arab nationalism was, of course, the sweeping return of Jewry. What then was to be the shape of the new Arab unity? What was to be its form, its centre, its authority, its weight? All were agreed as to its necessity, but few could agree as to its pattern or structure. Even at the outset, as early as the Alexandria conference, it was clear that there would be many internal differences. The fact that Arab states were neighbours did not in itself constitute automatic unity. The positive assets of common inheritance merely gave a start to the negotiations. There were at least three potential rivals for leadership—Egypt, the Hashemite family (Trans-Jordan and Iraq), and Saudi Arabia—and between these three there was little love lost.

Egypt claimed to be the most developed nation and thus held a right to lead the others. The King, Farouk, who fancied himself as a leader, had already made a bid to restore the Caliphate, and was encouraged by ample anti-British feeling to want to eclipse British authority in the Middle East. Egypt had other strong claims to leadership. Her size in population, in wealth, in volume of trade and experience in modern politics, all marked her out as a candidate for the role of leader. The Suez Canal alone put her in the world of international affairs and strengthened her hand. But even with all these qualifications Egypt had her rivals.

Ibn Saud, King of Saudi Arabia, was prepared to play second fiddle to no one. A proud and autocratic monarch, he was the leader of the Wahabis, a most powerful tribe in the Arabian peninsula. He had driven out his great rivals, the Hashemite family, and had taken from their control the sacred centres of Mohammedan allegiance, Mecca and Medina. If religion was to be the basis of the new-found Arab unity, then clearly Mecca had to be at the centre and spiritual authority would best radiate from a re-established Caliphate there. The centre of pilgrimage could claim to be the centre of Arabism; the home of the Prophet might well be a capital. But there were grave disadvantages. To the outside world Mecca meant little, except to the followers of the Prophet. It was off the beaten track and closed in any case to all non-Moslems. Furthermore, not all Arabs were devout Mohammedans and the more secular-minded much preferred the idea of a modern metropolis like Cairo as the future capital of the new Arab unity.

Thirdly, there was the Hashemite family to be reckoned with. The head of this family had been Sheriff of Mecca (till rusticated by Ibn Saud). His sons, Abdullah and Feisal, had become rulers of Trans-Jordan and Iraq—first as Emirs, then as Kings. Abdullah had dreamt of expansion and empire, a kingdom which might include Jordan, Syria and Iraq—a revival of the concept of the Fertile Crescent.

Meanwhile Iraq had begun to develop out of all recognition politically and productively. The oil found at Kirkuk in 1927 brought in untold wealth and gave a new impetus and importance to the Middle East area. Had the idea of the Fertile Crescent, the Greater Syria of Abdullah's dreams, ever materialized, there is no telling what the political consequences might have been.

In addition to the potential rivalry in leadership there were other dissident notes and undertones. Arabs in Asia were on the whole unwilling to allow too much political initiative and power to swing over to Egypt. In any case the more intelligent and cultured Arabs of Palestine, Syria, and the Lebanon tended to regard the average Egyptian as racially different and inferior and intellectually backward.

Then again there was the question of minorities—the many Christian communities—especially in Palestine and the Lebanon, and, far more disturbing to the Arabs, the steady infiltration of Jews into the Middle East. Here we come to the heart of the matter. The factor that really gave common cause for joint concern and action was that most Arabs regarded the prospect of Jews returning to Palestine in quantity with alarm, and the rate at which they were settling betokened the formation of a state. Zionism stood for nothing less than the right of every Jew to return to Palestine, and this involved a direct challenge to the Arabs in that country. The Alexandria Conference of 1944 tacitly concluded that any idea of a single political orientation of Arab states was out of the question. Far too many differences of outlook stood in the way. The Alexandria protocol, therefore, put forward the idea of a League which would bind together a group of independent sovereign states with the basic aim of mutual co-operation. It was to have a permanent secretariat and a Secretary-General, and its seat was to be in Cairo.

This was agreed upon at Bludan in March 1945. Bit by bit the League set to work to co-ordinate a political programme and to bring about a whole series of agreements between the neighbouring Arab states on all matters touching defence, communications, customs, criminal and commercial law, and higher studies. There

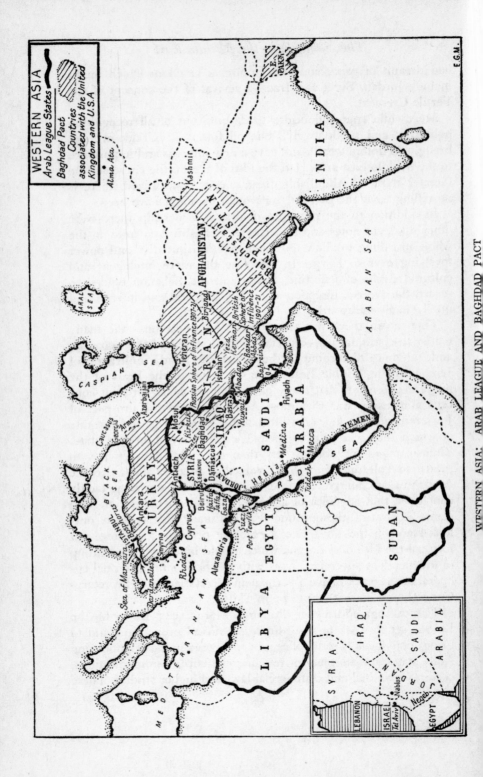

WESTERN ASIA: ARAB LEAGUE AND BAGHDAD PACT

WESTERN ASIA
Arab League States
Baghdad Pact
Countries
associated with the United
Kingdom and U.S.A

were distinct signs that Egyptian influence wished to dominate the League.

Soon after the fall of King Farouk in 1952 a new Secretary-General was elected to the Arab League, Abdul Khaliq Hassouna, a former Egyptian Minister for Foreign Affairs. Egypt struggled hard to keep the initiative in leadership in the Middle East from the Second World War onwards—under the ambitious Farouk, the moderate revolutionary Neguib and the astute Nasser.

2. THE NORTHERN TIER

But there was a group of states whose sympathies and affiliations could not be expected to fall into place within the Arab League or any purely pan-Arab conception. These were Turkey, Iraq, Persia, and Afghanistan. They all have this in common, that they lie as buffer states between Great Powers and thereby thwart expansion from each direction. Russia had for long been determined to break south into the warmer climes of the Mediterranean or the Persian Gulf. Germany had had hopes of penetrating through Turkey and even as far as the Persian Gulf. Britain had had a decidedly mixed relationship with all these countries.

The external dangers to these four states have been continuous and, therefore, it served their purposes well in 1937 to sign a non-aggression pact known as the Eastern or Saadabad Pact. Each country stood to gain, confident in the knowledge that none would be attacked by any within the alliance, but how did each country stand internally? Were there any weak links in this chain of friendship and how solid a political buttress was it between Europe and Asia or between the Communist North and the Arab South? Let us take each country in turn.

Turkey

Turkey had been remodelled by Kemal Ataturk, but her real strength had yet to be tested. So many reforms had been carried through with such thoroughness and in so short a time that no one could yet tell how far public opinion had supported the change-over to a new and Western way of life. Change had swept the country. Turkey had a new capital, Ankara; a dictator had ruled in the name of democracy, a contradiction in terms, and had decided at every turn what the will of the people should be. Members of the former Royal Family had been exiled. The Caliphate had been abolished. The Latin alphabet had been introduced, Turkish was encouraged, Arabic discouraged. The old traditional titles of courtesy, respect and office had been abolished and every family had had to adopt a family name of its own—a surname. Even the headgear of the nation had been officially and compulsorily altered.

Each and every change had been accompanied by uneasiness, some alarm and even revolt. The period of change had not been an easy passage by any means. Women had been given the vote, a revolutionary concept in the Middle East, and state ownership and control of many industries and public services on a Western pattern had become the accepted thing. The nation needed time to digest this new diet of change before it could be pressed to take more.

But fortunately the sense of national pride had also been greatly strengthened by a series of successes in foreign affairs. The Greeks had been expelled from Asia Minor to the great satisfaction of the new rule. The Italians, close as they were on the Island of Rhodes and in the Dodecanese, were Empire building for the moment in North Africa and later in Albania and Abyssinia. A treaty of non-aggression had been signed with Russia in December 1925, and soon after the outbreak of the Second World War in 1939 Britain and France together had signed a treaty of alliance with Turkey.

Turkey seemed secure behind her system of agreements and alliances. It is worth noting that the Saadabad Pact was signed in 1937, at a time when the forces of Fascism and Nazism were stronger than ever before. During the brief lull before the storm burst, Turkey began to look eastwards for friends from whom she could expect no danger.

A token of the new trust reposed in Turkey was the Montreux Agreement of 1936. By this new Straits Convention Turkey was allowed to re-militarize the zone of the Straits and the international commission came to an end. This was proof that Turkey was strong, stable and trustworthy in the eyes of the world. Kemal Ataturk died in 1938, but he had lived long enough to see the new republic through its first fifteen years of life.

The Struggle in the Middle East

Throughout the Second World War Turkey remained neutral. Some of the more influential politicians in Turkey sympathized with the Western European Powers, but they realized that public opinion in general was at least as much in sympathy with Germany as with the non-Axis world. Neutrality seemed to be the only solution and both belligerent sides were glad to have a neutral buffer state. Spies, literature and propaganda had a way to and fro, rather the same as Norway had provided in the First World War. It is typical of her plight than many young Turkish pilots were taught how to fly in Britain at the R.A.F. College at Cranwell, and then went back to Turkey to fly German aeroplanes. Both sides were doing their best for Turkey!

The real surprise came as the Second World War drew to a close. In March 1945 the Soviet Government declined to renew her treaty with Turkey as from the following November and made no attempt to draw up a new one. Once again Turkey feared the possibility of trouble from the north. The Eastern or Saadabad Pact, therefore, took on a fresh importance.

Iraq

Iraq, adjacent to Turkey, had been lopped off the old Ottoman Empire in the course of the First World War. For some time it had been doubtful to whom it should go, until the Peace Conference at Versailles decided that it should become a mandated territory under the supervision of Britain.

Meanwhile the British had decided to raise an Arab to power in Iraq and Feisal was the man of their choice. The Emir Feisal, son of Hussein, the Sheriff of Mecca, and brother of the Emir Abdullah of Trans-Jordan, had earlier made a bid for power in Syria, but Syria had been handed over to French administration in 1920 by the decision of Versailles. In a plebiscite Feisal gained 96 per cent. of the votes, with the result that the British High Commissioner in August 1921 proclaimed Feisal King of Iraq. The discovery of oil in 1927 began to bring in the wealth which the country needed. By 1932 the country showed sufficient political stability for the British to surrender the mandate and withdraw. Thus did Iraq become a sovereign independent kingdom, largely created by British encouragement and tutelage. In this way one branch of the Hashemite family acquired a kingdom and found some compensation for being driven out of Arabia. Of purer stock than the family of Ibn Saud, who had driven them out, the Hashemites could look upon the Iraqi kingdom as the reward of a just Providence.

In July 1937 Iraq was one of the four signatories of the Saadabad non-aggression Pact, linking herself defensively with Turkey, Persia and Afghanistan. Meanwhile the development of the oil industry eclipsed everything else. Pipe-lines carried the oil across hundreds of miles of desert to the Mediterranean coast at Banias in Syria and Haifa in Palestine. Vast royalties flowed into the Iraq Government and schemes were considered for improving the standard of living in the country.

Kirkuk, Mosul, Baghdad, and Basra became centres of world-wide interest and importance, and Iraq a country of political significance. As a new-born kingdom Iraq was ripe for development. Western Europe needed her oil and vied for the privilege of extracting it. The Iraq Petroleum Company kept an even balance between British, Dutch, American, and French interests. (Each country was allotted 23¾ per cent. of the annual output and the remaining 5 per cent. went to the Armenian magnate Gulbenkian.) In the modern age oil was absolutely vital and Iraq was lucky to have it.

A by-product of this commercial exchange was that Iraq was financially tied up with Europe and America and was, therefore, influenced by the ideas that came from these countries. She was progressive in official outlook, willing to trade, uninhibited and potentially wealthy. This progressive outlook was contrary to what one might have expected, for in the old order rule was despotic, and exploitation and self-interest were the usual concomitants of authority, especially among backward peoples.

Iraq was successful in fighting these dangers. When the Second World War broke out certain elements in Iraq endeavoured to ally themselves with Nazi Germany, feeling certain that Hitler would triumph in the end. His initial success in conquering Poland, smothering Denmark and Norway and his lightning capture of Holland and Belgium suggested military invincibility, but the revolution in Iraq was quickly squashed. It lasted throughout the month of May 1941, and was the signal for a similar revolt in Syria, though in the latter case the main object was to rid Syria of French control once and for all. In both instances British forces were used to restore order and stability and the military movements were directed from operational headquarters in Cairo.

As the war drew to a close Iraq quite naturally joined the Arab League and also became a member of the United Nations. In January 1948 she also confirmed her friendship with Britain by signing a twenty-year treaty of alliance and mutual assistance. In the aftermath of war Iraq found herself placed in an extraordinarily awkward position. Her politics depended upon her geography and her geographical location was embarrassingly near a multitude of warring factions. Her neighbours to the north-west, south, and west spoke Arabic, so they had language and literature in common. Her one and only neighbour in the east, Persia, had a different language. Nevertheless Persia was also predominantly Moslem, so the religious link cancelled out the linguistic difference. Iraq was committed to her alliance with Britain at a time when most of her neighbours were challenging and rejecting every semblance of dependence upon Europe.

Iraq was ready to be loyal to the ideals of Arab co-operation within the Arab League, but was wary of political twists some of which she found distasteful and mistrusted. A constitutional monarchy like Iraq might well be shocked at an Egypt which could exile a king and then put its hero revolutionary under house arrest within two years. More and more did her natural alignment seem to be with the Saadabad powers—her neighbours Turkey and Persia—an alliance which later grew into the Baghdad Pact.

Persia (Iran)

Persia is another country whose politics are largely governed by her geographical position—the perennial test imposed on all countries by nature. She is an ancient kingdom with a proud people and an independent tradition. Her large land mass occupies all the area between the Caspian Sea and the Persian Gulf, mountainous, rich in oil and capable of tremendous development. During the last century when France and Britain were extending their political authority into so many parts of Asia and the Middle East, Persia was one of the areas which was relatively free from outside interference, though never for long out of the political scene. Nor was she entirely free from pressure from Russia in the north. It is partly because there were so many rival interests that (somewhat like Switzerland and Siam) she was comparatively unmolested and it suited other countries to know that Persia was independent, vassal to no one.

Culturally she came within the Middle East area because her people were mostly Moslem and the system of life and thought was Islamic. Racially and linguistically, however, Persia was distinct from the Arab races that lay to her west and south. For this reason she had no claim to membership of the Arab League, which came into being in 1945, and she continued to find her natural affiliation with the Saadabad (or Eastern) Pact nations. She certainly had no desire to be swallowed up by anyone. But even mountains, desert, seclusion and autocracy could not prevent Persia feeling the fresh breeze of democracy. In 1906 (the same year in which the Duma met in Russia) the Shah agreed to the establishment of a National Assembly, or Majlis, and a new constitution.

This spelt the end of absolute rule and was in tune with the times. It offset for the time being the danger of revolt and revolution there had been in Constantinople in 1908, and in the whole of China in 1911. Persia was giving way to new ideas. Britain was always apprehensive that Russia would penetrate through Persia and endanger her position in India, and Russia was equally anxious that Persia should not be dominated by Britain. Britain and Russia, therefore, made their peace with each other as regards their respective attitude towards Persia by their agreement in 1907 (the Anglo-Russian Convention). The whole of the northern part of Persia, nearly half the country, was recognized as a Russian sphere of influence from 1907 to 1921 and approximately one-third of Persia bordering on India was recognized as the British sphere of influence, between the same dates.

Meanwhile there came a revolution of another sort—the discovery of oil at Masjid-i-Sulaiman in Persia in 1908. Though the start was small the repercussions were devastating. The new age of motors and mechanization, with its fantastic increase in each succeeding decade, beginning in the West and spreading throughout the world, drew the commercial and industrial attention of the more developed countries towards Persia and the Middle East. Oil in the next fifty years came to mean what gold and diamonds had meant in the previous fifty years. Abadan became the new Klondike, Kalgoorlie, or Kimberley. In respect of oil Persia was the pioneer. It was some years before oil was discovered in Iraq (1927), Bahrein (1932), Saudi Arabia (1936), Egypt (1938), and Kuwait (1938).

When Persia joined the Saadabad Pact in 1937 she was the largest oil producing country in the Middle East, a lead which she maintained until 1950, when a mis-controlled nationalist movement lost her her world market and temporarily disrupted her economy. The blame for this attached to the Prime Minister Moussadek. His determination to nationalize the oil industry in Persia appealed to large sections of his fellow countrymen who were ready to believe that they could operate the oil wells for themselves and thus reap the full benefit of its export. The outcome was disastrous. Persia had not the technical skill to carry out the work. The oil industry slumped calamitously. The goodwill of many countries was forfeited and Moussadek's plans for many reforms fell with him.

By 1954, when an international consortium was appointed to set Persian oil flowing again, Kuwait, Saudi Arabia, and Iraq had capitalized the opportunity and stolen the markets. British interests which had suffered severely in Persia found outlets for producing oil elsewhere in the Persian Gulf, and the United States consolidated her oil concessions in Saudi Arabia.

The general principle written into the oil agreements had been that 50 per cent. of all profits belonged to the Companies concerned and the other 50 per cent. went to the Governments of the countries in which the oil was engineered. Thus the natural resources of the Middle East had brought fabulous profits equally to both sides, but political interests were always liable to disrupt the commercial balance.

Throughout the later nineteenth century Russia had her eyes on Persia, and in 1918 the Soviet Government had gone so far as to declare that Persia must be captured. Persia well knew that the danger from the north was never far removed. In 1914 the Tudeh Party was formed, the policy of which was Communist, and in 1945 a 'democratic' party appeared in Persian Azerbaijan, and there was a tentative threat of a Communist enclave rooting itself in Persian territory.

Meanwhile in January 1942 a treaty of alliance was signed in

Teheran between Persia, Soviet Russia and Great Britain, by which the territorial sovereignty and political independence of Persia were to be respected. Russia had already concluded a treaty with Persia as far back as February 1921, and was to join with Great Britain and the United States in yet another declaration of good-will at the Teheran Conference in December 1943.

As already stated in an earlier chapter, suspicion of Russia rapidly increased in 1945 and 1946 when Russia, having under-taken to withdraw all troops from Persia within six months of the end of hostilities, neglected to remove them. Persia had to protest vigorously through the United Nations before Russia took the trouble to honour her pledges.

Later an attempt was made on the life of the Shah, Muhammed Riza Pahlavi (b. 1919, suc. 1941), and the responsibility for this was thought to be Communist inspired. In February 1949 the Tudeh Party was dissolved. The Shah himself had set a fine example in dividing up some of his own estates and giving them to the farming community and hoped that other great Persian landowners would follow his example. The official attitude was enlightened and progressive but Persia as a country was poised precariously in the diplomatic world.

In August 1953 Moussadek tried to maintain himself in power politically, and rally the nation around himself, by means of a referendum. His aim was to dissolve the Majlis, and whittle away the authority of the Shah. For a moment everything was in tur-moil. But prompt action by General Fazlollah Zahedi and loyal elements in the army saved the situation, and Moussadek was arrested, tried, and disgraced. Zahedi became Prime Minister, order was restored in the country, and diplomatic relations with Great Britain, which had been broken, were restored. The Inter-national Consortium acknowledged that the oil industry should remain nationalized, but Persia took over two small refineries, paid considerable compensation to the Anglo-Iranian Oil Company, and was apportioned two seats on a board of seven directors in the two companies which were to operate the oil industry. In return, the Consortium was to be entitled to buy up all the oil it required from the Persian owners. Both sides were satisfied. But the example which Persia had set in nationalizing a hitherto Western-controlled company was quickly noted by other Middle East countries.

The Struggle in the Middle East

Afghanistan

The fourth member of the Saadabad or Eastern Pact (1937) was Afghanistan. As with Turkey, Iraq, and Persia, the country was predominantly Moslem. The two main languages are Persian and Pushtu. Once again the geography of the country tended to direct its politics. British interests in India required that Afghanistan be either friendly or co-operative, or neutral, but if possible not hostile. This was sometimes a forlorn hope. Twice in the nineteenth century Britain had sent military expeditions into the country. In general Britain was content to ensure that no sudden attack was launched upon India from that direction and the North-West Frontier became traditionally one of the most carefully guarded frontiers in Asia—one of the garrison commitments of the British-officered Indian Army.

The country itself, partly secure behind mountain ranges, was undeveloped, lacked railways and had little contact with the outside world. It was not in the main stream of current events as Turkey frequently was. Nor had she oil to offer as Iraq and Persia had, but her position in Asia, poised between Russia, the Arab world and India, gave her a strategic importance which the other countries recognized and respected.

There were obviously strong reasons for Afghanistan to ally herself with suitable neighbours and in this quest the one natural direction was along the line of the Islamic countries to the west. A line from the Khyber to the Dardanelles may sound a trifle incongruous, but in 1937 there was almost no alternative. To the north was the momentum of a new political theory and economic change which ran counter to all that Afghanistan stood for. To the east were the Himalayas and Thibet. To the south-east were the embers of mistrust and animosity in British-controlled India. Only from the neighbours in the west, with certain cultural affinities, could there be useful association. These countries stood as a possible bulwark or buttress against the encroachments of Communism, which by its avowed atheism and anti-God movement was an offence to the religious instinct of the Mohammedan world, even to the somewhat secular modern Turkey.

Years later these countries came to be called collectively the Northern Tier—a rough and ready line from the Black Sea to the

Indian Ocean. But even this convenient description did not for long reflect the political stability or alignment of the area. The Arab League in 1945 reflected a new centre of gravity pivoting nearer the Eastern Mediterranean. Of the four Saadabad Powers only Iraq was a member, but the newly formed Arab League was something in the nature of a rival organization in some respects. The Arab League was an attempt to give political cohesion to a complicated set of forces—anti-Jew, anti-British, and anti-Communist. Its initial positive impetus rested largely on negative impulses, but not all of these impulses were shared in anything like the same measure by all the parties concerned. Turkey, Persia, and Afghanistan, for all their allegiance to the Koran, were not members of the Arab League. Islam had no overall political embrace. The dream of a unified Arab empire or federation in the Middle East was proving elusive and ethereal.

3. THE FATE OF PALESTINE

We must now turn our attention to the situation in Palestine as the Second World War came to an end in 1945. Britain had no desire to continue to govern the country under mandated authority as things were, but what was to be the alternative? Would the newly formed Arab League have sufficient political strength to bring about an Arab domination in the area and curtail Jewish infiltration, or would the Jews struggle to transform their footing in Palestine into a young nation?

The problem was a desperate one and no solution was either simple or acceptable. As long as Britain was responsible for the maintenance of peace and order she had the unenviable task of preventing both Jews and Arabs from carrying out their rival policies. Jews were pouring into the country in thousands and the tide had to be restricted and controlled. Limitation of entry only infuriated the Jews. Many of them as they arrived at Haifa were diverted to temporary encampments in Cyprus in order not to violate the monthly immigration schedule. Zionism, the return of the Jews to Palestine, reached fever pitch. Extremist groups like Irgun and the Stern gang threatened all manner of terrorist reprisals against British continuance in Palestine and British attempts to limit and restrain their activities. Sabotage, sniping and kidnapping were part and parcel of the move to disrupt normal life, intimidate the Arabs and lever out the British. It was obviously the prelude to a permanent settlement or even a military trial of strength if need be.

In view of all this the Arabs in Palestine and in the neighbouring countries began to prepare for the worst. Britain was in an extraordinarily awkward position. She had obligations to both sides. She had never promised the Jews more than a National Home, and this was naturally something less than a nation or state and, therefore, less than would satisfy the Jews. Furthermore, the rapidity and volume of Jewish settlement outstripped anything Britain had envisaged. On the other hand Britain had a set of understandings with the Arabs from the time of the MacMahon Correspondence onwards. With demobilization at home and garrison commitments in many parts of the world she was in no position to deal with the far-reaching and vexatious problem of Palestine.

Britain declared her wish to surrender the mandate. The problem passed to U.N.O. and became critical in 1947. The whole region of the eastern Mediterranean was volcanic. Turkey was undergoing a war of nerves at the hands of Russia. Greece was on the verge of internal collapse. Palestine was heading for war. The Secretary-General of U.N.O. (Trygvie Lie) did his utmost to bring into being a Guard Force such as was authorized by Article 43 of the United Nations Charter, which might act as an international police watch. It was a gallant attempt at a solution and was discussed by the military staff committees, but caution, timidity and preoccupation with the business of national reconstruction in the countries concerned talked the matter out until it was too late to take effect.

In desperation Greece asked the United States for help, which President Truman immediately agreed to provide, military and economic aid to Greece and Turkey. But this did not apply to Palestine, where the United States, like Britain, had sympathies with both sides. In April 1947 the United Nations set up a special committee on Palestine (U.N.S.C.O.P.) with a membership of 11 countries: Australia, Canada, Czechoslovakia, Guatemala, India, Persia, the Netherlands, Peru, Sweden, Uruguay, and Yugoslavia. This committee made three recommendations:

(*a*) Partition (7 to 3, with one abstention)

(*b*) A transition period under United Nations auspices
(*c*) Safeguards for the Holy places

The principle of partition had been frequently put forward before, notably by the Peel Commission in 1937, which allowed room for an estimated Jewish population of 2 million in the years to come. In 1947 the recommendation of partition was supported by the United States, Soviet Russia, all Europe and the British Commonwealth, in fact everyone except the Moslem countries.

On 29 November 1947 the principle was endorsed by the General Assembly of the United Nations by thirty-three votes to thirteen, with ten abstentions. Six Moslem states walked out—Syria, Lebanon, Iraq, Saudi Arabia, the Yemen, and Egypt.

The next operation was delicate in the extreme, the work of transferring political authority from Britain to the two new Governments which would take over. This responsibility was put into the hands of a United Nations commission composed of Bolivia, Czechoslovakia, Denmark, Panama, and the Philippines. It was hoped that the Commission would be able to transfer authority bit by bit, but two insuperable difficulties arose. The Arabs refused to recognize any right of the Jews to territorial or governmental sovereignty and, therefore, declined to co-operate. In addition to this Britain saw grave problems upsetting any gradual transfer and decided to fix a date on which she would relinquish all control. This announcement precipitated events one step nearer war, but it is doubtful if anything short of an international police or military force could have prevented an outbreak of war in any case.

On 15 May 1948 British authority was surrendered. The Jews immediately proclaimed the establishment of a State of Israel and the neighbouring Arab states invaded the new Israel. The vital need was to nip the war in the bud and to prevent it spreading or becoming a protracted campaign. It was also important to reassert the principle of arbitration and the authority of U.N.O. To this end Count Bernadotte of Sweden was asked to act as official (U.N.) mediator, and within a few weeks had arranged a cease-fire.

The Egyptian Army had penetrated well into Palestine and captured Gaza. Arab forces still held the centre of Palestine, but the Jews, to many people's surprise, held to the modern suburbs of Jerusalem, most of the coastline, together with the cities of Tel Aviv and Haifa, and the district of Galilee.

On 9 July the Arabs attacked again and a second cease-fire had to be arranged. Tempers were running high. On 17 September Jewish terrorists in Jerusalem assassinated both Count Bernadotte and his adviser, Colonel Serot. The State of Israel, through its Foreign Secretary Shertok, accepted the blame and denounced the desperadoes as 'outlaws, execrated by the entire people of Israel and the Jewish community of Jerusalem'. Dr. Bunche succeeded Bernadotte as mediator and after months of negotiation, deadlock and compromise, armistice agreements were signed at the U.N.O. headquarters on the Island of Rhodes between Israel and her Arab neighbours—Egypt (24 February 1949), Lebanon (23 March), Jordan (3 April) and Syria (20 July).

The re-establishment of peace, however uneasy, was a matter of gratification internationally, and a tribute to United Nations energy and tact. The Jews could boast of a sovereign state at last. They had endured centuries of wandering, humiliation and terror, strengthened by an invincible hope. In May 1949, less than a year after the British had left and only thirty years after the Balfour Declaration (November 1917), Israel became a member of the United Nations.

The first President of the Jewish nation was Dr. Chaim Weitzman, whose scientific services to the British nation promoted the Balfour Declaration, or rather gave the occasion for its formulation. Thirty years of patience had turned a dream into a reality. The triumph of Zionist aspirations involved the displacement of countless thousands of Arabs. It is estimated that over 750,000 Arabs became refugees, either in the Gaza strip or in the Jordan Valley and adjacent territory, or found themselves living in Israel.

The Grand Mufti of Jerusalem had hoped to be the acknowledged leader of Arabs in Palestine, but in December 1948 Abdullah was proclaimed King of a country now composed of Arab Palestine and the former Trans-Jordan—the new enlarged Kingdom of Jordan. In April 1950 an Arab security pact was concluded which stated that an attack on any one state would be regarded as an attack on the others. Next month, May 1950, Britain, France, and the United States, in an effort to prevent the possibility of war breaking out, undertook in a Tripartite Agreement not to provide weapons of war to either side concerned in the Palestine problem. The armistice was broken from time to time by a series of frontier incidents, most of which served to keep the countries on the alert, but never quite led to a renewal of war until 1956. Meanwhile the Jews probed deep into the Negeb, the triangular semi-wilderness that stretched south to the Gulf of Aqaba, an arm of the Red Sea.

4. EGYPT IN THE ASCENDANT

The advance of the armies of Egypt to Gaza filled her with momentary pride, but the inability to overthrow Israel was soon a matter of self-reproach. The result was a *coup d'état* in July 1952, in which King Farouk was forced to abdicate in favour of his son Ahmed Fouad II, and political power was in the hands of Colonel Neguib. In June of the following year the monarchy was dissolved and Neguib became Prime Minister of the new republic. Ten months later, in April 1954, Neguib, popular but too moderate, was forced by the Revolutionary Council to resign his post as Prime Minister and Military Governor. Gamal Abdul Nasser assumed power.

The new rulers of Egypt were determined to bring about some striking diplomatic success to confirm themselves in office. They had not long to wait. In October 1954 the Anglo-Egyptian Treaty of 1936 was terminated and a new agreement for the Suez Canal was drawn up. The British undertook to withdraw from the Canal area within twenty months, but Egypt promised to keep certain installations in working order and allow Britain to return if an outside power attacked. The terms of the Convention of Constantinople of 1888 by which the Canal was to be kept open as an international waterway were to be upheld. Nationalism rose high in Egypt. After seventy-two years of military occupation the British were finally on their way out. A new base had to be found for the British military headquarters in the Middle East and the only alternative choice was Cyprus.

Colonel Nasser began to demonstrate an initiative and energy which had not often been associated with Egypt. He tried to woo the Sudan to the idea of union with Egypt, as Farouk had tried before him; he established contact with the neutral states which preferred not to be identified too closely with either east or west. He allowed all manner of ill will to be propagated by press and radio against the colonial powers in order that he might the more prove to be Egypt's 'deliverer' from past tyranny. He certainly put new spirit into his people, and began to carry out a series of new reforms and building programmes for the economic development of the country. He made subtle bids for the leadership of the Arab states; extended the number and responsibility of Egyptian 'advisers' in other countries of the Arab League, and began to boast of triumphs yet unborn. Western statesmen feared the rise of another dictator, bent on capitalizing any and every diplomatic advantage and ruthless in the exploitation of every item of propaganda. A head of state so hostile to the West was the obvious ally, pawn, or associate of Soviet Russia. The association was quick to gather force, and eventually overreached itself, as we shall see in Chapter XIII.

X

THE FAR EAST

1. FROM WESTERN DEMOCRACY TO COMMUNISM IN CHINA

WHEN the Second World War came to an abrupt end in 1945 China had two leaders—Chiang Kai-shek in office and Mao Tse-tung biding his time. To follow the fortunes of the two men is to understand the transfer of power from Nationalist China to Communist China—a gigantic revolution, whose proportions and significance can scarcely be exaggerated. Its impact on the continent of Asia and throughout the world is likely to be felt for a long time to come.

Chiang Kai-shek had the satisfaction of knowing in the spring of 1945 that Britain and the United States would soon bring their full weight to bear against Japan as soon as Nazi Germany had been defeated in the West. The end was in sight. Chiang Kai-shek had led the nation for nearly twenty years and had been the Generalissimo throughout the struggle with Japan; he was idolized in the West as the defender of freedom, and was likely to emerge from the war with a reputation much enhanced by the prestige of victory. At the time China gave some appearance of unity, but this was not the real state of affairs. Ever since the Japanese had embarked on their imperialist expansion, the Communist organization in China had resigned itself to tentative alliance with the National Government. To do otherwise would have been treason. Political rivalries were patched over for the time being, but persisted all the same.

On 14 August 1945, just before the war with Japan ended, a treaty was concluded between China and Russia, and the two great nations reconciled themselves to neighbourliness in view of their common interest against a common foe. For a moment it really seemed that Communists and Nationalists in China might manage to sink their differences and stay at peace. Chiang Kai-shek him-

U Nu, Premier of Burma, with Mao Tse-tung in Peking (*see* p. 191)

Two Communist veterans, Mao Tse-tung of China and Ho Chi Minh of North Vietnam, at a reception in Peking (*see* p. 203)

Hiroshima—the sturdy new life of Japan replaces the destruction of
August 1945 (*see* p. 172)

self knew Moscow and Marxist policy and strategy at first hand, as indeed he had known Japan. He had known his enemies on their home territory and could guess what they must be up to, but even the treaty of friendship and all his personal experience could not save him from the consequences of the division that existed in China. Communism as a political creed had spread steadily during the war. Party membership had grown and had been carefully knit together in district institutions and the Army.

Communist policy immediately after the war was loyalty to the National Government (the Kuomintang) which, after all, had just concluded a treaty with Soviet Russia. But Chiang Kai-shek mistrusted their loyalty and continued to rely mainly on support from the United States. The Lease-Lend programme of American Aid had probably saved China. Personal, commercial, financial, and military links between China and the United States were powerful, and Chiang Kai-shek looked to Washington; Mao Tse-tung, his political rival, looked to Moscow. Which way would the nation go? Some advisers, including the Americans, tried to persuade Chiang Kai-shek to accept the compromise of a coalition government in order to retain the Communist alliance and maintain China's unity, but Chiang Kai-shek could not forget how nearly the Communists had captured the Kuomintang in its early days exactly twenty years before. Infiltration could so easily lead to domination.

Meanwhile there were sinister moves in the north. As the Russians gradually withdrew from Manchuria after the surrender of Japan, stacks of Japanese munitions and equipment were left behind and were taken over by the Chinese armies, including Communists. The Kuomintang Government had become corrupt. Faced with the problems of a nation exhausted by eight years of war and the ensuing widespread dislocation of life, also the need to resuscitate trade and an acute period of inflation, it failed to recover the popular support of all sections of the nation.

Mao Tse-tung on the other hand was soon in a powerful position. His followers were expert in guerrilla warfare. With daring and fortitude they had fought behind the Japanese lines in the north of China and were strategically placed astride the main railways when the war came to an end. The soldiers were politically indoctrinated as well as militarily competent. Mao Tse-tung was well placed to bargain with Chiang Kai-shek. General Marshall was sent by President Truman to bring the parties nearer together, but did not succeed.

In a cleverly worded manifesto Mao Tse-tung had set out in 1945 to win over support from the influential sections of society which most dreaded the prospect of Communism in China. The manifesto stated that imperialism and feudalism had been the root of Chinese troubles and that Communism, 'our new democratic system', was no enemy of individualism, private capital or 'honestly acquired' private property. This was enough to start winning over the middle classes and pacified the less wary amongst the wealthy. Mao Tse-tung, son of a well-to-do peasant and former librarian at Peking University, appealed also to other sections of the population—the politically disillusioned, the industrialists and the economically frustrated, the intellectuals, the debt-ridden peasants. These appeals amounted to a signal to revolt, and civil war broke out afresh. No further attempt at a united front was possible. The Kuomintang armies were defeated in the north and by 1948 Chiang Kai-shek's hope of regaining control had disappeared. Communist armies seized city after city and province after province and by lightning strokes imposed their régime in such a way as to make opposition futile. Chiang Kai-shek was driven from the mainland and took refuge on the island of Formosa (Taiwan), there to be the titular head of a Nationalist Government and still dependent on American protection.

On 21 September 1949 the People's Republic of China was proclaimed and Mao Tse-tung was elected Chairman of the Central People's Government. Peking, no longer called Peiping (Northern Peace), was to be the capital and a new national flag was adopted, a red flag with a five-pointed golden star in the top left-hand corner flanked by four smaller stars.

The Republic declared its hostility to imperialism, feudalism, and bureaucratic capitalism. It set out to create a system of peasant land ownership and to increase industrial development in a predominantly agricultural country. Everything was to be subject to scrutiny and revision. China, now a Communist state, was to launch out on a new social and economic programme which would affect more than 500 million people. This almost inevitably involved the closing of all frontiers so that this vast, wholesale

reindoctrination of the nation might go on behind closed doors
—the 'Bamboo Curtain'.

In February 1950 the new Government of China concluded
a treaty with Russia of a thirty-year alliance of friendship and
mutual assistance. Russia promised 300 million dollars in credits
and also undertook to surrender Russian interests in the South
Manchuria Railway and in the naval base at Port Arthur. All this
was preliminary. But the repercussions were self-evident and far
reaching. The extension and consolidation of Communist rule was
spectacular. Russia was indeed proud of her new partner. China
could do with a powerful ally. Politically they spoke the same
language. On paper the Sino-Russian treaty of 14 February 1950
was 'to prevent the recurrence of Japanese imperialism', but it
also covered any other threat or aggressive action 'instigated by
Japan or other nations'. This amounted to a joint warning to the
non-Communist world, a warning which some accepted on its
own merits and others resented. Before the end of the year 1950
the People's Republic of China was recognized by twenty-five
nations, including Soviet Russia, Great Britain, the Netherlands,
India, Pakistan, Ceylon, and Indonesia. The United States of
America hardened in support of Chiang Kai-shek in his island
fortress.

Meanwhile behind the Bamboo Curtain the internal revolution
was at work. Hostile elements were removed. Foreign consulates
were closed. Christian missionaries were turned out of the country
or interned. Foreign capital was frozen, property confiscated and
businesses taken over. The State left nothing untouched which
it had a wish to control. Arrests and kidnapping became normal practice, an experience to dread if one resisted authority or
discipline.

Many who had been taken in by the manifesto of 1945 were to
suffer in the régime which they had unwittingly or guilelessly
encouraged. As with Nazism so with Communism. Single party
rule came into operation. Looking back over the past the period
in China from 1911 to 1950 seems surprisingly transitory. The
work of Sun Yat-sen in overthrowing the Manchu dynasty and
establishing the republic was only the beginning and did not lead
to any really satisfactory settlement. In one way and another it
turned out to be an interval of civil strife between rivals and

competing forms of government, quite unresolved until Mao Tse-tung replaced Chiang Kai-shek. The endeavour to build a truly democratic China had failed. Another solution had to be tried.

2. JAPAN—FROM DEFEAT TO RECOVERY

On 10 August 1945 the Emperor of Japan broadcast an appeal for terms of surrender from the Allied Powers. Five days later the Second World War ended and the surrender of Japan was signed officially on board the U.S. Battleship *Missouri* in Tokio Bay on 2 September 1945.

Apart from her continuous reverses in battle in South-East Asia, the Pacific islands and elsewhere, Japan had been finally stung into surrender by the dropping of the first atom bomb on Hiroshima on 6 August, and the second on Nagasaki on 9 August. These final blows were struck by the Americans and as they had the largest fleets, armies and Air Force at their command in the Pacific area it was quickly decided that they should be entrusted with the military and occupational government of Japan. This decision spared the Japanese the burden of partition which Germany suffered and which later proved so intractable a problem. Japan was fortunate to be kept governmentally intact.

Countries which had fought and defeated Japan sent military missions to deal with all outstanding questions, but political and executive authority was vested in General MacArthur. Japanese soldiers abroad were soon repatriated and demobilized, except many held by Russia. The major war criminals were sent for trial.

General MacArthur set himself the task of governing the country through its own machinery and officials, but combined it with an attempt to re-educate the nation into ways more democratic and less chauvinistic.

The strength and unity of the Japanese Empire derived largely from a blind allegiance to the Emperor, approaching the old conception of Divine Right. Fanatical nationalism, militarism, imperialism all stemmed from this. Therefore it was vital to explode the myth and reconstruct the authority of the Emperor on the saner basis of constitutional acceptance, rather than mystical infallibility.

In a New Year's Day broadcast a few months after Japan's

defeat the Emperor himself disowned the suggestions of divinity with which tradition had surrounded his office. It was a radical change, which struck at the roots of Japan's past and needed time to become popularly accepted. In the new constitution which was drawn up in 1946 Article 1 declared 'The Emperor shall be the symbol of the State and of the unity of the people, deriving his position from the sovereign will of the people'. Thus he became a figurehead, but later on the article was amended to state that 'sovereignty resides in the people'.

The new constitution pledged Japan to renounce war for ever, abolish the secret police, drastically reduce the armed forces and create machinery for democratic government and representation. Men were given the right to vote from the age of twenty instead of twenty-five. Women were confirmed in their right to have a vote. Conscription was abolished and so was the peerage. A Bill of Rights was drawn up to offer guarantees of freedom and justice. Everything possible was done to make it less easy for Japan to become an aggressor nation again, but at the same time to encourage her gradual recovery and maintain her political integrity. American policy set out to ensure that Japan did not fall into the Communist sphere of influence.

The pre-war wealth of Japan had been in the hands of certain groups of nobles, industrialists and landowners. General Mac-Arthur estimated that too much control concentrated in the hands of too few people might lead to a return to semi-feudal oligarchy which had been Japan's tradition before. He therefore decided to break up these monopolies and cliques.

By a decree of December 1945 pressure was brought upon large landowners to sell parts of their estates in order that peasants might buy a parcel of land. In this way nearly 5 million acres were divided among $4\frac{1}{4}$ million tenant farmers. It is estimated that before 1939 several million families lived on the profits of small holdings of between one and two acres.

3. KOREA—PEACE AND WAR

On the defeat of Japan it was planned that Korea should be independent once again, having belonged by treaty to Japan from 1910 to 1945. First, it was necessary to accept Japan's surrender in Korea and for convenience sake it was agreed that Russia should treat with the Japanese authorities north of the 38th Parallel and that the Americans should deal with the situation south of the 38th Parallel. The Russians entered North Korea on 8 August and soon set up a Communist-led provisional government. The Americans did not arrive until 8 September, after the official surrender had been signed by Japan. Discussions took place in regard to the future of Korea but no agreement could be reached. These broke down in May 1946. In the autumn of 1947, against vigorous Communist opposition, a United Nations temporary commission was appointed to look into matters and of the nine members elected to the Commission one (Ukraine) refused to serve. Thus it came about that Korea became a U.N.O. commitment and responsibility.

In May 1948 a General Election took place in South Korea in the presence of United Nations observers. Approximately 90 per cent. of the electorate voted for a total of 200 representatives in a National Assembly which was intended to number 300. The remaining 100 seats were to be for members eventually elected from Northern Korea. Proportionately this was just, for the population of North Korea was estimated at eight to nine million as against about eighteen million in the South. This was a clear indication that Korea was expected to become unified in due course.

In July 1948 the constitution was adopted and Dr. Syngman Rhee was elected President. In August the republic of Korea was proclaimed. As if to counter any idea or suggestion of unity North Korea promptly declared itself a People's Republic in September 1948, with Kim-il-sing as its Prime Minister. It was immediately recognized by Soviet Russia and by December Russian troops were withdrawn, except for some advisers.

The 38th Parallel was now to all intents and purposes a fixed frontier and Korea had become two rival republics instead of a single independent state. Each side set out to win the other by propaganda, but in the meantime built up its armies to face any eventualities. The position during 1949 was uneasy.

In January 1950 the U.S.A., confident that Japan no longer constituted a menace to peace, and equally confident that Japan was resistant to Communism, adopted a new policy in the Western Pacific, accepting the fact that at Cairo and Potsdam, and under

The Far East

the surrender terms it had already been agreed that Japan should give up Formosa and Korea, it was decided that the U.S.A. had no further need or right to regard these two territories as within the American 'perimeter of defence'.

President Truman and Dean Acheson, the Secretary of State, were content that Formosa and Korea be left to find their own proper status by what means they could. This policy of partial withdrawal was tantamount to a recognition that the new régime in Peking had come to stay and that the future of Formosa at any rate was now a matter for internal settlement, even if it did mean the continuance of a state of war between Communists and Nationalists. The new policy raised an immediate hue and cry. Republicans in the U.S.A. accused the State Department in Washington of retreat, betrayal and folly. Senator Macarthy launched out into a campaign to prove the presence of Communists in the State Department who were distorting American policy in Communism's interest.

The cold war which had settled on Europe spread to Eastern Asia. The Americans' gravest suspicions had been aroused; they recollected the Berlin blockade, the establishment of a Communist régime in North Korea, the successful political conquest of China by Mao Tse-tung and now the declared withdrawal of the U.S.A. from Korea and Formosa. Were there to be no bases from which to keep a wary eye on Communist expansion? Had all the support given to Chiang Kai-shek in the past been wasted?

In June 1950 John Foster Dulles, newly appointed adviser in Foreign Affairs, flew to Tokio for discussions with General Mac-Arthur. The policy on China was completely reversed. MacArthur insisted that the United States must have bases in Japan and Korea and Formosa. This meant support for Syngman Rhee and Chiang Kai-shek.

The war in Korea broke out on Sunday, 25 June, and each side inevitably blamed the other for having started it. The invasion was obviously most carefully planned and premeditated. Two hours after firing started the North Koreans disembarked troops from a task force of twenty ships approximately twenty miles south of the 38th Parallel on the east coast. Such a force could not have been collected and despatched within this two-hour interval. The North Koreans 'beat the pistol', being as anxious that the

Tokio decisions just mentioned should not be put into operation, as Syngman Rhee was to drag in American forces in his support.

The Secretary-General of the United Nations, Trygve Lie, telegraphed at once to the United Nations Commission, which was in Seoul, the southern capital, and asked for immediate information and details.

Apprehension and alarm brought to memory the case of Manchuria in 1931 and within two days of the outbreak of the war the

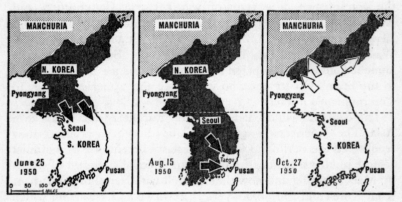

KOREA

United Nations had decided that international peace was seriously threatened and that only armed resistance could save the republic of Korea and restore peace and security in that area. The South Korean armies were no match for the northerners, who swept rapidly south. Fifty-three member nations of U.N.O. agreed that intervention was necessary and fourteen of them sent military units.

On 7 July all united forces were placed under the command of General MacArthur, but still the northern armies pressed south. By 15 September the South Korean and U.N.O. forces were cornered in a bridgehead in the south-east of the peninsula around Pusan. The northern armies had almost eliminated the opposition. In August MacArthur visited Chiang Kai-shek in Formosa and pledged himself to protect and restore his authority. The American

Seventh Fleet were already there to see that Formosa was not swallowed up while the attention of the world was focused on Korea. Then came the turn of the tide. Very cleverly MacArthur sent a large naval task force to land well up the peninsula in enemy occupied territory. This sudden move struck terror into the Northern Koreans who saw every likelihood of being cut off in the south. They turned and retreated quickly.

The North Koreans were rapidly pushed back and by 30 September the United Forces had reached the 38th Parallel. At this point Chou En-lai, Prime Minister and foreign secretary of the Chinese People's Republic, warned them to go no further. The British wanted to halt at this recognized frontier but MacArthur was determined to press on to the port of Wansan, 100 miles further north, and even possibly as far as the Yalu river, the boundary with Manchuria. This provocation brought in the Chinese.

From 26 November a vast offensive from the north was launched which drove the South Koreans and United Nations forces back to the 38th Parallel and beyond. In October President Truman had flown to Wake Island to confer with MacArthur. For another six months MacArthur retained his command, but in April 1951 he was superseded by General Ridgeway. No one questioned MacArthur's courage, brilliance or vast experience, but he had been successful in the Pacific arena for so long that he was in danger of directing affairs without sufficient recourse to advice or permission from Washington or New York. The tendency to take the law into his own hands led to his dismissal.

From February to June both sides launched attacks and the United Nations gained some ground, but on 10 July 1951, truce talks began at Kaesong, and later continued at Panmunjong. The negotiations dragged on from July 1951 till October 1952 before they reached deadlock and had to be suspended. They were reopened in April 1953 and eventually the Armistice Agreement was signed on 27 July.

The cease-fire talks had broken down in October 1952 after fourteen months of peace negotiation over the question of the repatriation of prisoners. The Communists had demanded that all prisoners should be returned. This would have meant the return of approximately 130,000 prisoners and internees held by U.N.O. But 47,000 of these asked not to be returned and the

United Nations authorities could not see their way to insist on their going home. The Communists on the other hand only held 11,550 United Nations prisoners, of whom only 359 (335 Koreans) wished not to be repatriated. The deadlock was later solved by agreeing that prisoners who resisted repatriation should be asked to allow the opposite side to explain their position and endeavour to win them over. These explanations were to be carefully supervised by a Neutral Nations Repatriation Commission for a period of thirty days.

The wholesale dislocation of life had been terrible. In March 1952 it was estimated that there were 2,600,000 refugees from Northern Korea in the southern republic, in addition to 4,300,000 destitute and homeless. Thirty-one U.N.O. nations contributed a total of 270 million dollars towards relief and rehabilitation. The American Senate authorized up to 200 million dollars. A few days later Soviet Russia announced a grant of about 250 million dollars for the same purpose in North Korea.

What can be said of the Korean War in retrospect?

(*a*) It pointed to the essential mistrust and antipathy between East and West.

(*b*) It proved that U.N.O. had some degree of determination and was likely to resist aggression in a manner not acceptable to the former League of Nations. Trygve Lie, Secretary-General of U.N.O., later wrote: 'Collective security has been enforced for the first time in the whole of human history'.

(*c*) It strengthened the conception of neutrality in certain nations and built up the idea of a third force (between East and West), or neutralism. India in particular was filling this role.

(*d*) It showed that modern atomic or nuclear weapons were not to be regarded as in any way normal to war. America, which alone had them at the time, refrained from using them.

(*e*) Korea remained divided.

If by any chance the Korean war had been designed as a test of the will of U.N.O. to meet force with force the answer was now clear, but it so alarmed public opinion in the United States that the American armed forces were increased from $1\frac{1}{2}$ million to $3\frac{1}{2}$ million—a big price to pay for mistrust and suspicion.

By 1956 the American forces were reduced to 2,900,000 and Russia offered in the same year to reduce her own forces by 1,200,000 to bring them down to the same level as the Americans. But by then nuclear weapons were becoming common property. Neither country any longer had a monopoly. Public opinion abhorred their use, and even more important, the attempt to win the world to a particular political viewpoint was switched from the battlefield to the home, the factory and personal allegiance. As the military factor receded, in spite of diplomatic ties and countless talks, the ideological factor became more and more important.

One particular mystery remained unsolved. In January 1950 Mr. Malik, the Russian representative on the Security Council, had protested that the Peking Government should be a member of U.N.O. and that he would no longer sit on the Security Council with a Nationalist China delegate as a fellow member. He walked out. He was still absent when the Korean war began in June. Russia was unable to exercise the veto. The Chairman for the month of June was Sir Benegal Rau, the Indian representative, and another Indian, Krishna Menon, happened to be Chairman of the U.N.O. Commission in Korea. The Chairman for July was a Norwegian and it was due to be the Russians' turn to preside for the month of August. Although the Nationalist China delegate was still on the Security Council Mr. Malik suddenly announced that he would be back in the Council and take his place as Chairman on 1 August. At that moment a North Korean victory looked more than likely, for the South Korean troops and United Nations forces were being pushed steadily down the peninsula. It is curious that during the vital months of the opening of the Korean war the Russian delegate should have been absent from his seat in the Security Council, and that the only reason he gave for going should not have still debarred him from returning at that crucial time.

4. THE JAPANESE PEACE TREATY AND THE PACIFIC ALLIANCES

It was not until 8 September 1951, six years after the defeat of Japan and after the Korean war had reached deadlock and armistice negotiations were in train, that a treaty of peace was eventually signed between Japan and the representatives of forty-eight other countries at San Francisco. Japan renounced her claim to all territories outside her main islands. She also agreed to U.S.A. trusteeship for the Ryukyu and Bonin islands. She had given some evidence that she had amended her way of life and adopted a more democratic mode of Government since her defeat in 1945. Elections in 1949 had already shown that Parliamentary rule was an accepted constitutional procedure again and further elections in 1952 and 1955 indicated that there was in the foreseeable future no likelihood of a recurrence of the militarist and imperialist expansion which had disturbed the peace of the Pacific so frequently from 1895 to 1945. It had been a phenomenal half-century for Japan. Her vanquishers might have treated her ruthlessly, the Americans in particular, but the bogey of Communism became an obsession in the United States, which far outstripped any fear of immediate danger from the Japanese.

It was clearly far wiser to rehabilitate Japan and forge a new alliance than poison the future with recriminations. Such was the mood in 1951. Within the next five years the pace of Japanese industrial and commercial development had so accelerated and boomed that she stood to capture some of the markets that she had lost since 1937. Japan's remarkable recovery—the outcome of zest, thorough planning and tremendous application—was paralleled only by that of her war-time partner Germany. Their resilience was incredible.

Pacific Alliances

The tension between East and West which reached its most critical phase during the Berlin blockade and the Korean war was worldwide in its impact. It was felt as much in North America and even in the southern hemisphere as in Asia and Europe. Proof of this can be seen in the set of agreements that were drawn up and signed at the time of the signing of the treaty with Japan.

On 30 August 1951 the United States and Philippines concluded a pact of mutual help. On 1 September Australia and New Zealand joined the United States in the A.N.Z.U.S. or Pacific Pact by which an attack on any one of these Powers was to be regarded as endangering the peace and stability of the others. On 9 September, the very day after the Japanese Peace Treaty, the United States and Japan entered into a separate security pact.

The attack on Pearl Harbour in 1941 may be said to have torpedoed American isolationism and to have ensured that there could be no easy retreat again into that particular policy or way of escape. Ten years later, in 1951, the four factors—Marshall Aid, the Truman Doctrine, N.A.T.O., and the Pacific Pact—showed conclusively that the United States was only too well aware that she was now internationally involved. She had accepted her new status and her new responsibilities—'the care of all the freedoms'. Even before these Pacific agreements were signed and sealed plans were put into full operation to advance the economic and material welfare of the less developed countries of South-East Asia.

This policy embodied in the Colombo Plan, which began the work in 1951, was later given military support by the South-East Asia Defence Treaty of September 1954. Inevitably it resulted in an outcry from Soviet Russia that she was being deliberately encircled and hemmed in. The Communist area of the world now extended across all Russia and Siberia, most of the countries from the Baltic to the Aegean, together with Manchuria, North Korea, and China. This spectacular increase of political sway alarmed the free nations of the world; none more so than where Communist parties were active, at bay or even outlawed.

5. THE NEW CHINA

When China established herself as a Communist state in 1949 she had need of help and advice from Russia, and Russia in turn was tremendously pleased to have China as a partner. Mao Tse-tung himself had visited Moscow to discuss the terms of the Pact of February 1950, but certain decisions were left undecided until 1952, and by then the situation had greatly altered. China found herself bearing a heavier burden than she had anticipated. The Korean war was costly and China needed the kind of equipment and financial loans which Russia might be expected to provide. China could produce small arms and guns, but for tanks, aircraft, and naval ships she looked to Russia.

Russia could ill afford to allow the Communist hold on China to weaken or to allow it to appear that Moscow and Peking did not see eye to eye. China, therefore, was in quite a strong bargaining position. In August 1952 she sent a powerful mission to Moscow to negotiate the next stage in the Russo-Chinese partnership. This time Mao Tse-tung stayed at home and the delegation was led by Chou En-lai in his double capacity of Prime Minister and Foreign Secretary. With him were Chen Yun, deputy Prime Minister and Chief Economic Planning Officer, and Li Fu-chun, the Chairman in charge of economic and financial affairs. All the indications were that much as each country was indebted to the other it was also a time for hard reckoning and hard bargaining. China was not going to be eclipsed as the lesser People's Republics had been, nor was she going to be made to dance to anyone else's tune. These are times when partners can also be rivals and the relationship between Russia and China contained the ingredients of tension. Russia numbered 200 million people. By 1952 China was nearer 600 million and rapidly increasing. Russia had based her revolution on the proletariat; China based hers as much on the peasants. But was this altogether in line with Marxist doctrine? If not, and if the experiment worked, then Mao Tse-tung could claim to be the equal of either Lenin or Stalin in originality and as an interpreter of Marxism.

It was obvious that the Chinese leaders were not ready to give any blind devotion or obedience to directives from the Kremlin; Peking was far too proud to play second fiddle to Russia. When China decided to cut herself off from communication with the outside world she was merely reverting to a policy common to her history and tradition, but behind this barricade of secrecy and detachment an iron rule gripped the country. The Land Reform Law of 1950 accelerated the process of land re-distribution, private businesses were hit hard by accusations of corruption and gradually brought under state control in 1952. Then China set out on her own first Five-Year Plan in 1953, setting targets for production for each year and in each industry. The whole country was divided into six regions to put these schemes into effect.

All opposition and resistance were ruthlessly eliminated and the Chinese people soon came to realize that the new Government was set to exterminate enemies of the régime on a scale never before imagined. The method differed from the Russian. Stalin and his secret police had usually removed citizens to Siberia to work in mines or forests as forced labour. In China, however, officials are said to have carried out public executions partly as a means of intimidating the nation and partly because in a thickly populated country life was dispensable and execution quick and cheap. Nevertheless it is also said that millions were moved or imprisoned as circumstances demanded. The twentieth century must go down in history as one of phenomenal and fantastic brutality in many countries. The Chinese leaders did not appear much in public or to the outside world until the summer of 1954. For their first five years in power they were absorbed in internal affairs, but a meeting of Foreign Ministers was held in Geneva in May 1954 to discuss the situation in Indo-China, and Communist China was represented by a delegation headed by Chou En-lai. During the conference the battle of Dien Bien Phu was lost by the French and the French Government fell. The British and Americans did not see eye to eye on matters of policy. China was seeing the Western Powers at their weakest. It was a further token that the surge of political strength in Asia had brought a new factor into world politics and that Europe alone no longer held the initiative.

XI

SOVEREIGNTY IN SOUTHERN ASIA

1. THE PATH TO FREEDOM

IN the history of Asia and even of the world 15 August 1947 may be as important a date as the discovery of America in 1492, the outbreak of the French Revolution in 1789, or the October Revolution of 1917 in Russia. It marks the end of an era and the beginning of another.

On that date the British Indian Empire came to an end and two new dominions came into existence, to take their place among the great nations of the world. This was no mere technical change of phrase or terminology. It marked the constitutional end of European domination throughout India and by implication challenged all European influence throughout the continent of Asia. It was only a matter of time before French, Dutch, and Portuguese authority were likewise challenged and overthrown, where they had not already given ground. In effect the day of European imperialism was over. Subjection in that sense was a thing of the past.

In Turkey and China the revolutions had been quite different in character. Kemal Ataturk had replaced the Ottoman Sultan. Sun Yat-sen momentarily succeeded the Manchu Emperor. These were internal adjustments, inaugurating entirely new régimes nevertheless. But in the case of India a European Power, albeit under fierce pressure, had voluntarily transferred political authority to the country which it had previously ruled. This was a decisive and responsible act, carrying with it a degree of goodwill which redounded to the credit of all concerned. Friendship between Britain on the one hand and India and Pakistan on the other not only remained intact in spite of many stresses and strains, but even increased and improved. The Commonwealth—an association of

Mahatma Gandhi and Pandit Jawaharlal Nehru in deep discussion in Bombay, August 1940, at the All-India conference when the 'Quit India' resolution was adopted (*see* p. 41)

Dr. Rajendra Prasad, first President of the Indian Republic, with Pandit Nehru, first Premier, at a meeting of the Constituent Assembly in New Delhi, January 1950 (*see* p. 184)

The Great Shwe Dagon Pagoda, Rangoon—a picture of grace and artistry; antiquity, devotion and poverty, with a modern pylon on the left—all symbolic of Modern Asia

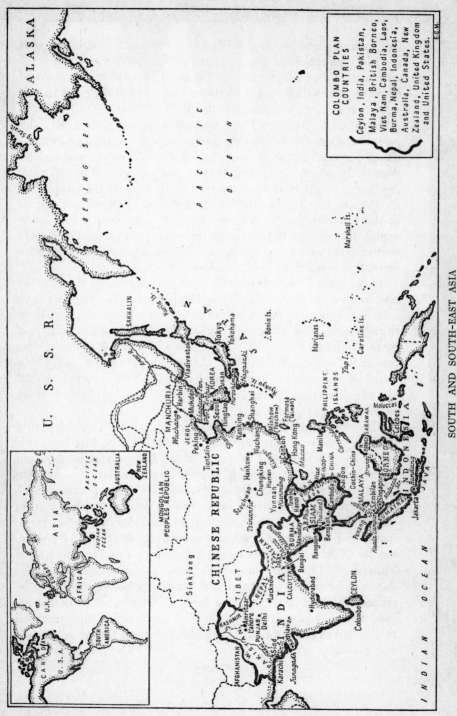

SOUTH AND SOUTH-EAST ASIA

COLOMBO PLAN
COUNTRIES

Ceylon, India, Pakistan,
Malaya, British Borneo,
Viet Nam, Cambodia, Laos,
Burma, Nepal, Indonesia,
Australia, Canada, New
Zealand, United Kingdom
and United States.

E.G.M.

free nations—was proving itself to be a constructive alternative to the old conception of Empire, and as such was a most hopeful constitutional development. But the steps that led to this transfer of power, and which resulted in the partitioning of the great Indian sub-continent, were themselves painfully difficult.

In 1945 the Congress Party had issued a manifesto before the general elections in which they had promised universal adult franchise, personal freedom, local autonomy, federation and indeed everything which was calculated to unify the country and allay any fears. In this way Congress hoped to draw in the support of the Princes, merchants, intellectuals and other community interests in the establishment of a new nation. It even went so far as to explain that though the social and economic policy would be largely that of state control, there would also be a guarantee of fundamental personal rights and freedom.

Though the Congress majority was overwhelming, the election also confirmed the strength of the Moslem minority. Early in 1946 a delegation of eight Members of Parliament was sent out to analyse the situation. This was closely followed in March of the same year by a Cabinet mission of three—Lord Pethick-Lawrence, Sir Stafford Cripps, and Mr. A. V. Alexander. They still thought in terms of a possible Union of India, but were instructed to find out whether or not India would accept such an ideal, or continue to press for partition.

Meanwhile the Viceroy endeavoured to rule the country with a Cabinet of fourteen, made up of six Hindus, five Muslims, two others and himself. This proved a failure. Congress refused to join in an interim government. Muslims were more than ever determined to press for the idea of Pakistan by direct action. On 16 August 1946 rioting broke out in many Muslim districts during 'Direct Action' Day, which was a public holiday in Muslim provinces. In September a new government was established in office, led by Nehru, but once again it failed to provide any united leadership. The situation was becoming desperate. Could the deadlock between the Hindu and Muslim points of view ever be reconciled? In a last attempt to bring about some kind of accommodation or reconciliation Lord Wavell, Nehru and Jinnah travelled to London to see if they could reach a solution. But no agreement was possible.

In December a constituent assembly met and in February 1947 Mr. Attlee, on the authority of the British Government, announced publicly that the British would withdraw from India in June 1948. The responsibility for seeing through this transfer of power was entrusted to Lord Mountbatten. His reputation in Asia was tremendously high. He had commanded the forces which had driven the Japanese out of South-East Asia. He had won the confidence of many Asiatic leaders by his wisdom, charm of manner and expedition. He was every inch a statesman, and withal a kinsman of the King of England and Emperor of India. He therefore spoke with an unusual personal authority.

Coming from him, with all this background of authority and prestige in mind, the transfer of power from the British Emperor to the people of India could be interpreted as an act of grace and goodwill, and not merely as the swan-song of a decadent and retreating Empire. The actual transfer of power came with great suddenness. The announcement was made on 3 June 1947, and an Indian Independence Bill was passed through Parliament at Westminster the following month. India was to be given self rule. Two dominions were to be created and individual states were to be free to join whichever of the two new countries they wished. Most unfortunately just at a time when hopes of a quiet transfer seemed likely communal riots, accompanied by extreme violence, broke out in the Punjab. In face of the bitterness and extent of the rioting Lord Mountbatten as Viceroy determined to bring forward the date of transfer from June 1948 to August 1947. This appealed enormously to the sense of pride and fulfilment on the part of both Hindus and Muslims. It is almost impossible for any European to realize quite what a great moment it was for them, or to appreciate the excitement and hope that underlay this promise of freedom.

On 22 July 1947 Nehru himself presented to the Constituent Assembly the flag of the new India. It was to have three colours—deep saffron, representative of Indian renunciation, white to represent the path of truth and dark green to indicate the relation of the people to the soil. Unlike the colours in the republican flag of China these colours in no way carried any communal significance. Rather did they serve to unify the nation in terms of tradition and religious reality. Superimposed in the middle was a wheel, the symbol taken from the Sarnath lion pillar which dates from about the first century B.C. and which is a symbol of India's ancient culture going back over a period of perhaps 5,000 years. The Sarnath lion pillar itself reminded Indians of a golden age in their history, the illustrious Asoka period, in which Indian ambassadors were men of peace and goodwill throughout a vast area of the world. At the same time the wheel, in a modern industrial age, represented movement and progress.

The presentation of this flag heightened the enthusiasm for independence which lay just round the corner. For Pakistan the new national flag was to be dark green with a white vertical bar at the mast, the white portion being one quarter of the total area. To emphasize the link with Islam a large white crescent was superimposed on the dark green, together with a five-pointed white heraldic star. On 8 August 1947 Delhi became the capital of the new India, which was to be predominantly Hindu, and Karachi became the capital of Pakistan which, of course, was predominantly Muslim. On the stroke of midnight, between 14 and 15 August, amidst great rejoicing, India and Pakistan became separate dominions. As a gesture of friendship and gratitude the new India invited Lord Mountbatten, the last of the line of Viceroys, to become Governor-General of the new dominion of India.

2. FULFILMENT AND CONSOLIDATION IN INDIA

Immediately the Constituent Assembly, together with the secretariat in Delhi, became the new Indian Legislature. In theory the Princes, who had hitherto enjoyed local autonomy, were free to accede to whichever dominion they wished, or even to remain independent, but in practice this was clearly impossible. Almost every Prince or Raja knew that he had no alternative but to submit his territories and much of his authority to the Central Government in Delhi.

Before partition and independence separate treaties had existed between the British Government and the individual Princes, but these were automatically at an end, the principle of paramountcy lapsed and each Indian ruler now had to come to terms with the new Indian Government. Many lesser states were quickly grouped together into six great unions and these amalgamations became viable states with their own separate representation. By way of compensation the most influential Princes in each region became Raj Pramukh (Prince President) for life. Many of the lesser rulers, though allowed to keep their titles and a big portion of their private wealth, were nevertheless removed from direct rule or political authority. The whole of India, which had consisted of more than 500 separate states, was now reduced in the first instance to sixteen operative units. The person chiefly responsible for this work of amalgamation of provinces and Princely states was Sardar Vallabh-bhai Patel. While this process was proceeding by stages, three territories proved actually resistant to any identification with the new dominion. One of these exceptions was Junagarh, which was ruled by a Muslim and which, therefore, had some desire to join Pakistan. The Nawab indeed fled to Pakistan and his state was quickly incorporated into Indian Kathiawar, becoming a member of the Indian nation. The second exception was Hyderabad, where the Muslim Nizam was determined to stand out for independence. Geographically this was bound to be an embarrassment to India, for his state lay in the very midst of Indian territory, surrounded by Madras in the south and the east, Bombay in the west, and the central provinces in the north. Many of the Hindu subjects in Hyderabad were perfectly content under their Muslim ruler, but the Government in Delhi awaited the first opportunity to engulf the state. In 1948, on the excuse that police action was necessary to rid the state of certain terrorist gangs, Indian troops moved in and Hyderabad was taken over. The third exception was Kashmir, to which we will return later.

In Delhi work began on the framing of the new constitution, which was eventually ratified and adopted in 1950. India was declared to be a sovereign democratic republic, established on a federal system, with a Cabinet responsible to Parliament and based on manhood suffrage. The new nation was confronted with problems of appalling magnitude from the start. It has been estimated that at the very time when the transfer of power was being put into effect no less than six million Muslims were on the move towards Pakistan in search of new homes and work, while at the same time five million Hindus and Sikhs were beginning to transfer themselves from Muslim territory to the new India.

A population of eleven million people suddenly on the move

presented the new Government with tasks which were beyond human control. Millions suffered; many died. This refugee problem, with all its communal antagonism, was a major calamity which blighted some of the rejoicing accompanying the transfer of power. Gandhi tried to use his enormous influence to improve the bitter relationships between the Hindus and Muslims and indeed began yet another fast—his fifteenth—in an attempt to persuade the rival communities to sink their differences. This further antagonized the Hindu extremists. On 30 January 1948 a young Hindu editor approached Gandhi in Delhi as he was actually on his way to one of his evening meetings, and after greeting him apparently loyally, shot him at point-blank range. Thus passed from the Indian scene one of the great architects of Indian independence and a great Asian. He had been the strangest mixture of astute politician, semi-mystic and fanatical patriot. In many ways he remains an enigma, but when he died men throughout the world realized that a great soul had passed from the daily scene. His body was cremated next day on the banks of the sacred river Jumna, and prominent among the vast crowd of mourners was the Governor-General, Lord Mountbatten, identifying the old régime with the suffering and sorrow of the new Indian nation.

We now come to some of the main problems that lay before the Congress Party which governed India. In the words of Mr. Chakravartri Rajagopalachari, who in June 1948 succeeded Lord Mountbatten as Governor-General of India: 'India is unchangeably committed to the policy of making everyone within her borders find pride and joy in citizenship, irrespective of caste, group or race.' This was easy to say, a genuine aspiration, but difficult to put into practice. The first question was one of frontiers. An English Judge, Sir C. (now Lord) Radcliffe, was responsible for deciding the delicate issue as to the future of such large cities as Calcutta and Lahore. His decision was that Calcutta should belong to the dominion of India, while Lahore in the Punjab should go to Pakistan.

In the meanwhile certain Communist elements in the country were agitating for separate language states, hoping that in some of the smaller, more backward districts they would be able to dominate local politics and by the process of sub-division and self-determination be able to set up Communist-controlled areas. But this policy was well known to the authorities in Delhi; when riots later broke out in West Bengal the Communist Party there was banned and many Communists were arrested all over the country.

The declared policy of the Indian Government was state control of the main means of production, and the general principle of socialism and nationalization. All industries were divided into four categories: those which should be state monopolies, such as railways, post and telegraphs and defence industries; secondly, industries like iron and steel, ship-building, aircraft manufacture and coal; thirdly, industries which would one day be brought under central control, such as textiles, sugar, transport, minerals, salt and so on. All remaining industries would probably be left in the hands of private enterprise.

Alleviation of poverty was the first concern and the gradual development of a welfare state along the lines already adopted in Britain. Side by side with this was the desire to educate the nation and remove some of the burden of illiteracy. A five-year plan also helped to regulate the need to industrialize the country systematically and also to develop food supplies.

One of the most encouraging features of the first year in the life of the two new dominions was the willingness to meet in a series of inter-dominion conferences. In April 1948 at Calcutta, both India and Pakistan agreed no longer to agitate either for reunion or for territory which they considered had unjustly been taken from them. They also agreed to reduce import and export duties and to improve communications between the territories. In May at Delhi they further agreed to the mutual exchange of a long list of essential foodstuffs and other commodities, and in August came to a satisfactory agreement as to the treatment of evacuated property and exchange of civil prisoners.

In this way they demonstrated to the outside world that they could reach common agreement on a wide range of outstanding issues and thus restore a degree of goodwill which had partly been lost at the time of partition. In 1949 both countries were represented at the Prime Ministers' Conference in London and decided to remain within the Commonwealth as equal partners within the free association or family of nations. On 26 January

1950 India was officially proclaimed a sovereign democratic republic and Dr. Rajendra Prasad was elected as President. In the elections which were held at the end of 1951 and early 1952 it was estimated that the electorate, now that manhood suffrage was granted, had increased from 30 million to 176 million. Of these no less than 107 million people recorded their votes.

In the central Parliament the Congress Party won 362 seats out of 489, and in the constituencies they won roughly two-thirds of the seats (2,085 out of 3,055). There were Communist victories in several districts in the south, especially in the Telangana area of Hyderabad. Fortunately India had built up a body of experienced politicians and administrators in the days of British rule and, therefore, found herself perfectly capable of continuing the system of Parliamentary Government which she found thoroughly workable and suitable to India's needs.

Fortunately also, unlike some other parts of Asia, the army refrained from interfering in politics and professional politicians were left to do their own job. In Foreign Affairs Nehru set his heart on steering a course between the Great Powers and steadfastly refused to take sides either with the East or the West. He knew Russia, and Moscow in particular. He knew Britain intimately and had had many dealings with Europe and America, but he was determined that a policy of non-involvement was the right course for India, and added to this (somewhat difficult) attitude of neutralism the positive one of trying to create a wide peace area in Asia.

Sound in principle, this policy was nevertheless difficult to operate in practice. It is tremendously to his credit that he has been as successful as he has. France was quick to realize that she had little hope of continuing her rule over the few small bits of territory she held in India and was not slow to surrender them. Portugal on the other hand became uncommonly obstinate and was to prove a thorn in India's flesh for years to come.

In 1950 Chinese troops invaded and occupied Tibet. This was enough to antagonize Nehru at the time and upset Indian trust in her great Asiatic neighbour China. It was not until four years later that India agreed to recognize Tibet as an integral part of Communist China and to withdraw certain military guards which were stationed there.

In July 1954, when representatives of Communist China agreed to go to Geneva to discuss the future of French Indo-China, India was invited to become Chairman of the International Supervisory Commission for Vietnam, Cambodia and Laos in recognition of her desire to remain neutral. The other two members of the Commission were Canada and Poland. On his way back from this Conference, the Chinese Prime Minister, Chou En-lai, paid a visit to Delhi and invited Nehru to return the visit in Peking. In the course of their public utterances each spoke of the 2,000 years of peace which had so far existed between their two countries. Meanwhile both publicly acknowledged that they represented quite different systems of government and yet saw no reason why they should not abide in peace as neighbours.

During the visit Nehru pleaded for the release of certain American airmen who were held captive by the Chinese, who partly in deference to his persuasion and prestige granted them their release. Jawaharlal Nehru was rapidly gaining a reputation for neutrality and mediation. But this neutrality was not at all passive, or negative. It was a deep-seated and urgent conviction that to side unequivocally with either East or West would merely be to heighten alarm and suspicion and to contribute nothing to the peace of the world or the future of Asia. This policy opened Nehru to criticism from all sides. Some thought he was merely sitting on the fence; some thought that he was changing sides, but other events helped to prove that his motives were genuine.

First, there was the case of Korea. Indian diplomatic circles did everything possible to prevent the Korean war from spreading and gave warning at intervals to both sides in the hope of encouraging a settlement. Secondly, with regard to Pakistan, the relations with India were poisoned by friction in Kashmir, and this in turn had been referred to the United Nations. In time this might have been solved, but in 1954 Pakistan accepted American military aid and thus took sides in the struggle between East and West, a move which aggravated Nehru very considerably. By having American military strength right into the midst of a trouble area he thought for a moment that his hopes of extending the area of peace were rapidly being threatened. When Pakistan also joined S.E.A.T.O. and became a member of a defence pact with the Western Powers, Nehru was once again put out. It is not without significance that one of his chief visitors at this time was Marshal Tito, representing a country which at that time was similarly neutral— Yugoslavia.

It may seem too much to believe that India can keep on terms of equal friendship with the Commonwealth, with Soviet Russia, with Communist China and with the rest of the world, but to a very remarkable degree Nehru succeeded in keeping in touch with all of them and inspiring mutual trust. With one country he had a particular grievance—with South Africa, on grounds of racial discrimination. Pandit Nehru's stature as an international statesman has grown with the years, and reflects the position attained by India as a new republic with considerable moral weight.

3. FULFILMENT AND CONSOLIDATION IN PAKISTAN

15 August 1947 was as great a day of rejoicing in Pakistan as in India. A new dominion had been given birth. But a very awkward situation was created by the fact that the country existed in two quite separate sections. In the West, by far the larger area, the population numbered approximately thirty-five million and included the provinces of the Sind, West Punjab, Baluchistan and the North-West Frontier province. It was really from this area that the idea of Pakistan had originated. The majority of the people spoke Urdu. The country itself was open to development and included some of the richest wheat and cotton areas of the sub-continent. Even more important in some respects was the fact that it was near the centre of the Muslim world and, therefore, might have been expected to look for affiliation to Arabia and the other Arab regions.

The eastern portion of the new dominion was small in comparison and incorporated eastern Bengal and part of Assam, but it had a total population of forty-two million, of which a large proportion—estimated at eleven million—were Hindus, and greatly resented the division of the state. A similar resentment in 1905, it will be recalled, led to a subsequent reunion. The bulk of the people speak Bengali. The main products are rice and jute. The most pressing problem in both areas was the vast influx of refugees, who clamoured for settlement and compensation. It is estimated that West Punjab alone received something in the region of $5\frac{1}{2}$

million refugees. Little wonder that a state of emergency had to be declared.

Whereas the dominion of India had inherited the seat of government, together with a trained secretariat, files, equipment and experience, the new dominion of Pakistan had to set to work to build her civil service, Government secretariat, and headquarters from scratch. Experience could only come by trial and error and this was bound to take years. Some experience had of course been inherited from the previous régime, but to nothing like the extent in which India had profited.

In the early days of the new dominion an attempt was made to set up Pakistan as an Islamic state founded essentially on Muslim culture and with the backing of the new Shariat movement. The local authority of the Mullahs grew rapidly and there was every indication that Pakistan might soon become a theocratic state, possibly lapsing into something which was out of touch with the new trends of the twentieth century. The leading politicians and statesmen, therefore, took steps to ensure that the new state did not get too much into the hands of the Muslim authorities.

The Governor-General of Pakistan, Mahomed Ali Jinnah, was appointed in August 1947, but did not live long enough to see the country through its early development. He was worn out by thirty years of strenuous work and died in September 1948. So torn was Pakistan by internal rivalries and external friction that in 1948 almost any opposition to central authority was viewed not as healthy criticism, but with profound suspicion. The criticism came not only from the Mullahs, but also from the Red Shirt leader, Khan Abdul Ghaffar Khan, who had instituted the Pakistan People's Party, and who was suspected of treachery.

Both he and his brother, Dr. Khan Sahib, who had been Prime Minister of the North-West Frontier, were arrested. Friction continued in Kashmir, and a movement, said to have been instigated from Pakistan, put forward the suggestion that the Pathans who lived on the borders of Pakistan and Afghanistan should declare the formation of a separate state to be known as Paktoonistan. Nothing came of this.

With so many thorny problems to deal with it is little wonder that Pakistan failed at the time to make a satisfactory bid for the leadership of the Arab nations. Meanwhile she tended to look for help from the West, especially in the development of her industries and commerce. Here again she came up against her neighbour India. The problem lay in the fact that the five great rivers which flow through the Punjab are the basis of the economy and prosperity of Pakistan. These waters if diverted into canals could be made to irrigate a vast area not yet brought under full cultivation. Friction was bound to arise over the diversion of these waters and the development schemes involved. It was a question of how to be fair in the apportionment of water-power.

In 1954 Nehru opened the Bhakra Nangal irrigation scheme on the Sutlej River. Pakistan meanwhile also had her own irrigation schemes on foot, especially the Thal project in the Punjab and the lower Sind barrage at Kutri, which were designed to provide water for a total territory of no less than $4\frac{1}{2}$ million acres. A famine crisis in 1953 had threatened a terrible collapse of the national economy but the United States and the Commonwealth countries were exceptionally generous in coming to the rescue of Pakistan.

On the death of Jinnah in September 1948, Liaquat Ali Khan, who had been Prime Minister, now became Pakistan's second Governor-General. But in October 1951 he was assassinated and his place as Governor-General was taken by Ghulam Mohammad. In April 1953 the latter had to dismiss the Government of Nazi-Muddin for inability to deal with contemporary problems, and Mohammed Ali was put into office together with a Ministry of more progressive-minded moderates.

In East Pakistan in 1954 Communist agitation had led to the Communist Party being outlawed and many leaders arrested. In the same year Pakistan had concluded a treaty of friendship with Turkey and accepted military aid from the United States, and had joined the South-East Asia Treaty Organization (Manila Pact). One danger into which Pakistan fell, but which India had avoided, was that the Army tended to interfere in politics. Both in 1950 and in 1953 Pakistan had had to face trouble from three separate quarters at the same time; the Mullahs, who were gaining authority; the Army who were putting pressure on the Government; and the Communists who were working for subversion. Internal stability was not easy to acquire.

In 1956 Pakistan became a republic within the Commonwealth, and Suhrawardy, the Prime Minister, continued the policy of his predecessors, whereby Pakistan linked together S.E.A.T.O., the Baghdad Pact, and the Commonwealth.

4. THE NEW BURMA

It is as easy to deal with Burma in a chapter on India as it is to include it in a chapter on South-East Asia. Burma had after all been administered under the general supervision of the Viceroy; Burmese delegates had attended Parliamentary sessions in Delhi; and Burma was indeed a part of the vast British Indian Empire so far as government had been concerned. But racially and nationally it was precisely the prospect of possible incorporation in India which Burma most dreaded.

This separation from India was promised her in 1937. No sooner had Britain promised India that one day she would become independent than Burma suspected that this involved subordination to British rule after Indian independence had been achieved. Her fears had gone full cycle. On the outbreak of war Burma offered to help Britain against Japan, but the offer was rejected and Burma therefore looked to Japan hopefully to rid her of British domination. In 1940 U Aung San was invited by the Japanese to go to Japan and only returned to Burma when the Japanese armies invaded the country. He was put in command of Burma's national army and became the head of the A.F.P.F.L.—Anti-Fascist People's Freedom League, the pre-war Thakin revolutionary movement. Although the Japanese promised the Burmese independence in 1943, and although a puppet government was set up in Burma, the Burmese soon realized that the Japanese had no intention whatever of honouring this promise. Their treatment of the Burmese was contemptuous, haughty and most humiliating.

In 1945 Burma was successfully liberated by the Fourteenth Army under the command of General Slim, and U Aung San realized that he had far more hope of achieving independence for his country by co-operating with the British and Indian liberators than he had ever had from the Japanese. In May 1945 the British promised to grant self government and trusted that Burma would remain within the British Commonwealth, but U Aung San was satisfied with nothing less than complete independence.

In August 1946 General Sir Hubert Rance became Governor

of Burma in place of Sir Reginald Dorman-Smith, and his attitude towards freedom for Burma was far more sympathetic. In October U Aung San became leader of a new Council of Ministers dominated by his own party, the A.F.P.F.L., and his first action was to dismiss all Communists in responsible places. In January 1947 U Aung San headed a delegation to London and was so impressed by the desire of the Government of Mr. Attlee to grant to Burma the fulfilment of her national aspirations that he returned to his country on the crest of a wave of confidence and hope. At the General Elections in April the A.F.P.F.L. party won 173 of the 210 seats, the Communists gaining seven.

The minorities in the country, and especially the Karens, the Shans, the Kachins and the Chins, became troublesome at the prospect of being engulfed by the Nationalist Party. In June 1947 the Constituent Assembly declared that Burma would become an independent republic and should leave the Commonwealth of Nations. A month later, on 19 July 1947, U Aung San and six of his Cabinet Ministers were assassinated at a Cabinet meeting. U Saw Ba Mau and seven other conspirators were immediately arrested and executed. U Nu, a man of deep religious piety and culture, who had been U Aung San's deputy as Vice-President of the A.F.P.F.L., succeeded him in control of the Government.

The new constitution was passed in September 1947. The Burma Independence Bill passed through Parliament at Westminster, and on 4 January 1948 Burma left the Commonwealth and became the Republic of the Union of Burma. Its first President was Sao Shwe Thaik. Burma adopted a two-chamber system of government—a Chamber of Nationalities or Senate, in which non-Burmese were given ample representation, and a Chamber of Deputies, twice the size of the Senate. As a proof of good faith and goodwill Britain liquidated the debt owed by Burma to Britain and thus helped to give the country a good start financially.

Although Burma was as determined as other countries to set out on a policy of nationalization, she found herself heavily committed in a succession of rebellions in district after district. In 1948 a Communist Conference in Calcutta had provided the signal for many Communist groups to stir up trouble, and in March Burma's Communist Party was in open revolt against the Government. The 'White Flags' seized control of the district between Rangoon and Mandalay, and the 'Red Flags' operated south in the Irrawaddy delta. As if the trouble with the Communists and Karens was not enough, an offshoot also grew in the A.F.P.F.L. party, known as the People's Voluntary Organization.

Had all these factions taken the trouble to unify their operations it is doubtful if the central Government could have maintained its authority, but gradually U Nu gained command of district after district and began to restore confidence throughout the country. In 1952, in the first elections held after independence, the A.F.P.F.L. gained 180 seats out of 233. The Communists were rash enough to demand expropriation of property and to deny any compensation to previous owners. This was so contrary to all sense of justice that by the end of 1953 the Government declared the Burma Communist Party unlawful. In the same year an Asiatic Socialist Conference was held at Rangoon at which Mr. Attlee was present as a distinguished guest and delegate. In 1954 a new and separate Karen state was inaugurated within the Burma Union. Matters of foreign policy, taxation, defence, and communications remained the responsibility of the Central Government but otherwise the Karen state was self-governing.

The Central Government was by now in a position to undertake its programme of village welfare, mass education, land reform and industrial development. In 1950, when the Korean war broke out, Burma supported U.N.O. and thus indicated her general support of international authority and Western democracy. Nevertheless it was equally incumbent upon her to develop friendly relations with her neighbour in the north, the Communist government of Peking. China laid claim to certain border territories, where the frontier had long been uncertain, which Burma had no intention of surrendering. This source of friction persisted for years.

In 1956 U Nu resigned the Premiership, and retired to a life of meditation. His statesmanship and advice were still to be available to his successors. But early in 1957 he was back again in office, the one outstanding figure who could hold the country together and negotiate with others. While U Nu was enjoying his temporary retirement Chou En-lai had visited Burma on his extensive goodwill tour of many countries in the winter of 1956-57. His visit and the return of U Nu greatly eased and accelerated a frontier settlement.

Asia Speaks for Herself

5. THE NEW CEYLON

In the course of the Second World War Ceylon managed to remain free from the wide sweep of Japanese occupation which threatened the Indian Ocean territories. At the same time, in 1943, Britain promised Ceylon full internal civil administration as soon as conditions allowed. The island became the headquarters of the South-East Asia Command, under the leadership of Admiral Lord Louis Mountbatten. As soon as the war was over a commission was set up under the Chairmanship of Lord Soulbury to work out the constitution for the island, and a Ceylon Independence Act was passed through Parliament in December 1947, which gave Ceylon dominion status. In February 1948 this Act came into operation and Lord Soulbury became the first Governor-General, with D. S. Senanayake of the United Nationalist Party as first Prime Minister.

Ceylon's position was somewhat embarrassed by her proximity to the mainland. For fear that the immigration of Indians might increase and upset her internal political plans, Ceylon restricted the franchise to her own Singhalese nationals. This was interpreted by India as a deliberate affront to upwards of a million Indians resident on the island. Ceylon, like India, did her best to steer her foreign policy in the direction of neutrality, but found this increasingly difficult. On the one hand Soviet Russia constantly vetoed Ceylon's application for membership of U.N.O., probably because Ceylon still allowed Britain to have the use of certain military bases; and on the other hand there were Left Wing influences within the island whose avowed policy was to break with the Commonwealth and go over to Russia.

On the death of Mr. Senanayake in 1952 Sir John Kotelawala became Prime Minister. He pictured Ceylon as the Switzerland of Asia, and Colombo, as he said, the Geneva of the Orient. A patriot, an ardent supporter of the Commonwealth and an internationalist, he nevertheless endeavoured to negotiate for Ceylon a middle path between the rival groupings among the nations. Ceylon favoured neutrality as much as India. In 1954 Nehru persuaded Sir John Kotelawala to go so far as to register all Indians in Ceylon who hoped one day to acquire Singhalese citizenship. This seemed to be the first step in claiming the right to a vote. In the elections in 1952 the United National Party gained fifty-four seats, the Left

192

Wing parties twenty-one, and the Independents eleven. For the time being nationalism held power secure.

At the Bandung Conference in 1955, when the leaders of Communist China did their best to woo the neutral countries of Asia and North Africa and assume the political leadership of the continent, Sir John Kotelawala was one of the most outstanding advocates of non-Communist democracy. He went so far as to suggest that the Communist Powers were now the new Imperialists.

At the next elections in 1956 voting swung very much to the Left and a coalition of Left Wing parties, headed by Mr. Bandaranaike, took over the Government from the United Nationalist Party. At this point some people quite expected that Ceylon might opt out of the Commonwealth, but on the contrary, Mr. Bandaranaike represented his country at the Prime Ministers' Commonwealth Conference in London in July of the same year and expressed no wish for Ceylon to leave the Commonwealth at this stage. Britain was allowed to use one naval and one air base, but in 1957 even these were willingly surrendered.

6. KASHMIR

The State of Jammu and Kashmir has been the greatest bone of contention between India and Pakistan ever since partition in 1947. Both countries expected to acquire it, and made anxious bids for its possession and allegiance. For nearly 150 years (1820 to 1947) Jammu and Kashmir were Hindu-dominated and linked with the Punjab. Muslims were often miserably treated and severely taxed, so much so that in 1930 a Muslim Conference party was formed to resist the decrees of the Maharaja. In 1938 a new party was founded, the National Conference Party under Sheikh Abdullah, which associated itself with the Congress Party of India. Both parties were eventually suppressed. At the time of partition the Maharaja was placed in an impossible position. His Muslim subjects hoped to join Pakistan. Geographically there was a connexion, for the Indus and Jhelum rivers ran into West Pakistan. The Muslims had strong grounds for hope. But the Maharaja himself discountenanced such a prospect and played for time, refusing to commit himself. This heightened the tension, and in October 1947 armed tribesmen attacked the country from outside. The ruler fled, appealed to India to help him, and assigned his State to the Dominion of India. Pakistan refused to recognize the accession or to accept any responsibility for the attacks on the territory. India therefore turned to the United Nations for arbitration. It was not until December 1948 that both sides agreed upon a cease-fire, which became operative in January 1949. The controversy over possession continued. India refused to accept an American (Admiral Nimitz) as mediator. From April 1950 till April 1951 Sir Oswald Dixon did his utmost to reconcile the differences, to be followed by Dr. Graham. Neither succeeded. India complained that the Azad frontiersmen who troubled Kashmir were encouraged and supported by Pakistan.

In 1951 the Maharaja (Hari Singh) resigned in favour of his son, Karansinghji Bahadur, and in November 1952 Kashmir was proclaimed a republic. A movement for independence gained support, until the Prime Minister, Sheikh Abdullah, was arrested. Fresh talks opened in Delhi in July 1953 but little progress was made. When Pakistan then accepted military aid from the U.S.A. the situation was further complicated, India became increasingly indignant and the Kashmir Assembly declared that it could not go back on its accession to India. The controversy dragged on and on with neither side willing to give way. A plebiscite was suggested from time to time, and it was reliably estimated that the result would be favourable to Pakistan in the ratio 60 : 40, but a plebiscite was thought to be of no avail as neither party would be likely to accept an adverse result. The result was deadlock.

Early in 1957 Kashmir fell to India by lapse, and default of settlement. Two-thirds of the country was already occupied and held by Indian forces, the remaining third by Pakistan troops. Pakistan appealed to U.N.O., and a neutral negotiator, Hr. Jarring of Sweden, was despatched to find a possible solution. For the fifth time the effort to mediate failed, and the marvel is that high spirits on both sides were held in check, and this critical issue did not break out into wholesale warfare. Like so many other parts of the world Kashmir had suffered partition.

XII

INDEPENDENCE IN SOUTH-EAST ASIA

1. THE CHRYSALIS PERIOD 1942-45

By a strange twist of history Japan may be held responsible for producing a whole crop of new governments in South-East Asia between 1942 and 1945. It was Japan's invasion and occupation of this vast area which further undermined the eastern Empires of Britain, Holland, and France. European domination was challenged, came to an end and was temporarily replaced. There were new incentives to nationalism and new leaders came forward to fight for the freedom of Asians from any subservience to imperial rule.

The three short years of Japanese occupation gave all the territories of South-East Asia just long enough to review their position, to determine not to go back to the old pattern of subjection to Europe and to press on towards the ultimate objective of one day governing themselves. The temporary overthrow of imperial authority provided an interval of time, as it were a cocoon stage, during which something entirely new was being born. Countries which had been relatively docile and had accepted foreign rule were forced to think about their future afresh, to produce new leaders and forge their own way ahead. Nowhere was it a light task. Generally speaking these countries resented Japanese military control, and not even the propaganda of joining with Japan in creating a co-prosperity sphere could convince them that the Japanese Empire would be any more acceptable than the imperial rule they had already known. In some places they co-operated with the Japanese invader. In others they adopted a policy of passive accommodation, but in most cases they were quick to realize that a great opportunity had been given them to make a bid for independence.

2. MALAYA

At first sight it may seem strange that Malaya did not follow Burma, India, Pakistan, and Ceylon in being granted self government within a few years after the end of the Second World War. One of the reasons was that the other countries had all been part of the British Indian Empire, but Malaya was a separate administration. There were also other and deeper reasons: Malaya had been a collection of Sultanates and the native rulers were the local authorities; political parties had not yet evolved and there was nothing to compare with the Kuomintang, the Indian Congress or the Muslim League. However anxious, therefore, Britain might have been to welcome Malaya as yet another equal partner in the free association of the Commonwealth, such an eventuality was ruled out by the lack of any experienced and tested political body which could safely be entrusted with the responsibility of government over the whole area.

There was another problem—that of race and language. The Malays naturally hoped and expected to maintain control of affairs in their own country when the day of independence should come. But the Chinese by rapid infiltration were threatening to outnumber them and there was the danger that they might indeed become the dominant influence in the country. This applied even more in Singapore than it did in Malaya. Meanwhile the Indian community were hoping for at any rate minority recognition and representation. It was not going to be easy to work out the right constitution for such a fluid and multi-racial populace.

As soon as the Second World War was over and the British had taken over the administration from the retreating Japanese, the essential task was to bring about some kind of Government which would give Malaya an administrative unity and prepare her for eventual self-government. This task was entrusted to Sir Harold MacMichael. The outcome was the publication in January 1946 of a Government White Paper setting out a plan for Malayan Union, to come into operation in April of the same year.

The plan was that all nine Malay states, plus Penang and Malacca, should be members of the Union; that the Sultans should retain their thrones and that Singapore should remain a separate Crown Colony. Treaties were to be signed with all the rulers and legal sovereignty surrendered to Britain. But the idea of a Malayan Union collapsed. The Malays suspected all manner of dangers in any transfer of power and even imagined that the British in turn might ultimately be persuaded to favour the Chinese because of their majority, at the expense of Malayan interests. This ill-starred project nevertheless bore useful fruit in an unexpected direction: Malaya woke up to the need to create political organizations. So emerged a United Malaya National Organization, U.M.N.O., born at Kuala Lumpur in 1946. Dato Onn bin Jafaar was elected its first President.

Less than two years later a new scheme proved more acceptable and came into operation. This was the promulgation of the Federation of Malaya on 1 February 1948, administered by a High Commissioner and assisted by Executive and Legislative Councils. The latter consisted of fifteen officials and sixty-one elected representatives. There was no territorial difference from the Union plan of 1946, but the new Federation constitution had the merit of having been worked out by thorough consultation between all the main parties concerned—the rulers of the Malay States, the United Malay National Organization and the British Government. Each ruler continued to govern his own state with the help of an Executive Council and a Council of State, but also continued to accept advice either from the High Commissioner or the British adviser appointed to each state.

The franchise was given to those who qualified by birth in federal territory or by residence (fifteen years), and this covered Chinese, British and Indians, as well as Malays. Then came trouble. In June 1948, coinciding strangely enough with the Berlin Blockade and also with rebellion in other parts of Asia, a wave of violence broke out. Rubber planters were murdered. Rubber trees were attacked and ruined. Chinese who were known to be loyal to the Kuomintang Government were assassinated, as well as the British. Ambushing, sniping and raids became frequent. It soon became apparent that the origins of this unrest and turmoil were Communist-inspired and that the terrorists hoped to capture sufficient control of at least one area so as to be able on 3 August 1948 to declare the existence of a Communist Republic of Malaya. The Communists had two advantages. Some of them had served in the jungle and fought against the Japanese and were well accustomed to that particular kind of guerrilla warfare. They also had stubborn leaders, one or two of whom had even been decorated by the British Government; one of them, Chin Peng, Secretary-General of the Malayan Communist Party, had even taken part in the Victory Parade in London in 1946. At the end of the war these rebels were thought to have disbanded and to have surrendered their arms, but this was wishful thinking. In the lull between 1945 and 1948 the Communists had been very busy carefully organizing cells in many of the Trade Unions, notably in Singapore, and planned to disturb the economy both of Malaya and Singapore if and when the situation allowed. When the test came and the Government began to take action against them many of the Communist leaders fled. Others were arrested, but terrorism pervaded the land. Tremendous efforts were made to restore civil order and produce a sense of security. Settlements of Chinese immigrants were thought to be the main centres of disaffection, and one recommendation of the Briggs Plan, which was drawn up to deal with the emergency, suggested that new villages should be made available to them in the hope of winning over their loyalty.

Far stronger security measures were put into effect with police, home guard and military support, especially after the appointment of General Sir Gerald Templer as High Commissioner in January 1952. Gradually the guerrilla forces were pushed further and further back into the thick jungle and confidence in Government authority and security began to return. But the danger merely receded, it was not eliminated.

By 1955 Chin Peng and his terrorists were known to be operating from the border districts of Malaya and Siam. Meanwhile the desire for political independence in Malaya had increased steadily and a new constitution was adopted in 1954. Elections to the Legislative Council were held in July 1955, and the United Malays National Organization, working in close alliance with the Malayan Chinese Association and the Malay Indian Congress, together won fifty-one of the fifty-two seats. This indicated a unity of policy and action which could not have been foreseen ten years earlier in 1945, and was a big step forward towards the granting of complete independence, which was eventually promised in the early days of 1956.

The Communists made one last desperate attempt to identify themselves with the movement for independence and Chin Peng asked for an opportunity of discussing the matter with a Malayan deputation. The meeting took place in the heart of the jungle as Chin Peng was in hiding at the time, but with no satisfactory result. The Malayan leader, Tengku Abdul Rahman, came to London in 1956 to work out with the British Government the final details of the transfer of power; Malaya was to be independent from August 1957.

Singapore

Singapore became a separate Crown Colony in April 1946, when the previous Straits Settlement Colony was dissolved and when Penang and Malacca were incorporated in the Malayan Union —later to become the Federation of Malaya. A new constitution was proposed by the Rendel Commission and elections took place in April 1955. The Labour Front gained ten of the twenty-two seats and no less than four other Parties shared the remaining twelve seats. Singapore began to clamour not merely for independence, but possibly even for dominion status, but the British Government felt that it needed time to make sure that sufficient political stability existed before she felt ready to grant the measure of self government demanded.

The wilful eloquence and flamboyance of the Chief Secretary, David Marshall, kept Singapore in the forefront of public notice until his replacement in 1956 by Lim Yew Hoch, whose discretion and more patient ways paved the way towards constitutional change.

3. INDO-CHINA: VIETNAM, LAOS, CAMBODIA

The struggle for political independence in French Indo-China is not as complicated and difficult to follow as it would seem at first sight. During the main period of Japanese occupation, the years 1942–44, the Japanese 'allowed' the officials of Vichy France to continue their administration of Indo-China. Their opposite numbers in France were collaborating with the Germans, and a similar collaboration with the Japanese military authorities went on in French territories in the South China Sea area. But in the spring of 1945 all this was changed. France was once again free from German occupation in Europe and would soon be free to 'liberate' her colonial possessions in the East. Japan, therefore, took over control from the French in Indo-China on 9 March 1945.

By way of easing alarm and in an attempt to give the impression that the change-over was locally welcomed and supported, the Emperor of Annam (Bao Dai), the King of Cambodia (Norodon Sihanouk) and the King of Laos (Sisavong Vong) were all encouraged to issue declarations of independence. The impression was deliberately created that French rule was over, independence had been established and a certain degree of gratitude was owed to the Japanese for their act of liberation and their protection during the war. This did not last.

Throughout the Second World War Ho Chi Minh had been carefully and systematically building up the organization of a Communist Party designed to overthrow both the French and the Japanese and to restore the Annamese sovereignty in Indo-China. For a time he had to organize his forces from China, but in the autumn of 1944 he moved his headquarters into the Red River area of Tongking, well placed to seize power as soon as the Japanese were defeated or left the country. Thus in August 1945, just as Japan surrendered so suddenly and dramatically, Ho Chi Minh captured Hanoi, the capital of Tongking, and to him accrued all the kudos of a liberator. Without delay his forces took over Saigon, the capital of Cochin China, and Ho Chi Minh's authority began to run the full length of the country from Tongking in the north, through Annam in the centre, to Cochin-China in the south.

The Emperor Bao Dai had little alternative but to abdicate and Ho Chi Minh declared the three countries (Tongking, Annam, and Cochin-China) a republic to be known henceforward as Vietnam. With clever realism Ho Chi Minh appointed Bao Dai Supreme Councillor of State, for the Emperor's name would lend respectability to the new Government and give every appearance to the outside world of a return to tradition and order, and thus disguise a political revolution. For a moment the issue looked as though it had been settled. The Japanese had been expelled, the French had not returned to power, genuine nationalist forces within the country seemed to have discovered a workable compromise pattern of Government. The defeat of Japan, having been brought about in the main by the armies, navies, and air forces of Britain and America and their attendant allies, it was therefore their statesmen meeting in Berlin who made the operative decisions which for the time being were to govern the liberation and the immediate destiny of countless millions of people in Asia as well as in Europe. These statesmen met at Potsdam in July 1945 and evolved their own policy in regard to the former French Indo-China.

The most urgent decision was as to the method of accepting the Japanese surrender. They decided that the Chinese Nationalist forces were to occupy the territory north of the 16th Parallel and that the British were to take over the situation south of this line. These were temporary measures to give the French time to recover their breath before taking over their Far Eastern colonial territories again. The attitude looks unrealistic in retrospect, as if the great Western Powers were thinking only in terms of putting the clock back to pre-war administration, but their real concern in the first instance was to safeguard against a period of chaos and also (in July 1945 the war in the Pacific was still not yet concluded) to ensure that someone would be available to accept the Japanese surrender and deal with the immediate aftermath.

On 13 September 1945 the British Commander, General Gracey, arrived in Saigon. He was quick to realize how completely the republican Vietnam Government was in control. General Leclercq, the French military commander, realized the same thing and in March 1946 came to terms with Ho Chi Minh. The French agreed to recognize Annam and Tongking as one autonomous territory. Ho Chi Minh assented to France's wish to send troops back into the country, but it was stipulated that they were to be removed within five years. Meanwhile the future of Cochin-China was to be settled by plebiscite. Ho Chi Minh needed time to consolidate his influence. He could expect no help from any neighbouring country at the time, neither from Chiang Kai-shek's China, nor from Siam, nor from any other quarter. His future success depended on winning the confidence of all sections of the community—troops, peasants, workers, industrialists, business interests, French officials, and Roman Catholic nationals—a tall order for a new and Marxist régime.

He promised almost everything—religious toleration, the right to private possession and a remarkable degree of accommodation. Later in 1946 Ho Chi Minh visited Paris. It was a gesture of conciliation and delighted French officials while disgusting Annamese nationalists. His visit resulted in a *modus vivendi*, with a good deal of give and take on both sides, but this delicate equilibrium was soon upset. The French High Commissioner, Admiral d'Argenlieu, who had arrived early in 1946, was determined to oust Ho Chi Minh, whom he regarded as a tool of the Kremlin and a menace in the Far East. Furthermore the new French constitution, adopted by a referendum in October 1946, incorporated all the overseas territories and associated states belonging to France within a far-flung French Union. In this constitution Vietnam, Laos, and Cambodia were counted as associated states.

The fundamental principle in the constitution was close federation and the Union was part and parcel of the republic. The constitution, therefore, offered little prospect of real independence or local sovereignty and certainly no hope of anything approaching the offer of dominion status which Britain was already offering India within the Commonwealth. Mistrust flared up again and negotiations failed. In December 1946 French garrisons were attacked and a long period of guerrilla warfare set in. There was a faint hope in March 1947 that if Ho Chi Minh could have been promised independence, friendship between France and Vietnam might have been established, but French politicians abhorred such a concession. They were convinced that it would be the beginning of the end. If Vietnam was to be granted independence, then Laos, Cambodia and possibly Morocco, Tunis, Algiers, Madagascar, and elsewhere would demand the same—the collapse of yet another Empire. France was doing her best to stave off the inevitable.

There seemed to be no end to the deadlock until France hit on the idea of trying to persuade Bao Dai, who was now in retirement on the island of Hong Kong, to come back to his throne in Vietnam. If his demands for certain assurances had been granted speedily it is possible that he might have gone back with greater confidence than he did, but the French took a year and a half to conclude the preliminary negotiations with him before he was reinstalled in his capital at Hué, and by then the situation had changed.

The Communist Government of Mao Tse-tung was now in control of the Chinese mainland. Chiang Kai-shek had been chased from China on to the island of Formosa (Taiwan). Ho Chi Minh could, therefore, expect military aid from the new Government in Peking and this was not slow in coming, but as soon as China began to support the Vietminh Government of Ho Chi Minh it was only likely to be a matter of time before the United States would be invited to support the French and Bao Dai forces in the south. Britain and the United States, among other powers, recognized the Bao Dai régime as soon as it was established, the immediate consequences of which were that China and Russia gave full diplomatic recognition to Vietminh. Towards the end of 1950 the appointment of General de Lattre de Tassigny brought new vigour and success to the campaign against Vietminh and it was at this point that the French invited the United States to come to their assistance.

By now the war in Korea had also broken out and Asia was faced with two small countries, Korea and Vietnam, divided almost equally into halves and each locked in combat. Both threatened to develop into war on the fullest possible international scale. The Berlin blockade had been serious enough. The Korean war had become a United Nations commitment and the situation in Indo-China might equally have flared up into a Third World War. The year of crisis was 1954.

With the death of General de Lattre de Tassigny in 1952 French influence appeared to disintegrate and the Vietminh forces became sufficiently successful not only to conquer garrison after garrison of French forces, but also to aim a thrust into the neighbouring territory of Laos, in the direction of its capital Luang Prabang. In an attempt to break this line of advance and to embarrass the attack the French military authorities decided to hold the fortress town of Dien Bien Phu at no matter what cost. It was at a time when the battle was raging fiercely around this frontier fortress in the far north of Tongking that arrangements were made for a meeting of Foreign Secretaries to discuss the position in Indo-China. By great good fortune the Foreign Secretaries of Britain, Russia, the United States, and France had been meeting in Berlin to discuss issues arising out of Germany and Austria when it was suggested that they should try to solve the deadlock in Indo-China. Russia agreed to come to such a meeting on condition that the Peking Government was also represented, and the other countries assented. This conference met in Geneva in April 1954, and it was the first time that Chou En-lai, as Foreign Secretary of Communist China, attended such a conference. Russia was as eager to watch her new partner in delicate negotiation with the West as indeed the Western authorities were to test China's goodwill and readiness to co-operate.

Almost as soon as the conference had convened Dien Bien Phu was captured by the forces of Ho Chi Minh, and this was a great feather in the cap of the Communist camp. In Geneva East and West stated their terms and once again it seemed as though the conference would end in deadlock. There was little hope of compromise. Mr. John Foster Dulles, the American Secretary of State, had refused to attend the conference in any case and had sent a deputy. He had protested already that the only hope for peace in the East lay in military talks with powers which the United States could trust. Military talks had in fact just taken place in Singapore between the Anzus powers (Australia, New Zealand, and the United States). Mr. Anthony Eden had attended a meeting of the Colombo powers (India, Pakistan, Burma, Ceylon, Indonesia) and hoped to gain their support in any decisions that were made at Geneva. He was prepared to trust the new nations which had been given complete independence and which he felt sure would be ready to co-operate.

In the very middle of the Geneva Conference Mr. Anthony Eden had to fly to Washington for a conference and the other Foreign Secretaries took the opportunity to go home and consult their respective Governments. Molotov flew back to Moscow; M. Bidault returned to Paris and Chou En-lai went back to Peking via Delhi and Rangoon. Before the conference broke up the Vietminh government tried to suggest that recognition should be given to the resistance movements that were at work in Cambodia and Laos respectively. This would have meant a further collapse of French authority in these territories.

When the conference foregathered for its second stage there were two significant changes. France was represented by M. Mendes-France, who insisted that a solution to the problem of French Indo-China should be reached within nine days, otherwise he would have no alternative but to resign and France would have to appoint a new representative. This added an unexpected note of urgency to negotiations which had already dragged on long enough. Secondly, Molotov and Chou En-lai were far more conciliatory and accommodating than they had been during the first session. Mr. Dulles, afraid to let the Indo-China question touch off an international war, may possibly have had something to do with this more reasonable attitude from Moscow and Peking.

By the middle of July it was obvious that a solution could be reached. Vietnam was partitioned, roughly along the line of the 17th Parallel. This left the country sadly divided, very much as was the case in Korea. Cambodia had already been declared independent in 1953 and under the Geneva Agreement elections were held in September 1955. All the seats were won by the popular Socialist and Community Party, formed and led by Prince Norodon Sihanouk himself. In the case of Laos, the two northern provinces were held by the Pathet Lao rebel forces and it was impossible to bring about agreement with them as to the matter of the elections, but elections were nevertheless held in the southern provinces in December 1955, and both Laos and Cambodia were recognized as neutral territories.

So far as Southern Vietnam was concerned it was agreed that elections should take place in two years' time, in 1956, but these never took place. The general outcome, therefore, of the Geneva Conference was that Ho Chi Minh's government established itself securely in the north and France gave up all hope of removing it. Communism in Indo-China for the time being appeared to be held at bay, but at the cost of partition. This was yet another stage in the gradual folding up of the French Empire. In Asia France had already surrendered Syria and the Lebanon and the small enclaves in India. Her hold in the former Indo-China was rapidly loosening. Almost immediately France became further embarrassed by trouble in North Africa, where Tunis, Morocco, and Algiers each in turn began to demand independence.

4. INDONESIA

The Dutch were as reluctant as the French to lose their Empire in Eastern Asia. Although before the Second World War there were assurances that the Dutch East Indies would one day be granted self government, the processes of preparing the country for such an eventuality were slow indeed, and uninspiring. The islands which composed the Dutch East Indies were so closely linked to Holland in trade and commerce, wealth and prosperity, that the reluctance to lose them is understandable. They were essentially part of Holland.

Dutch families not merely found their business interests in those islands, but lived there, knew the people intimately, often inter-married and were proud of their Empire. The thought of losing it was wholly repugnant and partly explains their obstinacy and resistance when the time for surrender came. It is true that between the two World Wars there had been a mild development of political consciousness, including an embryo Communist Party, but to all intents and purposes the Dutch East Indies had as yet no effective organized political units. Government was in the hands of the Dutch. In the course of Japanese occupation, from 1942 to 1945, nationalist incentives became coherent and organized and this concentration of nationalist feeling was as much anti-Dutch as anti-Japanese.

As the Second World War came to an end the Japanese made one desperate bid to guarantee that the Dutch islands would gain their independence and not be recovered by the Dutch. They invited several Indonesians to a conference in Saigon to discuss the setting up of a nationalist government, and indeed on 17 August 1945, independence was proclaimed in Java. By this time Holland had been freed from Nazi occupation, but the Dutch were still in no position to send military forces to take over control in the East Indies. The British were, therefore, asked to undertake the re-sponsibility of landing on the islands, disarming and repatriating more than a quarter of a million Japanese and other nationalities and also of guaranteeing civil order to the islands.

One of their first responsibilities was to release some 200,000 prisoners of war, most of whom were Dutch, and many of whom were civilians. The British discovered that the new nationalist authorities were more than likely to challenge the return of the Dutch and so they had little alternative but to recognize them as the *de facto* republican government for the moment. It was generally hoped on the British side that the Dutch and Indonesian republicans would later be able to meet in conference and decide in mutual discussion the best constitutional future for the territories. The Dutch Governor-General, Dr. H. J. Van Mook, who had been appointed in 1942, soon arrived to take up his responsibilities, but refused to have dealings with the republican leader Sukarno. A more moderate Indonesian, who, unlike Sukarno, had not collaborated with the Japanese, Sutan Sjahrir, replaced Sukarno and was later invited to go to Holland for discussions, but there were wide differences between Dutch policy and Indonesian hopes.

The Indonesian Communist Party (P.K.L.) came to the fore and made several attempts to infiltrate into trade union circles and also into the remoter districts, where they stimulated unrest. On one occasion an attempt was made to kidnap Sutan Sjahrir and several of his friends, but Sukarno, now President of the Republic, managed to prevent the attempt. So impossible was the relationship between Dutch and Indonesians in 1946 that Lord Killearn was asked to become Chairman of a neutral commission which met at Ling Gad Jati, near Cheribon, to thrash out some kind of agreement.

Eventually the Dutch recognized the republican government of Sukarno as the *de facto* government for the three islands of Sumatra, Java, and Madura. This commission further brought about their agreed aim that there should be a united states of Indonesia, a part of a yet wider Netherlands Indonesian union, which would also include Surinam and Curacao in the Caribbean area. These terms, reached in November, were passed through the Dutch Parliament and the Central Indonesian National Committee in December 1946.

The Dutch never really trusted the goodwill of the republicans, nor were they willing at heart to accept them as equal partners in the newly formed union. On the Indonesian side the agreement was hotly contested by the Masjumi Party, which was the Moslem bloc in Indonesia. This federal system of government lasted through 1947 and 1948, but proved in the end to be only an interim solution. Fighting broke out in many places and on two occasions, in July 1947 and December 1948, the United Nations were asked to intervene in what was considered an international matter, and on each occasion demanded a cease-fire.

In October 1948 the Dutch Governor-General, Dr. Van Mook, resigned. For several months during the year the civil war had proceeded, not between the Dutch and the Indonesians, but between the moderate republicans and the Communist elements. There were, therefore, two separate issues at stake all the time. First, would the Dutch recognize the genuine independence of Indonesia, and secondly, which political orientation would take the place of the Dutch? The second alternative was not only between moderate republicans and Communists, but was far more complicated, because almost every political complexity from fanatical Moslem and extreme Right Wing nationalist, to varying degrees of orthodox Trotskyist or Titoist Communist, and everything in between was present in the Indonesian situation.

Politically the whole area was unstable and lacked coherence. In the circumstances the Dutch did not contribute to a solution by their lack of realism and delaying tactics. In the meantime India and Pakistan, as well as Burma and Ceylon, had gained full independence, making the Indonesians all the more determined to continue to fight for the principle of self-government and independence. They looked to India for encouragement, and not in vain. In January 1949 Nehru summoned a conference at Delhi to try to suggest some way out of the impasse. He himself supported the Indonesian republicans and, largely as a result of his influence and leadership, the Dutch Prime Minister flew to Indonesia. The republican leaders were themselves reinstated in office in Jakarta in May, and from August to November a conference was held at The Hague to work out the final details of self-government.

In December 1949 Indonesia became a sovereign independent state, associating with the Kingdom of the Netherlands on a voluntary and equal basis; Sukarno was elected President, and Dr. Hatta became first Prime Minister. In September 1950 the republic of Indonesia was admitted to membership of the United Nations. But all was not quite settled; the Dutch still maintained their possession of Dutch New Guinea (Irian) and refused to consider it in any way a part of the republic of Indonesia. This was to lead to more trouble. Sukarno himself preferred to follow the Nehru policy of neutrality, and a strong national government seemed to be well placed in office, but rivalry between the National Party, the Masjumi Party (the Moslem Party) and the Communists

President Sukarno at a reception in Indonesia (*see* p. 208)

A Jordan-Israel frontier post, Jerusalem—a picture of dejection, the price of partition (*see* p. 156)

President Nasser with President Sukarno in Cairo, 1956 (*see* p. 209)

became increasingly acute, the Communists regaining more and more control through trade union organizations, and in one coalition government the Defence Minister, a trained and expert Communist, was accused of packing the ranks and leadership of the Army with trained Communist Indonesians.

In the elections held in September 1955 the Parties were remarkably evenly divided. The National Party (P.N.I.) gained fifty-seven seats, the Masjumi Party fifty-seven, the Nahdatul Ulama gained forty-five, and the Communists thirty-nine.

In August 1956, immediately following Egypt's nationalization of the Suez Canal Company, the government of Indonesia cancelled all financial obligation to pay off old debts outstanding to Holland's credit. Goodwill between Indonesia and the Netherlands had evaporated, but Indonesia had still not been successful in putting her own house in order. The government of Sastro-amidjojo, who succeeded Dr. Hatta as Prime Minister, had difficulty in holding the country together politically and economically. From time to time army commanders assumed control of provincial administration and ignored the decrees of the central government. Indonesia was threatened with internal disruption. Meanwhile, Sukarno went on a tour of a number of countries to study their forms of government, from which experience he hoped to discover one suitable to Indonesia. Early in 1957 he announced a plan for a new constitutional experiment, 'guided democracy', expressing the hope that rival groups would be willing to coalesce in the national interest. Some interpreted the new plan as the first step towards enforced dictatorship, citing his admiration of what he had seen and learnt in Peking. Moslem nationalists had no desire to co-operate with local Communists, and to add to the confusion army units in Sumatra, Borneo, and a number of islands continued to defy the central administration, headed by a cabinet of 'experts' under Dr. Djuanda. The future of Indonesia as a political entity became an open question and a state of emergency was declared. What was to be the fate of the country? If Indonesia has to pass through a long period of unsettlement as China did, it might be disastrous to her hope of maintaining unity. On the other hand, a strong influence with a limited objective might still manage to spare Indonesia the tragedy of internal division.

5. THE PHILIPPINES

The Philippines became an independent Republic on 4 July 1946. It might almost be said that the United States were as anxious for the Philippines to accept independence as the Filipinos were to have it. The American conscience had never been quite happy about its acquisition of the Philippines in 1898 nor did Americans care to be accused of 'Imperialism'. As early as 1916 the Jones Act had introduced a measure of independence and the Tydings-McDuffie Act of 1934 carried the process a stage further. The Philippines had become a Commonwealth in November 1935 and embarked on a ten-year period of transition during which to learn the art of self-government. Thus the Filipinos were promised political freedom first among the Asiatic territories, at approximately the same time that a procedure for increasing independence was being worked out for India at the Round-Table Conferences.

In December 1941 came the lightning attack by Japan, with a force estimated at 200,000. The American Commander-in-Chief, General Douglas MacArthur, suspecting that such an attack might come, had already organized a vigorous defence system and was determined to make the Japanese pay the highest possible price in men and equipment for any success they might gain. From January to May 1942 the Japanese besieged the Bataan Peninsula and it was only after four months of terrible fighting that American forces surrendered at Corregidor (May 1942). General MacArthur escaped to Australia, there to prepare for a gradual liberation of all Japanese-occupied territory and the eventual defeat of Japan in the Pacific. Some sections of the Philippine populace refused to collaborate with the Japanese and guerrilla warfare continued in many districts. During this occupation period a People's Liberation Army (the Hukbong Bayan Laban sa Hapon) was formed and led by Luis Taruc. This organization, more generally known as the Communist Hukbalahap, was officially formed to fight the Japanese, but later became the political rival of the Nationalist and Liberal parties and a sore trial to the police and government. As soon as the Japanese were defeated the Hukbalahap asked for formal recognition, but this was refused. The leader himself, Taruc, was elected a member of the Legislature but was not allowed to take his seat. The Communist Party was banned in October 1948.

Manuel Luis Quezon, virtually a father of the Republic, had been President from 1935 till his death in 1944, i.e., from the formation of the Commonwealth almost till the end of the ten-year transition period and the end of Japanese occupation. He was succeeded by President Roxas who had collaborated with the Japanese. Then came the Liberal President, Quirino, whose efforts to appease the Communists only resulted in an intensified civil war. Meanwhile, the Nationalist leader, Magsaysay, realizing that social and economic reforms alone would undermine the appeal which the Communists had put before the peasants and workers, set in operation new resettlement and agricultural schemes and also kept watch on the activities of Chinese traders who were suspected of feeding the Filipino Communists with arms and ammunition. Only then did the government begin to gain the upper hand. In the presidential election of 1953 Ramon Magsaysay gained an overwhelming victory over President Quirino and, to all outward appearances, the new Republic has hopes of a more stable era.

The link with the United States was not entirely severed. A ninety-nine year military agreement was signed in 1947, whereby the United States were to be granted the use of certain military, naval and air bases and undertook to give military assistance to the Philippines. The fact that the United States has these rights and bases in the South China Seas means that she cannot be disinterested in whatever happens in the whole of South-East Asia. The argument equally holds the other way round. South-East Asia has to take account of American forces in the vicinity. It was from Manila in September 1954 that the idea of a South-East Asia Defence Organization was floated, and the Philippines became one of the founder-members of S.E.A.T.O.

The death of Magsaysay in an air crash in March 1957 was a sad blow for the nation. His energy, integrity, and vision had given new hope to the Philippines, and there is little doubt that he would have been re-elected President for another term in the following autumn. He was only forty-nine when he died. His leadership has been described as 'active rather than intellectual, proletarian rather than parliamentarian', for his interest in social reform and

the personal happiness of his people meant that he never allowed
affairs of State to degenerate into sterile bureaucracy.

6. THAILAND (SIAM)—
FROM AUTOCRACY TOWARDS DEMOCRACY

The politics of Siam or Thailand are as complicated as any in
Asia, and reflect most of the diverse elements that are jostling each
other for pride of place and authority. Thailand is the one sizeable
nation in Asia which has managed to keep clear of European
domination and has therefore not passed through the same stages
of agitation or liberation as so much of the rest of Asia. Thailand
has known Western rule on every side and yet has known that it
was to other nations' advantage that Thailand should be left unmolested as a most convenient buffer-state, and if possible ally.
Her monarchy, the Chakri dynasty, reigned serenely from 1782
until 1932, in which year a new constitution was introduced which
put an end to absolutism. This opened the way to ambition and
personal power and the two leaders who represented left- and
right-wing interests were respectively Nai Pridi Panomyong and
Field Marshal Luang Pibul Songgram. Around these two leaders
Siamese politics have since mainly revolved.

Pibul Songgram, doubtless influenced by his respect for the
German military tradition of which he had personal experience,
staked his future on an appeal to nationalism, strong personal
authority and the support of the army. He saw the advantage to
himself and his country of allying himself with the Japanese as
they swept over Eastern Asia in 1941 and 1942. Thailand thus
joined the Fascist powers and stood to gain much if Japan, Germany and Italy had won the Second World War. In return for her
friendly co-operation Thailand was given certain territories in
Indo-China, ceded to her by the Vichy Government of France in
1941 and also four Malay and two Shan states ceded to Thailand
by Japan in July 1945. But Pibul's Government collapsed in
July 1944, and when the Japanese were defeated the annexed
territories were handed back to France and Britain in 1946. With
the fall of Pibul, Pridi Panomyong, the left-wing leader who had
led an underground movement against the Japanese, came back

into power. In 1933 the Communist Party had been outlawed, but this order was repealed in October 1946.

Then came a period of rapid change, verging on turmoil—there were two civil wars and three *coups d'état* between 1945 and 1951. The post-war constitution of May 1946 had promised free elections and the prospect of democratic government, itself a new venture for the Siamese. The result was a frequent change of government—Seni Pramoj (January 1946) Kuang Abhaiwongse (March 1946), Pridi Panomyong (August 1946) and Thamrong Nawasawat (November 1947). In June 1946 the young king Ananda Mahidol was found dead, presumably murdered or poisoned, but the mystery was never satisfactorily cleared up. He was succeeded by his younger brother, Phumipol Adulyadej.

In 1947 (8 November) Pibul Songgram was restored to power by a *coup d'état* with promises of a new constitution and programmes of educational, military and social reform. Pridi fled the country, to become a thorn in the flesh of the Pibul government. With Communism in the ascendant in China and Annam, and also aggressive in Burma, Pridi had good reason not to lose hope and concentrated on developing the idea of a Free Thai movement in the north. The racial affinities existing between the Siamese, the Burmese and the people of Yunnan provided a chance of creating a separatist state on the China-Siam border territory and of keeping alive the hopes of Communism within Thailand. The new constitution promised in 1947 was promulgated in 1949 and offered representative government for Thailand; the following year, 1950, saw the outbreak of the Korean war and Marshal Pibul Songgram committed Thailand to support the United Nations against the aggression of the North Korean Republic. This action ran counter to Thailand's traditional policy of neutrality, but was consistent with Thailand's membership of U.N.O. which dated from 1947. It was also proof of the government's determination to withstand Communism both in and out of the country. But the establishment of a Communist government in power in Peking and growing Communist influence in Indo-China convinced Pibul that the latest constitution opened the path too wide to rival interests and endangered his own position. On 29 November 1951, by yet another *coup d'état* he abolished the 1949 constitution and restored the 1932 pattern in its place. This constitution provided for a

Asia Speaks for Herself

single chamber assembly of which half the members were elected
and the other half were nominated, i.e., appointed by the king on
the recommendation of the government. This meant, in effect,
that Pibul was secure as Prime Minister and his Nationalist government had little to fear from any of his opponents. Every effort was
made to restrict Communist activity, especially amongst the
Chinese sections of the community where it was most rife. But
he promised that there would be a fully elected assembly in 1962,
saying that Thailand needed an interval of ten years (a so-called
trial period) in which to prepare herself for democratic government.

In 1953 it was announced from Peking that a 'Thai autonomous
region' had been established in the Province of Yunnan, and the
successes of Vietminh forces in Indo-China further alarmed the
Thailand government. Therefore in May 1954 the U.N. Security
Council was asked to send observers to keep watch against any
possible Communist advances across the Siamese frontiers and in
September 1954 Pibul was most willing that Thailand should be
represented at the Manila conference at which the principles of
an anti-Communist South-East Asia Treaty Organization were
discussed. Thus Thailand linked herself with the anti-Communist
front and accepted military assistance offered by the United States.

In 1955 Marshal Pibul Songgram went on a world tour and on
his return felt that the time had come for the return of party
politics. His régime had often been described as a dictatorship,
partly dependent on the favouritism and severity that usually
accompany personal rule. He was eager both to explode this idea
and to side with Western democracy. In 1956, therefore, political
leaders like the former Prime Minister, Kuang, entered the field
of politics again in the hope of building up a party strong enough
to contest elections.

Thus between 1932 and 1957 Thailand has passed through the
vicissitudes of absolutism, Japanese occupation, Liberal left-wing
and nationalist governments and a sequence of about five changes
in constitution. Her sense of nationalism has arisen not so much
from any necessity to discard foreign rulers as from the need to
discover in what way best to rule herself. In the process of experiment she is apprehensive of Communism, cautious not to be over-
indebted to the United States, wary of China and desirous of
consolidating her nation, being loyal to the king, the Buddhist

214

religion, Western democracy and the international family as embodied in the United Nations. At a time when many of the countries of Asia are republics, most of them secular and some Communist, Thailand stands out as one of the great exceptions.

XIII

THE ROAD TO BANDUNG

1. THREE FUNDAMENTAL ISSUES

THE victories throughout Asia of nationalism over Western imperialism in the period from 1945 to 1950, fortified by strong press and radio propaganda, stimulated an almost continent-wide elation. 'Imperialism' and 'colonialism' were the catch-phrases trotted out by government spokesmen in many countries to arouse vocal support for the resurgence that was sweeping Asia and to denounce the political supremacy which Europe had commanded for so long. It was as if the leaders of Asia could scarcely bring themselves to believe that the era of self-rule had really arrived: it was still too good to be true. Their first and paramount need was to realize exactly what had been accomplished. In 1947 Sukarno of Indonesia in a powerful speech had reiterated the truism, that the lifeline of imperialism had been the long route that ran from Gibraltar, through the Mediterranean, the Suez Canal and the Red Sea into the Indian Ocean, the South China Seas and the Sea of Japan. 'The territories on both sides of this lifeline were colonies, the peoples were unfree, their futures mortgaged to an alien system. Along that lifeline, that main artery of imperialism, there was pumped the life-blood of colonialism.' Here was one voice, a customary analysis, an inflection of the voice of Asia—rightly emphasizing the maritime nature of the eastward advance of Europe in the past, but not entirely just in its overall spirit of exaggeration, envy and resentment. This was the overtone of reaction, but it was an impulse so commonplace and shared by so many that it helped to weld together many of the countries of Asia in the general direction of mutual interest and regional collaboration.

In 1947 the Indian Ambassador, Asaf Ali, had called together the

Asian and African members in the United Nations in an endeavour
to unify their policy over the question of Israel, and this initiative
had within it the principle of a new alignment, a re-grouping of the
nations. The three Yalta Powers, Great Britain, the United States,
and Soviet Russia, which had dominated the scene in 1945, were
now split; their war-time alliance had not held; and their rival
doctrines were irreconcilable. A world thus divided gave ample
scope for the emergence of a group of revived nations. In 1945
the vast continent of Asia provided only nine foundation members
of the fifty-one which constituted the United Nations. They were
China (Nationalist), India, and the Philippines; and the six Middle
East countries—Turkey, Lebanon, Syria, Iraq, Persia, and Saudi
Arabia. By 1950 seven more Asian countries had been admitted
to membership—Afghanistan (1946), Thailand (1946), Pakistan
(1947), Yemen (1947), Burma (1948), Israel (1949) and Indonesia
(1950). These additions gave Asia sixteen members out of a total
which had grown by 1950 to sixty, 26 per cent. of the total.
Nations great and small sat as partners within the United Nations
Organization. Politically India began to take the fore, and sometimes stood out as the spokesman for much of Asia, but vote for
vote even a small country like Yemen counted as much as Soviet
Russia or the United States.

But the backwash of imperialism persisted. Although the United
States and Britain had freely left the Philippines, India, Pakistan,
Ceylon, and Burma, France and Holland still clung desperately
to the hope of keeping their Far Eastern possessions, against
impossible odds. Thus in 1949 a conference was held in Delhi of
Asian and African nations to protest before the world against the
injustice of continued Dutch oppression and recalcitrance in Indonesia. This moral support provided by the Delhi conference
greatly strengthened the hands of the nationalist leaders in Indonesia in their negotiations with the Dutch, and consolidated the
feeling of co-operation among the non-European countries. In
face of this growing pressure the Netherlands had no alternative
but to concede sovereignty to Indonesia in December 1949.

Nevertheless, this process of severing the shackles of Europe had
its own limitations and restraints. The time was long past when
Asia could lapse into her former seclusion. A multiplicity of commercial ties, treaty obligations and personal connections bound

Asia closely together with the rest of the world, and any drastic break of such vital links could only be unrealistic and foolish, as certain events were to prove.

The first necessity, therefore, was for the leaders of each country to arrive at a judicious appraisal of the entirely new situation which had so closely followed the end of the Second World War. Among other features, sea power, as a means of holding empires together, was eclipsed by the new forces of nationalism, racialism, and one might almost say, a new continentalism. The new nations that had arisen had no navies of any great size, nor did they feel they needed them. They were land powers, with internal lines of communication, requiring sea-routes primarily for trade and commerce and dependent upon the acceptance of international law to keep the ocean-lanes open and safe. The old type of empire was receding. Only gradually was it being realized that the mid-twentieth century harboured yet more virulent imperialisms under other guises—the doctrines of world-wide revolution and organic change inherent in Marxism, to which we shall refer again.

The second basic problem was how each country could make the best possible use of the new opportunity given it, for political independence could prove to be an empty victory unless it was vindicated by economic stability and general progressive well-being. This was to be one of the tests. But to carry out the necessary programmes of agricultural and industrial development required technical experience and advice which many Asian countries for the moment lacked. There was no alternative in most cases but to look abroad for big amounts of capital, equipment, and contractual responsibility. Economic progress was the most pressing priority and underlay all political strength or advance. Markets had to be secured. Possibilities of famine had to be anticipated and forestalled. Natural resources had to be discovered, harnessed and used. Modern hydro-electric schemes had to be initiated, and all these developments needed a readiness on the part of the new nations to accept the techniques which usually only the Western powers could teach them. Some of the 'old' powers could be trusted; some could not. What often mattered so much was the motive that lay behind material assistance.

Here we come to the third overriding issue—the choice of ideology. As before, Sukarno of Indonesia was one of the leading statesmen to sound the alarm. 'Colonialism,' he said, 'has also its modern dress, in the form of economic control, intellectual control, actual physical control by a small but alien community within a nation. It is a skilful and determined enemy, and it appears in many guises. It does not give up its loot easily.' This was a warning frequently to be echoed by the spokesmen of other nations: permeation and subversion were the hall-marks of twentieth-century upheaval. The particular aspects of the danger were quite different in different places, and to evidence a few of them is to oversimplify and belittle the magnitude of the principle. In the Middle East it was a matter of oil concessions. In the Far East it was connected partly with the tidal wave of an increasing Chinese population overflowing into the whole region of South-East Asia. But far more delicate and subtle were the inroads of trade and thought. In the latter respect Marxism was clearly the most subversive and ruthless. The dream of world-wide revolution was no idle theory. It was intended to be practical politics—when the moment was ripe.

2. CONSPECTUS 1950–55

The political map of Asia had changed radically between 1945 and 1949; national flags were now flying where Western empires had once held sway. The next five years witnessed the attempt by Communism to be considered the rightful successor to Western imperialism of the old style, a challenge which set in train a series of civil wars and which threw into clearer relief the distinctions between the rival creeds. The civil war in China ended in a resounding victory for Communism in 1949, a *fait accompli* which marks as important a turn of events as the partition of India (1947) or the creation of the state of Israel (1948), so important in fact that Peking may supersede Moscow as the dynamo of the communist machine, and China may inherit the political leadership of the entire Marxist system. Her overwhelming population, her racial calibre, and inherent patience are among her qualifications for this role. Western Europe and the United States had been too preoccupied with events in Central Europe, the Balkans and the Levant to give adequate attention to what was happening in the Far East. Nor did their policies agree. The independence of Chiang

Kai-shek and the corruption and ineffectiveness of the Kuomintang government were partly responsible for the loss of British
sympathy in the East, while the Americans went to the other
extreme in support of a lost cause. This divergence of policy was
temporarily repaired by the outbreak of war in Korea in June 1950.
The crushing initial successes of Communist North Korea had the
effect of unifying most of the non-Communist world in moral and
material support of South Korea. Immediate and spontaneous
intervention prevented the whole of Korea becoming Communist
in one fell swoop. The eventual deadlock along the 38th Parallel
was a moral victory for the West, no less important than the failure
of the Berlin blockade of 1948–49.

The switch of events from Europe to the Far East had yet another consequence. The United States, New Zealand, and Australia
hastened to conclude an arrangement for mutual defence in the
Pacific, the A.N.Z.U.S. Pact, in September 1941. Yet this consolidation of military strength could do nothing to prevent Communism spreading on the mainland. Civil war in Indo-China
loosened the grip of French possession, and the military conflict
that ensued had every appearance of a desperate European rear-
guard action. The harder the French fought to retain their Far
Eastern empire, and the more they looked to the United States
for funds or equipment, the more they strengthened the sympathy
countries felt for one another. It was in August 1953, when the
struggle in Indo-China was acute, that the Prime Minister of
Indonesia, Sastroamidjojo, suggested that it was time that countries
both in Asia and Africa began to work together in unison, for only
in co-operation could they stand against the remnants of 'imperialism'. This principle of collaboration was endorsed by a conference of five Asian Prime Ministers in Ceylon in April 1954,
and the process of mutual discussion among Asiatic statesmen
was thus carried another stage forward. High-level conferences,
hitherto, had presented the spectacle of Soviet Russia in the
person of Molotov confronting the representatives of Britain,
France, and the United States. This three-to-one balance was
completely altered by the doubling of the Communist front.
The Peking régime which had cut itself off from the outside
world for nearly five years in order to consolidate its hold on China;
which had depended very much on the support it derived from

Russia; and which had been denied membership of the United
Nations, now came out into the open, somewhat shyly at first, to
feel its way into the arena of international diplomacy. The prospect was both hopeful and alarming. It was unrealistic for a
country the size and power of China not to be a member of the
family of nations. Sooner or later the position would have to be
resolved. The Geneva conference was a sign, therefore, that the
isolation was breaking. But the gigantic proportions that the new
Communist bloc presented to the world filled the hearts of many
with the grimmest forebodings.

The grip of militant Communism in such widely-separated areas
as Korea, Vietnam and East Germany, where bisection was becoming a common pattern, and the emergence of China into the
open, greatly increased the feeling of apprehension. No one could
tell where the next probe or rebellion might occur. In these circumstances new diplomatic and military fronts developed apace.
In August 1954 Turkey—always wary of her giant neighbour
in the north—became a partner with Greece and Yugoslavia in
a Balkan Pact, thus creating a bridge between three countries
remarkably distinct and different in constitution, politics, and
ideology, but fearful of the powerful embrace of the Russian bear.
A similar dread, generated by the existence of Communist cells
and movements at work throughout South-East Asia drove the
countries threatened by subversion to look for security in a
regional defence organization.

The direct outcome of this was the Manila Pact and the South-
East Asia Treaty Organization. Beginning in September 1954, a
line of non-Communist countries stretching from the Philippines
in the Far East, and coming through Thailand, by way of Ceylon
to Pakistan in the West began to form the latest of the regional
defence schemes, projects which were constitutionally permitted
by the Charter of the United Nations. As was to be expected, the
governments of Peking and Moscow promptly denounced
S.E.A.T.O. as a deliberate attempt to intimidate and contain the
Communist bloc, and the cry and accusation of 'encirclement' was
raised once again. The new treaty of friendship between Pakistan
and Turkey virtually linked S.E.A.T.O. with N.A.T.O. and lent
force to the complaint. However much such organizations demonstrated the intention of the countries concerned to resist the

inroads of Communism they could not in themselves either eliminate the infiltration of Communist doctrine or the subversive activity of Communist agents. The real battle was as much in the realm of propaganda as in any treaty alignment. Never was this to be more in evidence than in the next three years, when the Communist front made a concerted effort to pretend that a new benevolence had taken hold of despotism and the Siberian wolf had become a docile lamb. The deception cut both ways, as we shall see.

Meanwhile, the willingness of Chou En-lai to travel out of his own country and negotiate with the outside world had also led to a closer relationship between China and India. After the first phase of the Geneva conference in May 1954 Chou En-lai visited Delhi, and the terms of a Sino-Indian Pact were concluded. By this Pact, signed in June 1954, the two most powerful nations in Asia reached agreement on five paramount principles:

1. Mutual respect for each other's territorial integrity.
2. Non-aggression.
3. Non-interference in each other's internal affairs.
4. Recognition of equality.
5. Peaceful co-existence.

These principles charted a new political future, and gave hope of some compromise in Asia. The pact was an endorsement of confidence in Communist China's emergence from behind the bamboo curtain, and an act of encouragement at a time of tension. It indicated, for example, that India was now reconciled to China's subjugation of Tibet, and was willing to let by-gones be by-gones. By this rapprochement Nehru and Chou En-lai towered more than ever over the Eastern scene. Moscow may have viewed with gratification the welcome recognition now being given to the Peking government but probably watched with interest, not unmixed with concern, the growing stature of Mao Tse-tung and Chou En-lai and their tendency to set their own course of action. Nor did Nehru escape criticism and misunderstanding. Many people in the West were bewildered by his willingness to treat with Peking, and regarded it as a betrayal of Commonwealth loyalty and sympathy with the 'free' world. Some doubted his honesty of purpose, and saw him only as an opportunist, an enigma, or at worst a traitor. Such accusations were often a misreading of his position. An over-close identification with the West was clearly out of the question; it was sufficient that India still desired to retain her place within the Commonwealth. But equally India's traditions, spirit and development did not lend themselves to the acceptance of Communism; her instincts were far too naturally democratic to resign themselves to the dictates of a totalitarian order. India came somewhere between the two, and yet had a desire to be correct and sensible in her relations with both, and be a counterpoise between them. Thus had India been manoevred into a position of neutrality between the rival systems, and in this situation Pundit Nehru had set his course. He aimed at creating a wide area of peace on the continent of Asia as occasion allowed, even though at times his actions and policy appeared to blur the vision he advanced. The idea, nevertheless, of a community of peaceable neighbours was soon to become almost a political doctrine—*Panchsheel*. He aimed at keeping doors open wherever possible, for to slam them was only to provoke hostility. More and more did he come to assume the role of a mediator with all the risks attendant on such a position.

Meanwhile, what had been happening in the Middle East? In 1950 stalemate existed between the State of Israel and her Arab neighbours. The first phase of their war had been halted by an armistice, and, by a Tripartite Agreement of May 1950, Britain, France, and the United States had hoped to prevent the two sides flying at each other's throats by restricting or prohibiting supplies of war potential to the belligerents. But the Arab-Israel conflict was only one issue in a vast area seething with unrest. The Middle East had no vestige of real unity. Turkey, Iraq, and Persia were hypersensitive to the threat from Russia, and this nightmare governed all other considerations. This provided a certain identity of purpose. Then there was the Arab League, which was designed to be a major political factor in the Middle East, but which was shot through and through with the self-interest of each of its component parts. In spite of all the common concerns which justified the inception of the League each member-state tended to prize its own traditions, sovereignty and independence to such a degree as to deny the League the full impact it might have had in the area.

In June 1950, for example, the Arab League concluded a Collective Security Pact, which was signed by Egypt, Saudi Arabia, Lebanon, Syria, and the Yemen, but the Pact was not complete. Iraq joined belatedly in February 1951, but Jordan still remained outside it. She hoped for better terms of settlement over the Palestine question by keeping clear of too many awkward commitments. In any case she still had her alliance with Britain, on which she depended considerably for military advice and an annual subsidy of £12,000,000. King Abdullah's dream of enlarging Jordan at the expense of Israel or even by extension of Hashemite influence was a live issue until his assassination in Jerusalem in July 1951.

The surge of nationalism in the Middle East touched off another crisis—this time in Persia. The government's desire for a greater share in the profits from oil, the need of the country for revenue and reform, and a burst of new-found confidence culminated in a decision to nationalize the oil industry. The Persian Prime Minister, Razmara, who had opposed the idea of nationalization, was assassinated in March 1951; his successor, Hussein Alai, had persuaded both houses of parliament to pass the necessary legislation for nationalization; but it was left for Moussadek, the next Prime Minister, to carry out the plan—with disastrous consequences. All the properties of the Anglo-Iranian Oil Company were seized, including the refinery at Abadan, and the Persian government discovered that without the technical experts and the tanker fleets she was in no position to export the oil to markets abroad which hitherto she had supplied. The International Court of Justice ruled itself unqualified to pass judgement, and missions from Britain, the United States and the International Bank also failed to bring about a reconciliation. In 1952 diplomatic relations between Persia and Britain were broken off; the oil output from Abadan slumped badly; and oilfields in other countries reaped markets which Persia was losing. Nationalism had overreached itself in this mishandled act of nationalization. Two years were to elapse before a new agreement was reached. The oil companies accepted the principle of nationalization, but the government gave them a share in the future production and refining of the oil.

There was a state of unrest from the Persian Gulf to the Eastern

Two Arab Kings—Hussein of Jordan and Saud of Saudi-Arabia in 1957
(*see* pp. 249–250)

Premier Chou En-lai of China welcomed at the airport by Premier Ali Sastroamidjojo of Indonesia, when arriving for the Bandung conference, April 1955

Five Prime Ministers on a balcony at Bandung—U Nu, Nehru, Mohammed Ali, Sir John Kotelawala and Sastroamidjojo

(see pp. 230-239)

Mediterranean; everywhere, just exasperations and provocations. How could stability be restored?

Three steps were taken in September 1951 to try to recover the situation. In the first place Turkey, the one consistent and most stabilizing influence in the area, had joined the North Atlantic Treaty Organization, thus committing herself militarily and ideologically with the West. Secondly, the British, French, American, and Turkish governments announced their intention of trying to form a Middle East Command (Middle East Defence Organization—M.E.D.O.), and that the support of other countries in the Middle East would be invited. Thirdly, it was suggested that the Suez Canal zone should become the joint responsibility of the countries represented in this Middle East Command, and would thenceforth cease to be a British base. Each announcement generated yet more wrath from Soviet Russia, and the Kremlin promptly issued a warning that any Arab state which became a party to the realization of a Middle East Command under the aegis of the West would thereby forfeit the friendship of Russia. The warning found favour in high places, especially in Egypt. King Farouk took the opportunity of paying off old scores by cancelling the 1899 Condominium agreements as to the joint control of the Sudan, and immediately had himself styled 'King of Egypt and the Sudan', an ill-advised act of presumption which put the Sudan on its mettle against the day of its independence. Egypt also proceeded to abrogate her 1936 treaty with Britain, a treaty which in any case was soon due for revision. The prospect of a Middle East Command coming into being vanished as quickly as it had appeared. A Middle East in which the West might once again call the tune was anathema to Egypt and Syria in particular. A Middle East weak and divided, yet hostile to the West, suited Russia well. Active participation in the area was only a matter of time and opportunity.

The year of turmoil, 1951, ended with one encouraging achievement—Libya became an independent kingdom under Seyid Idress, the head of the Senussi tribe. The territories of Cyrenaica, Tripolitania and the Fezzan, a lengthy stretch of the North African coastline including the ports of Tobruk, Benghazi and Tripoli, were joined together in this embryonic kingdom, now to be ruled by an Arab chieftain. Till 1911 it had been Ottoman. From 1911 till 1941 it had been Italian. For the next two years it had been the scene of Rommell's uneasy occupation until his defeat by Field Marshal Montgomery's Eighth Army. In 1945, to the dismay of all concerned, Molotov had requested Tripoli as part of Russia's war-spoils, the first hint that Russia was territorially interested in Africa. Libya's subsequent membership of the Arab League connects her consequentially with affairs in Western Asia.

For the next three years, from early 1952 to early 1955 (the date of the conference at Bandung) the main focus of attention in the Middle East is the revolution in Egypt. A complexity of forces—including a discredited monarchy, a nation disappointed over the deadlock with Israel, and known corruption in official circles—led to a military coup in Cairo in July 1952 which brought about the abdication of the king. Farouk found exile in Italy, and was succeeded by his infant son, Ahmed Fuad II. Colonel (later General) Neguib, the leader of the revolutionary committee, assumed office as Prime Minister, and in February 1953 negotiated an agreement with Britain, whereby the Sudan might become independent after a period of transition and trial. Four months later Egypt ceased to be a monarchy, and was proclaimed a Republic with Neguib as its first President. Many Egyptians still hoped that once the British had withdrawn from the Sudan the latter would be willing to countenance union with Egypt, thus bringing about a unity in the Nile valley, and the fact that Neguib was half-Sudanese gave force to this aspiration. But when the time came the Sudan chose to be independent, and Egypt did not find it easy to forget the disappointment.

It was imperative, meanwhile, that the young republic of Egypt should have some signal diplomatic success wherewith to consolidate its authority and enhance its prestige, as much among its own nationals as in the outside world. This triumph was the signing of the Anglo-Egyptian Suez Canal agreement in October 1954, by the terms of which all British troops were to leave the Canal Zone within twenty months, but were to be entitled to return if certain eventualities of war obtained. Rejoicing in Egypt at the prospect of Britain's departure was unbounded. Not since 1882 had Egypt been free of British garrison forces. In spite of the satisfactory conclusion of this agreement President Neguib was considered too moderate a leader to satisfy the ardent nationalism that galvanized the more ambitious of the younger potential Egyptian leaders, political and military. In November 1954 he was deposed from the Presidency, and Colonel Gamal Abdul Nasser became the Head of State, a strong and determined will bent on carrying nationalism as far as it would go.

Throughout 1954 the ideological division of the world into the two blocs—Communist and non-Communist—was as clear-cut and understood in the Middle East as it was elsewhere. Never a month passed without some vituperation or incident to confirm the impasse. The Iron and Bamboo Curtains were as much realities in the public mind as they were realities in matters of travel restriction, trade negotiation, and diplomatic suspicion. Compromise was unthinkable or unworkable. And yet many of the countries of the Middle East did not properly belong to either side and were party to no entirely satisfactory grouping. It was out of this predicament that two alternative offers of solution emerged. In 1954 Iraq suggested the formation of a powerful bloc among Asian nations, for the purposes of mutual protection, which might include India, Pakistan, Turkey, Afghanistan, and the Arab states. But this project failed to win the support of Pundit Nehru, and was later scorned by Colonel Nasser. Nasser was bidding hard for the headship of the Arab nations, and could not afford to let this leadership slip to Nuri es Said, the Iraqi Prime Minister, whose initiative in this new formation would boost the prestige of Iraq and detract from Egypt's bid. Iraq, therefore, turned to Turkey and had no difficulty in reaching agreement on fundamentals. The first intimations of this agreement so enraged Nasser that he summoned the Arab Prime Ministers together to review the situation, and thus hoped to spike the new alliance. Neither Turkey nor Iraq were deterred. In February 1955 their Pact of mutual co-operation was signed at Baghdad, a pact much resented by various members of the Arab League, but a pact which was destined to grow in strength and importance in the next few years. Within a week Egypt tried to offset or unbalance the Pact by a new alliance with Syria, a rival alignment, whereupon Britain became a party to the Baghdad Pact. A race had started.

The other alternative idea was the conception of a Third Force, which for a time represented a certain reality but found no coherent expression. It was a drawing together at a personal rather than a government level of the leaders of certain nations and political parties who were groping their way towards a balancing 'middle' force. Tito of Yugoslavia stood out as an example of one who had defected from one major bloc and had resisted the temptation to be swept into another. He represented the possibility of a Third Force. At one stage it seemed that Yugoslavia in Europe, India in Asia, and Egypt in Africa might lead the way in such a venture, and become pioneers of a gigantic 'neutralist' buffer between the other two. Political parties in other countries toyed with the idea of supporting the project, though the main appeal of the conception was to a variety of smaller nations, including the so-called 'uncommitted' parts of the world.

3. PREPARATION FOR BANDUNG

But if the Baghdad Pact had a contested start, and the idea of a Third Force failed to mature, there was one suggestion which gathered momentum and became a landmark in the history of two continents. This was the plea for Asian and African co-operation, advocated by Sastroamidjojo, the Indonesian Prime Minister, as early as August 1953, and endorsed at a conference of five Asian Prime Ministers held in Colombo and Kandy in April and May 1954. In December 1954 a further meeting was held at Bogor in Indonesia, at which the Prime Ministers of India, Pakistan, Ceylon, Burma, and Indonesia specified the four purposes of the conference which it was proposed to hold at Bandung in April 1955. The purposes were:

(a) To promote goodwill and co-operation among the nations of Asia and Africa; to explore and advance their mutual as well as common interests; and to establish and further friendliness and neighbourly relations.

(b) To consider social, economic and cultural problems and relations to the countries represented.

(c) To consider problems of special interest to Asian and African peoples, problems affecting national sovereignty, and of racialism and colonialism.

(d) To view the position of Asia and Africa and their peoples in the world of today, and the contribution they can make to the promotion of world peace and co-operation.

The Road to Bandung

The composition of the coming conference was clarified. No European nation was invited; in that respect the Bandung conference was an assertion of complete independence from the apron-strings of the old imperial powers. The decisions which had been taken by the European powers in Berlin in 1884 as to the overall parcelling out of Africa, Asia, and the Pacific islands among themselves had largely become dead letters, especially in Asia. Bandung marked the recession of 'Europe in Asia' and the challenge that was coming in Africa. As no European nation was to attend at Bandung, Soviet Russia was excluded. This fact had one inescapable consequence. The Marxist position was to be put forward by China, standing on her own—without the nursing hand of Russia. China has never looked back from that position of responsibility. As Communist China was to be at Bandung, Nationalist China was to be absent. Israel also was omitted, doubtless in deference to the Arab League. Six African countries were to attend—Egypt, Ethiopia, Gold Coast (now Ghana), Liberia, Libya, and the Sudan. Their views at this conference are set out in the next chapter.

XIV

THE BANDUNG CONFERENCE

1. HISTORIC SIGNIFICANCE

THERE can be no understanding of modern Asia—or Africa—without a grasp of what happened at the Bandung Conference, for Bandung marks one of the greatest and most crucial turning-points of modern history. It amounted to more than a declaration of sovereign independence for the continent of Asia from the bondage of Europe. It was not a post-mortem on what had gone before, so much as an expression of a new vitality which had inspired half of Asia and most of North Africa. It was an outburst of racialism, for the moment eclipsing even the force of nationalism, and it marked a new solidarity between a vast group of emancipated nations. It demonstrated the power and resilience of their new-found confidence, largely kept in control at the conference itself by the responsible attitude of experienced statesmen, and admirably harnessed to the needs of the countries concerned by important decisions as to how they were to work together when the conference was over. So much was agreed and so many practical resolutions were adopted that the rest of the world was at first tempted to dismiss the results as over-ambitious and idealist. But they were wrong. Bandung was the touch-stone of a new age, the articulation of a new dynamic. Early morning had broken over the East. Some may have hoped that evening was settling over the West, for resentment and ill-affected memory were in the air. Bandung challenged the supremacy and superiority of the white races, for in general terms the coloured races were agreed about this. The day of Western imperialism was condemned and all lingering traces of it were called to account. By implication Soviet imperialism did not escape notice or rebuke, and the Russian-owned half of Asia was conspicuous by its absence. This deliberate exclusion was significant for the future; it invited a change of diplomacy and strategy, as we shall have reason to see later.

But for all the strands of agreement in principle, and for all the new solidarity it crystallized, Bandung spoke to the world with many voices, not one. Though new friendships were forged which governed events in later years, and which explain much of what has happened since, there were, nevertheless, many cross-currents and points of difference which deny to the conference the overriding quality of unanimity. Policies were shown to differ, and differ widely, but the remarkable phenomenon was the courage and honesty with which each country stated its position, pressed its case, and assumed a readiness to understand and co-operate. No less remarkable is the fact that Asian and African loyalties did not blind the delegates to the importance of strengthening the authority of the United Nations as the focal centre of the greater family of nations. In this respect there was nothing narrow or irresponsible about the deliberations at Bandung; it was tantamount to the recognition of international law and debate as the final arbiter, and the subjection of even racial and continental interests to world judgement.

Twenty-nine countries were represented at Bandung: Afghanistan, Burma, Cambodia, Ceylon, Communist China, Egypt, Ethiopia, Ghana (Gold Coast), India, Indonesia, Persia, Iraq, Japan, Jordan, Laos, Lebanon, Liberia, Libya, Nepal, Pakistan, the Philippines, Saudi Arabia, Sudan, Syria, Thailand, Turkey, the Democratic Republic of Vietnam, the State of Vietnam, and Yemen. Most of the countries had in common that they had come through a long period of struggle and had recently attained political and constitutional freedom. The only country to decline an invitation to attend was the Central African Federation.

2. UNITY AND DIVERSITY

The atmosphere and candour of the conference are best conveyed by a glimpse of the statesmen who attended and a brief mention of some of the points they raised. Only in this way can one appreciate the tremendous range of the issues that were considered and the complexity of them. Most of the five sponsoring nations refrained from speaking at the opening session, leaving it to the invited nations to put forward whatever they saw fit. Alphabetically, Afghanistan came first. Here at once was the problem of a nation hanging between the fires of Communism and Western democracy. The tension between East and West was a reality to her. What had Bandung to offer?

Cambodia was unique in having its ex-king, Norodom Sihanouk, speaking as Prime Minister. Paying special tribute to Pandit Nehru, one of the promoters of the conference, as 'this great Asiatic', Norodom Sihanouk went on to declare that Cambodia based her national policy on the general principles laid down in the agreement between India and China, the five pillars—*Panchsheel*—of mutual respect, mutual non-aggression, mutual non-interference, mutual help, and peaceful co-existence. In this gradual establishment of a community of neutral nations Cambodia's natural gravitation and affiliation was towards India and Burma.

Sir John Kotelawala, Prime Minister of Ceylon and one of the chief sponsors of the conference, spoke as an idealist and as a devout Buddhist. 'The great teachers of all religions,' he declared, 'are agreed that it is not through hatred and violence, but through compassion, peace, and goodwill, that mankind can find salvation.' It was a salutary note. He also solemnly denounced Communism.

Chou En-lai, speaking as Prime Minister and Foreign Minister of the People's Republic of China, and as the mouthpiece of Asiatic Communism, cut across all susceptibilities, and did not hesitate to specify and enumerate the problems and plague-spots which he regarded as most urgently in need of attention. He ranged from Morocco, Algiers, and Tunis in North Africa, to the Suez Canal, Palestine, Goa, and Korea. He condemned the principle of apartheid; rebuked the Netherlands' persistent occupation of West Irian; warned the Bandung delegates against United States' 'colonialism', in particular America's 'protection' of Taiwan (Formosa), and spoke of the Thai and Chuang minority problems. Almost no controversial issue or area escaped his survey. On the subject of religion, so vitally related to Asian politics, Chou En-lai was explicit about his government's official policy but at the same time tried to allay fears and suspicion. 'We Communists are atheists,' he admitted, 'but we respect all those who have religious belief. . . . There are in China, not only seven million Communists but also tens of millions of Islamists and Buddhists, and millions of Christians and Catholics.' Included in the Chinese delegation was an imam, a Mohammedan leader, a fact which appealed immensely to the Arab world and to the large Islamic population in Indonesia. Chou En-lai also claimed that 'In China every national minority has its autonomous region,' thus putting China forward as the champion of minorities and the protector of lesser nationalities. By this speech he made it clear that China was alive to current issues in every part of the world.

Gamal Abdul Nasser, Prime Minister of Egypt, made the most of the Bandung opportunity to establish himself as a statesman and as one of the leading spokesmen of the Arab world. 'Only political stability, economic development and social justice' can bring about a 'healthy world society'. No one would cavil at such a judicious generalization. Even the stings in his speech were moderated by objectivity. 'It is regrettable that racial discrimination is still practised in South Africa.' Great force was given to this protest by quoting the considered opinion of a United Nations Commission which had described it thus: 'The doctrine of racial superiority on which apartheid policy was based is scientifically false, extremely dangerous to international peace and security, and contrary to the dignity and worth of the human person.' Among the leaders and nations emboldened to move forward in quest of national fulfilment by the assurance of popular Bandung support Nasser and Egypt were certainly among the foremost.

Ethiopia, represented by Yilma Deressa, chairman of the Ethiopian delegation to the United Nations, alone spoke as a Christian country, albeit reminding the conference that even the Koran paid tribute to Ethiopia. Yilma Deressa appealed for tolerance, and adherence to the United Nations Declaration of Human Rights, and denounced regional pacts which had become so much the fashion. In line with most other delegations Ethiopia condemned colonialism, having suffered from it at the hands of Fascist Italy. Special mention was made of the pleasure of having small, new nations present such as Libya, Sudan, and the Gold Coast.

The Gold Coast was represented by Kogo Botsio, Minister of State, on behalf of the Prime Minister, Dr. Kwame Nkrumah. He explained that the Gold Coast also shared the sense of elation, the 'stir of fellowship', which was the common property of all the

Bandung delegations, but he made it abundantly clear at the same time that Britain had never hindered the process towards self-government but rather had encouraged it. Britain wanted the Gold Coast to have full nationhood, and this was to become reality in March 1957 (when the Gold Coast became Ghana).

Ali Amim, Minister of Finance for Iran (Persia), pleaded for progress on the basis of equality. No solutions to the problems of the world could be found either in antagonistic blocs, or in an attitude of supremacy, or in isolation.

A vigorous speech from the Iraqi delegate, Mohammad Fadhil Jamali, suggested that the three really disturbing influences in the world were crumbling colonialism, Zionism, and Communism. He referrred to Algeria as an example of the first; branded Israel as an 'illegitimate state and aggressor'; and summarized Communism as a 'one-sided materialist religion'. In the presence of the Chinese and other Communists he declared:

> Communism is a subversive religion. It breeds hatred amongst classes and peoples. Thus the Comintern, and later its offspring the Cominform, represent the great centre of command for the agents of this new anti-God religion and no nation on the globe is left untouched by their activity and subversion . . . Today [1955] the Communist world has subjected races in Asia and Eastern Europe on a much larger scale than any old colonial power.

No punches were pulled at Bandung.

The violent attack on the very existence of the state of Israel was reiterated in the speech by the delegate from Jordan, Sayyed Wahid Salah, Minister for Foreign Affairs. He claimed that Israel owed its existence directly to the influence of the Bible on the Protestant nations, Britain and the United States. He substantiated this suggestion by quoting an extract from the memoirs of Dr. Weizmann, who contended that much support for the Jewish cause came from the sympathy of Biblical Protestantism, and commented 'This is very regrettable indeed.'

The Prime Minister of Laos, Katay Don Sasorith, followed somewhat the same line as Cambodia, in saying that Laos endorsed the five principles already set forth in the Sino-Indian Pact of June 1954.

The Lebanese Prime Minister, Sami Bek Solh, also joined in

the denunciation of Israel, but made a strong plea for some solution to be found for the Arab refugee problem.

A much more pacific speech then came from the acting Secretary of State for Liberia, Momolu Dukuly. He introduced Liberia as 'the second oldest Negro republic in the world and the only Republic in West Africa'. Freedom and friendship were the keynotes of his contribution.

Mahmoud Muntasser, Libya's ambassador in London, represented his country at Bandung, and gave the usual warnings about colonialism, racial discrimination, and dangerous interference from outside by other nations, including the danger of intellectual slavery.

The Foreign Secretary of Nepal, Sovag Jung Thapa, reminded the conference that the Buddha had been born in Nepal, and implied that Buddhism was perhaps Nepal's greatest contribution to the cause of peace among the nations. Nepal also supported *Panchsheel*, but also advocated an enlargement of the Colombo Plan for material assistance in undeveloped areas.

Pakistan was represented by her Prime Minister, Mohammed Ali, the bulk of whose speech stressed the principles of national sovereignty; equality; non-interference; non-aggression; right of self-defence; self-determination; and settlement by negotiation. There was no strong mention of Islam, which had been the *raison d'être* for the creation of Pakistan.

Carlos P. Romulo, representing the Philippines, pointed out that his country had been the first new nation to appear after the Second World War. He counselled the nations not to allow themselves to become anti-white, and went on to warn them of the real danger of Communism.

This kind of power, once established, roots itself more and more deeply, gets more and more committed to perpetuating itself. Moreover—and the whole logic of human experience throws its weight into the scale—this system of power becomes inherently expansionist. . . . It seeks, and must seek, to crush all opposition, wherever it exists. This road is open before many of us. The gateway to it is strewn with sweet-smelling garlands of phrases and promises and high sentiment. But once you march through it the gate clangs behind you. The policeman becomes master, and your duty thereafter is forever to say 'aye'. Even those who enjoy the role of mastery must know that this system devours its own.

The Prime Minister of the Sudan, Sayed Ismail El Azhari, explained that this was the first appearance in the outside world of the newly-born Sudan, which had only just attained independence.

The Syrian Minister for Foreign Affairs, Khaled El Azu, repeated many of the charges which had already been made—against Israel, French possessions in North Africa, apartheid, and Western Irian.

The Thailand Minister for Foreign Affairs mentioned the religious structure of his country, with the majority of its eighteen million people Buddhist, but also containing three million Moslems. Thailand, he said, was delighted that Laos, Cambodia, and the State of Vietnam had regained independence, but dreaded the intentions of the Chinese and Communist minorities in the country. Three million Chinese in Thailand constituted a potential menace. To whom did they really owe their allegiance—China or Thailand? It was only because Thailand feared infiltration and subversion by Communists that, for reasons of self-defence, Thailand had chosen to put its trust in a collective defence system, as permitted by Article 51 of the United Nations Charter. This was the Manila Pact.

A similar argument for the principle of defensive alliances was taken by Turkey, whose spokesman was the Deputy Prime Minister, Fatin Rustu Zorlu. With much tact he referred to mistrust of a certain 'neighbour', and pointed out how all too easily the countries of Eastern Europe had fallen prey 'to a country which had entered their territories as liberators. Remember Benes and Czechoslovakia.' Therefore, Turkey had seen the necessity of joining N.A.T.O., and the Balkan Pact; it had signed treaties with Pakistan and Iraq, and become a member of the South-East Asia Treaty organization. It was common sense in the face of danger.

Pham-van-Dong, the Deputy Prime Minister for the Democratic Republic of Vietnam, expatiated at great length on the struggle against the French in Indo-China. He ended by endorsing the five principles of *Panchsheel*, especially the theory of peaceful co-existence.

For the State of Vietnam, the Minister of Planning and Reconstruction, Nguyen Van Thoai, gave a brief summary of the struggle, and added a solemn warning against the insidious nature of Communism.

The Bandung Conference

The speech of Emir Seif El Islam Al Hassan, Prime Minister of the Yemen, returned the conference to trust in the United Nations and in the Charter of Human Rights, a hopeful note after all the dust of controversy that had been stirred up.

After these opening speeches the delegates settled down to committee work, and Pandit Nehru scarcely exaggerated when he said that Bandung might almost have been the capital of Asia and Africa for those few days. Over half the population of the world was represented at this conference, and the topics discussed in committee covered the widest possible range—major problems such as human rights, peace, co-operation, colonialism, and such detailed subjects as trade, raw materials, banking, shipping, exchange of information, development of atomic energy, and price control. This intricate committee work, this sharing of hopes and fears, and this thrashing out of resolutions and recommendations can only have resulted in a strengthening of mutual interest between the countries concerned. It found expression in the feeling of solidarity Bandung gave to the Afro-Asian countries.

3. THE FINAL COMMUNIQUÉ

The communiqué issued at the close of the conference was a lengthy and comprehensive document. The first main section dealt with economic co-operation, and recommended the fullest possible assistance and exchange between member-nations. It greatly encouraged the exchange of trade delegations and groups of businessmen. Soviet Russia and China made full use of this opening without delay, and trade missions suddenly increased in vogue.

The next section concerned cultural co-operation, and it was agreed to develop the exchange of all cultural links as speedily and thoroughly as practicable.

The third section was on human rights and self-determination, followed by a section on the problems of dependent peoples. In each case the French government was urged to bring about a peaceful settlement of the issues in Algeria, Morocco, and Tunisia.

The fifth part of the communiqué, dealing with 'Other problems', declared the support of the Conference for the rights of the Arab people in Palestine, thus virtually ignoring the existence of

Israel, and giving tremendous encouragement to the Arab nations in their campaign.

The Netherlands government was invited to honour certain promises and agreements previously concluded with Indonesia, and was asked to surrender West Irian to the new republic. Much more delicately the conference pledged its support of Yemen 'in the case of Aden and the southern parts of Yemen known as the Protectorates'. It was one of the first real indications of a coming pressure in this quarter. Britain was not mentioned by name, nor directly criticized, but the inclusion of this item in the communiqué was a warning of what was to come in the Arabian peninsula.

The next section took up the subject of World Peace and Co-operation, and pressed for the admission to U.N.O. of a number of countries present at Bandung which seemed to be qualified for membership under the terms of the U.N. Charter. Of these, Cambodia, Ceylon, Jordan, Laos, Libya, and Nepal became members of the United Nations in the same year as the Bandung Conference (1955) and the Sudan and Japan were admitted in 1956. Morocco and Tunisia, which were not represented at Bandung, were also admitted in 1956, so that the total Afro-Asian increase was ten countries, compared with an increase of six in Western Europe (Austria, Finland, Ireland, Italy, Portugal, and Spain) and four in Eastern Europe (Albania, Bulgaria, Hungary, and Rumania) in the same period. The continent of Asia had nine members of the United Nations Organization at its inception in 1945. By January 1957 it had twenty-two. Africa and Asia taken together in 1945 had a total membership of only thirteen, but by 1957 this had reached a total of thirty, which is some indication of the rapid increase in the number of new self-governing nations considered to have arrived at some degree of constitutional maturity and political stability.

But the Bandung Conference was not content merely with the prospect of additional Afro-Asian representation at U.N.O. The final communiqué pointed out that the Security Council bore no adequate or equitable geographical distribution, and protested that the Afro-Asian powers would never be able to make an effective contribution to the maintenance of international peace until they were allowed into the Security Council.

The communiqué then went on to plead for the prohibition of

the production and testing of nuclear and thermo-nuclear weapons, and for the limitation and reduction of armed forces everywhere. It ended with a further enunciation of basic principles and rights, to which the assembled delegates could give unqualified support.

The tone of the Conference was largely set by the speech of Dr. Sukarno, President of Indonesia, who begged the delegates to go about their deliberations with the right spirit of trust and common endeavour. 'Let us not be bitter about the past, but keep our eyes on the future.' In very much the same spirit Pandit Nehru in his speech at the concluding session remarked:

> We mean no ill to anybody. We send out our greetings to Europe and America. We send our greetings to Australia and New Zealand. And indeed Australia and New Zealand are almost in our region. They certainly do not belong to Europe, much less to America. They are next to us and I should like Australia and New Zealand to come nearer to Asia. I would welcome them because I do not want what we say or do to be based on racial prejudices. We have had enough of this racialism elsewhere.

Here was the true instinct of great statesmanship, and a token of the breadth of vision prevalent at Bandung.

Finally, the Conference recommended that the five sponsoring nations should be authorized to convene another such conference when the occasion warranted it, and Nehru, reporting to the Lok Sabha (the Indian Lower House) a week later, put the conference in its true setting when he said:

'It would be a misreading of history to regard Bandung as an isolated occurrence and not part of a great movement of human history.'

It will be interesting to see in the next half-century the direction this movement takes. The example of Asia has greatly accelerated similar trends throughout the whole continent of Africa already.

XV

AFTER BANDUNG

I. THE FIRST REPERCUSSIONS

THE Bandung Conference should have ushered in a peaceful era of constructive progress. The programmes outlined provided ample scope for the entire energy of the nations concerned to evolve together a way of life, and a sense of fulfilment, best suited to each. New incentives were backed by the promise of mutual help. But idealism was soon sullied by new complications, and all hope of a settled future was scattered to the winds. Too many unresolved issues were left untouched, or merely analysed and not concluded. Israel, Taiwan (Formosa), Kashmir, were among the most critical. But the more important issue was ideological. Soviet Russia had followed the discussions at Bandung with acute interest and concern. Not to be present was hard enough to bear; to be constantly and severely castigated was insufferable. To be represented, as it were, by her partner China was reassuring up to a point; but there were distinct signs that Communist China was attaining a stature and prestige which amounted to leadership in her own right. In Asia, Peking might soon count for more than Moscow. It was, therefore, inevitable that Soviet Russia would quickly have to recover the initiative, and establish herself again as the dominant protagonist of the Marxist cause. How was this to be done? Clearly, Russia—already the proud possessor of more than half the continent of Asia—would have to make a bid for closer friendship with Asiatic nations. This, in itself, was not difficult so long as one was in a position to denounce the colonialism of others, offer financial and technical assistance, and protest a longing for friendship to those most open to such overtures. But Russia could not embark on such a scheme until it was quite certain that the situation in Europe was quiet and calm. Hence, in July 1955, the Heads of government of Russia, Britain, France, and the United States met in Geneva to confer on the international situation, and Marshal Bulganin (Prime Minister) and Mr. Khrushchev (First Secretary of the Communist Party in the Soviet Union) were careful to bring with them the outward tokens of a new relationship—abiding cordiality, an apparent desire to agree or compromise, and a fresh endorsement of the doctrine of peaceful co-existence. The latter phrase was nothing new, but its hourly reiteration began to persuade the world that the Cold War, which had run its course almost uninterruptedly since 1948, might now be at an end. The outcome of the Geneva conference, at any rate, was a temporary period of blissful relaxation. The countries of Eastern Europe showed no sign of internal upheaval for the moment, and an effort was made by Bulganin and Khrushchev to woo Marshal Tito, President of Yugoslavia, back to the Kremlin fold. The effort failed, but the tactics they used were more encouraging—persuasion rather than force. In order to maintain the period of easement and relaxation a meeting of Foreign Ministers was fixed for the following November, and it was surmised by many that nothing untoward was likely to occur in the interval, if such a meeting was already projected. This confidence was sadly misplaced.

As early as June 1955—within a few weeks of the gathering at Bandung—Egypt began her sabre-rattling offensive against Israel once again. 'Israel will not exist long in the land of Arabism.' 'We will fight you across every inch of Palestine.' 'The Egyptian, Syrian, and Saudi Arabian armies will fight with determination to exterminate Zionism in the second round of the Palestine war.' The verbal offensive over press and radio was violent, abusive and unchecked. If Nasser did not count himself among the mighty after his fraternizing with Sukarno, Nehru, Chou En-lai, Kotelawala, Mohammed Ali, and a galaxy of Asian and African notables, clearly Egypt at any rate saw him as the Protector of Islam and the hope of the Arabs. It was openly boasted that Egypt was training 'millions of Commandos' (*Fedayeen*) for the attack against Israel, and frontier incidents began to suggest that the day of reckoning was not long to be delayed. Then, on 27 September 1955, Colonel (later President) Nasser announced the shattering news that an agreement had been reached with Czechoslovakia by which Egypt was to be supplied with arms. Shiploads arrived at once. The

Tripartite Agreement between Britain, France, and the United States by which the contracting powers agreed not to provide arms either to Israel or the Arab neighbours in order to prevent an arms race and the possibility of war, was rendered useless. In a wholly irresponsible and reprehensible spirit Soviet Russia had inflamed an already precarious situation, turned the tables on her own recognition of Israel, planted a stake for herself not only in the Middle East but on the continent of Africa, and forfeited in one single action the goodwill which had been quietly accruing since the Geneva Conference of July. Once again she had baffled the non-Communist world by the emptiness of her pledges, and proved the duplicity inherent in the doctrine of peaceful co-existence. Much more was to come.

2. KHRUSHCHEV TO THE FORE

In November and December 1955 the two Russian leaders, Bulganin and Khrushchev, set off to tour vast areas of Asia—first India, then Burma, back to India and finally to Afghanistan. This remarkable hop, skip, and jump performance had an incalculable propaganda effect and importance. In India the opportunity was taken of attacking Britain and all colonial powers, of intensifying the friction between India and Pakistan in their dispute over Kashmir, and of offering the friendship of Russia to the people of India. Burma likewise received promises of material support, and so did Afghanistan. The tour was one way of putting Russia back into the centre of the picture after being left out at Bandung. It was clearly a means of warning other Asian nations from joining up with S.E.A.T.O., and even more, an attempt to diminish the influence of such defensive pacts by wooing the so-called 'uncommitted' nations of Asia to closer friendship with the Communist world. But here again there are signs that the Bulganin-Khrushchev tour had the ulterior motive of ensuring that China's new position in Asia, following the 1954 treaty with India and her enhanced prestige after Bandung, did not eclipse the role that Russia had marked out for herself in leading the world Communist front. Russia had good reason to envy China, and clearly foresaw that the day was not far distant when China might make a bid for the

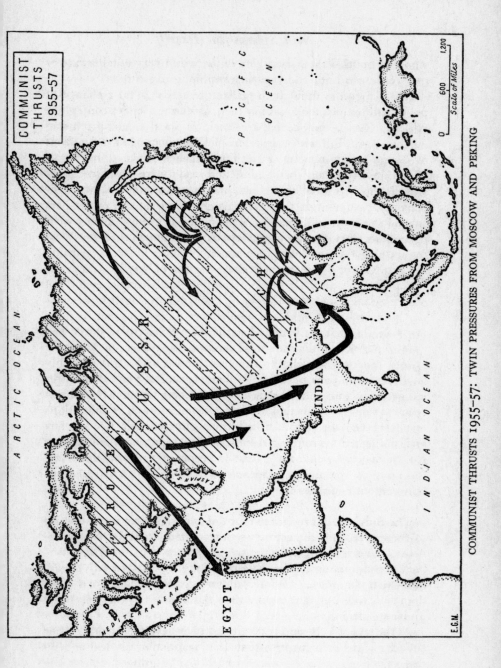

COMMUNIST THRUSTS 1955–57: TWIN PRESSURES FROM MOSCOW AND PEKING

whole of South-East Asia, a part of the world very much aware of new responsibilities and very susceptible to overtures.

It is sometimes difficult to realize quite how great a change of policy and outlook took place in 1955. Until the Geneva conference of July, Russia had been her usual cautious, uncompromising defensive self. But with the arrival of Khrushchev in the forefront of Soviet policy-making a fresh turbulence broke upon world affairs. Joviality, hard-bargaining, and insult were never so closely wed. He looked an affable clown one moment and breathed irredeemable vituperation the next. His cleverness at the outset persuaded the more gullible that 'peaceful co-existence' means what it suggests. But he was also adept at out-manœuvring the West by jumping the Northern Tier, touching down in Africa, earning the gratitude of Egypt and stretching the arm of Russia as far as the Indian Ocean—all in a matter of months. But Khrushchev did not only play the diplomatic game; he knew only too well how economics affect politics, and how vital a part trade can play. In 1955, for example, it is estimated that the Sino-Soviet bloc purchased over 26 per cent. of Egypt's total exports, 21 per cent. of Turkey's, 15 per cent. of Persia's, 12 per cent. of Burma's, and probably anything up to 50 per cent. of Afghanistan's. Each of these figures indicates a vigorous trade mission in each country, and Russia was quick to seize on the idea of trade exhibitions as well as delegations to consolidate the links. In his very forthright way Khrushchev once informed a group of American Senators who were visiting Russia that 'we value trade least for economic reasons and most for political reasons as a means of promoting better relations between our countries'.

The Bulganin-Khrushchev tour did as much harm as good, both to themselves and the countries they visited. In India Nehru redressed many an overstatement, and recovered many of Khrushchev's indiscretions. The Russian visit was welcomed, largely because it augured a new inter-communication of ideas and freedom to travel, but at the same time the motives of the visit came under suspicion.

At the end of February 1956 Khrushchev gave the world another shock, no less of a surprise than the Egyptian arms deal and no less calculated than the Asian tour. In a lengthy speech at the

After Bandung

Twentieth Congress of the Communist party of the Soviet Union he denounced Stalin as a traitor to the true Marxist position and vigorously deflated his overtowering prestige. Stalin had become an idol in the public mind and so epitomized one-man rule that this full-scale attack was launched from the Kremlin by warning Communists against the cult of the individual or the cult of personality. For a time public opinion was bewildered by the attack, in and outside Russia. Was Khrushchev trying to enhance his own authority at the expense of his former master? Was he trying to pose as the champion of the oppressed? Was this a back-handed way of denigrating the leaders of Soviet Russia who had been Stalin's closest advisers, and who by implication were being likewise denounced? Or was it a clever way of preparing himself for his forthcoming visit to Britain by undercutting all criticism of previous Soviet administration? Britain might after all still be in the mood to claim enormous compensation for losses incurred by the Bolshevik revolution in 1917. To dissociate from Stalin would be to disown earlier obligations and liabilities. It gave Bulganin and Khrushchev a clean slate on which to write the interpretation of Marxism afresh. It half suggested that the days of tyrants were over, and that Russia wished for nothing better than to be *persona grata* with the rest of the world. With this *volte face* behind them the Russian leaders visited Britain in April 1956, a visit calmly respected if not enthusiastically welcomed.

Two events showed the way the wind was blowing. The Commonwealth Prime Ministers met in conference in London as usual in the Summer of 1956, and no weakening in the bonds of Commonwealth loyalty were detectable. India had not been weaned away from her partnership within the Commonwealth. Not even the Kashmir dispute prevented the Prime Ministers of India and Pakistan sitting round the same conference table. But in contrast to the unique freedom which characterized the Commonwealth the new wave of liberalization which swept through the Soviet countries began to create more problems than the dethronement-of-Stalin policy had anticipated. The sluice-gates were opened and the still waters of docile obedience became the flood waters of criticism and self-analysis. Students felt free to discuss as rarely before. Foreign visitors were allowed into Communist countries, which in turn permitted certain citizens and delegations to travel abroad. Ideas and experiences crossed and re-crossed frontiers and comparisons became possible again. National feeling in the satellite nations began slowly but surely to turn against the iron-rule of the Kremlin, and narrowed itself to the demand that Russian occupation forces should be withdrawn from non-Russian territory. The momentum of reaction took time to work itself out, but the trend was unmistakable. It burst in the early autumn, first in the Poznan riots in Poland, then in Poland's demand for self-government (albeit on Marxist principles), and later in the national rising in Hungary in October. Russian policy had suddenly to be put into reverse. The threat to Russia of losing her grip over Eastern Europe was nipped in the bud, but the trials of strength both in Poland and Hungary were carefully noted by the rest of the world. The nature of international Communism was revealed in all its naked fury and revolutionary determination. What applied in Europe could also apply in Asia; hence the cause for considerable alarm. Luckily for Russia events in the Middle East stole the attention of the world, and prevented any direct action being taken, even by the United Nations, in Eastern Europe.

3. THE MIDDLE EAST EXPLOSION

A set of local crises, backed by years of frustration and antagonism, culminated eventually in a gigantic explosion in the Middle East. By continuous incitement Greek-speaking Cypriots worked up their agitation for union with Greece (*Enosis*), and the British, determined to maintain their last stronghold in the Middle East, sent out a Field Marshal, Sir John Harding, as Governor to try to restore civil order and break up the terrorist campaign. The situation grew so serious that in 1956 Archbishop Makarios, the leader of the movement, was suddenly whisked off into exile in the Seychelles, but his removal rather sharpened the crisis than otherwise. Britain came in for a succession of slights from many sides. The possession of Aden by the British was challenged. Sheiks along the coastline of Arabia began to denounce British protection and suzerainty. The British Commander of the Arab Legion in the State of Jordan, Glubb Pasha (later Major-General Sir John Glubb), was dismissed, and Jordan partially came under the influence of Egypt for a time in the general reorientation.

In June 1956 the last of the British troops left the Suez Canal Zone, in strict accord with the 1954 agreement. This departure was marked by exuberant rejoicing in Cairo, celebrations which were attended by the Russian Foreign Secretary, Shepilov. Until this moment there had been no talk of any change of status or ownership of the Suez Canal Company, and the Canal concession was not due to expire till 17 November 1968. France still provided sixteen of the thirty-two directors of the Company, Britain nine, Egypt five and the United States and Holland one each. But already Egypt was anticipating the day of her possession and control of the Canal, and adopted certain attitudes which were clearly contrary to International agreement. She had already impounded ships which were in transit to Israel, and in spite of protests and resolutions from the United Nations had refused to release them, thus breaking faith with the U.N. Charter as well as with the Constantinople Convention of 1888. All manner of provocation crept into the affairs of the Canal organization. Egypt took to withholding visas from newly-appointed foreign pilots, demanding that more and more Egyptian pilots be introduced and making it difficult for certain other nationalities to be employed by the company. Events began to move fast. Colonel Nasser had had notable successes to his credit—the exit of the British; the retention of vast stores in the Canal Zone; and preparation for the defeat of Israel in the near future. He proceeded to abolish the authority of the Revolutionary Council, offered himself for election as President (his was the only name offered), conferred in July with the leading 'neutralists'—Marshal Tito and Pandit Nehru—and was in no mood to be balked in any plan. With the sympathy and frendship of Russia, India, and the Arab League, Egypt was in a strong bargaining position.

Then came the blow which turned her sour. Britain and the United States, having previously promised to help Egypt with financial aid in building the Assuan High Dam, now withdrew their offer on 20 July 1956. Six days later President Nasser at a carefully-staged demonstration in Alexandria dramatically announced the immediate nationalization of the Suez Canal Company. The repercussions were far-reaching. Even Britain's ally, Iraq, approved the sudden decision. Indonesia promptly cancelled her obligations to pay any debts to Holland, and the whole episode gave the impression of being a signal victory for the Bandung powers over the fading authority of Europe. Everything that Britain and France did subsequently was interpreted as retaliation or reversion to 'imperialism'. In part this snub to Britain and France made up a little for the earlier failure to incorporate the Sudan. The British Prime Minister, Sir Anthony Eden, branded President Nasser as a dangerous dictator, who must be brought to account. August 1956 was a month of anxiety, disorganization, and conference. Twenty-two nations were invited to London to discuss the future of the Canal; eighteen agreed that there should be some form of international control. Mr. Menzies, Prime Minister of Australia, led a delegation to discuss terms with President Nasser, but negotiations broke down. A Canal Users' Association was set up, and canal payments were withheld from Egypt. The result was deadlock, and gross uncertainty shrouded the Middle East. The Secretary-General of the United Nations, Hammarskold, paid rapid visits to the area in the hope of preserving peace, but all to no avail.

On 29 October 1956 the tiny State of Israel attacked her neighbour Egypt, routed her forces, captured huge quantities of equipment, took thousands of prisoners and very nearly reached the Suez Canal within a matter of days. The very day after the Israeli attack the British and French governments issued an ultimatum to the combatants to stop fighting; Egypt ignored it. On 1 November Britain and France entered the fray and captured Port Said, declaring their object to be the separation of the warring factions. The situation was fantastically complicated. If Israel had been left to fight Egypt alone it is almost certain that neighbouring Arab countries would soon have joined in against Israel, and the war would have become an all-out affair of the Arab League versus Israel. Where this would have stopped no one can say. Equally, had Britain and France not shown a strong hand at the very outset Egypt might have 'invited' Soviet Russia to fly in to her assistance; Russian arms and equipment were already in Egypt. Man-power could quickly be supplied. This was prevented by Britain's action in bombing Egyptian aerodromes and rendering them unserviceable. All this, and more, coincided with the devastating rising and brutality in Hungary. After repeated appeals from Britain and France the United Nations resolved to create an international police force to send to the Suez area, and the British and French forces accepted a cease-fire proposal forthwith. Their 'war' had lasted less than a week. The U.N. police force, composed of contingents from all over the world, was quick to arrive and was put under the command of a Canadian, General Burns. This principle of arming U.N.O. with its own Force had been strongly advocated by Trygvie Lie during his seven-year term as Secretary-General, and the refusal of U.N.O. to accept the idea had been an acute disappointment to him. It is doubtful if it would have come into being even in November 1956 had there not been a double crisis to demand it. The danger in Hungary probably helped to deflect Russia from any temptation to intervene in Egypt, while Russia's predicament in Eastern Europe probably emboldened Britain and France to re-enter the Suez area while Russia was pre-occupied. The prompt action of U.N.O., and the willingness of the British and French to hand over to the international police force, served to contain the war. Once again the outbreak of hostilities which might so easily have developed into a chain-reaction, leading ultimately to large-scale warfare, was held within a narrow compass, the area around the Sinai Peninsula, just as it had in Korea and Vietnam. Nor had any side in any conflict dared to use nuclear weapons. A few weeks after the removal of British troops from Port Said Sir Anthony Eden was forced by a breakdown in physical health to resign as Prime Minister, to be succeeded in January 1957 by Mr. Harold Macmillan. Nasser, meanwhile, enjoyed the position of being the 'innocent' victim of direct aggression; failed to call in the half-million rifles he had allowed to be issued at random during the crisis; and began to state his own terms as to the future settlement of outstanding issues. All the blame was made to appear to be on the attacking side, irrespective of all provocation and declared hostility. Israel retired, as bidden by the United Nations, behind the previous armistice lines, and asked only to know whether Egypt and the other Arab nations would be willing to recognize her territorial sovereignty, and drop all idea of exterminating her. Meanwhile, in the Arabian peninsula the reduced prestige of Britain caused further trouble, chiefly in the Yemen. Minor skirmishes instigated by the Yemen betokened future difficulty for the Aden Protectorate and the Hadhramaut. The United States, uninvolved in the attack on Egypt and the

Canal, strengthened her oil concession rights in Saudi Arabia and made sure of her base at Dharan. As the dust of battle settled Egypt drew close again in alliance with Saudi Arabia and Syria, and together these three promised Jordan financial aid to the amount hitherto granted by Britain. In the North and East Turkey, Iraq, Persia, and Pakistan remained firm and pledged their allegiance to one another in the Baghdad Pact. Britain was re-admitted to the Conference table, and the United States joined its councils. Nevertheless, one of the overriding factors remains the character of President Nasser. If he is mellowed by the lessons of November 1956, and can restrain and discipline the emotions of his people and act constitutionally over the settlement of the Suez problem, he may well carve out a place in history for himself and Egypt as great as that of Kemal Ataturk and modern Turkey—a fine and lasting achievement. If, on the other hand, his ambitions are as far-reaching as is sometimes suggested—a desire to lead the Middle East and sway the North African coastline—he may go the way of most dictators and overreach himself. Egypt would then pay the price of any disaster. So great was this uncertainty that President Eisenhower made a bid to re-establish stability in the Middle East and offset the intrusion of Communism by offering enormous material help to all who wished to accept it. Several nations immediately suspected the motives of this 'Eisenhower doctrine'. Others accepted the offer, including Israel. American influence was thereby counterpoised against other contenders for power or protection.

4. THE MASSIVE STRENGTH OF CHINA

This book cannot end without reverting to the importance of remembering what is happening in China. At a time when most people were thoroughly preoccupied with events in Poland, Hungary, the Middle East, and Kashmir, the Chinese Prime Minister, Chou En-lai, was carrying out a painstaking and patient tour of South Asia. He was in no hurry. He was given none of the excessive publicity that accompanied Bulganin and Khrushchev. He blew no trumpets nor inflamed sensitivities. Nor did he confine himself to India, Burma, and Afghanistan. Chou En-lai accommodated himself with typical acumen to the atmosphere and tradition of each country he visited, and left a deep impression of friendship and under-standing. He also visited Burma and India, Ceylon and Pakistan. Nor did he play upon differences that existed. His object was to bridge gulfs, not to arouse indignation. The impact of his visits will be felt at a deeper level than the more superficial tour of his Russian opposite numbers. And indeed they needed his help precisely at that moment. The risings in Poland and Hungary carried the implication that the force of nationalism might be stronger than international Communism. This had to be corrected at all cost. Soviet Russia was in no position to state the case when she was doing everything possible to smother the force of national-ism. Therefore, Chou En-lai was hurriedly invited to Moscow, and reasserted the solidarity of all Marxist states within the single doctrine. But he was astute enough to take the opportunity of visiting the countries with which Russia was having such difficulty —Poland and Hungary. In this way his reputation spread, his personality became known and trusted, and he was put in the position of being an arbiter, a peace-maker and an international statesman. Chou En-lai's personal prestige in much of Asia, like that of Mao Tse-tung, is one of the great factors of the moment, and partly offsets the stigma of China's not being a member of the United Nations. For this very reason China can be a law unto herself, without worrying unduly what the United Nations may think about her actions and policies—not a wholesome state of affairs in the world of today, when a new international order is being evolved. Her neighbour, Japan, was admitted to member-ship in December 1956. China still waits and can afford to be patient.

SELECTED BIBLIOGRAPHY

GENERAL

Bell, Gertrude, Letters of. E. Benn, 1947.
Beloff, Max: *Soviet Policy in the Far East,* 1944–51. Oxford, 1953.
Calvocoressi, P. (with Wint, G.): *Middle East Crisis.* Penguin Special, 1957.
Chiang Kai-shek, Gen. and Madame: *China at the Crossroads.* Faber, 1937.
Coast, John: *Recruit to Revolution.* Christophers, 1952.
De Gaury, G.: *The New State of Israel.* Verschoyle, 1952.
Dulles, Foster Rhea: *America's Rise to World Power.* Hamish Hamilton, 1955.
East, W. G. (and Spate, O. H. K.): *The Changing Map of Asia.* Methuen, 1953.
—— *The Changing World.* Harrap, 1956.
Fabian International Essays. Hogarth, 1956.
Froembgen, Hanns (trans. K. Kirkness): *Kemal Ataturk.* Jarrolds, 1937.
Furnival, J. S.: *Netherlands India.* C.U.P., 1939.
Gathorne-Hardy, G. M.: *Short History of International Affairs,* 1920–39. Oxford, 1950.
Hall, D. G. E.: *History of South East Asia.* Macmillan, 1955.
—— *Europe and Burma.* Oxford, 1945.
Harrison, Brian: *South-East Asia.* Macmillan, 1954.
Hopkins, Harry: *New World Arising.* Hamish Hamilton, 1952.
Hourani, A.: *Syria and Lebanon.* Oxford, 1946.
Kahin, G. M.: *Nationalism and Revolution in Indonesia.* Cornell, 1952.
Kirk, G. E.: *Short History of the Middle East.* Methuen, 1948.
Latourette, K. S.: *A History of Modern China.* Pelican, 1954.
Lie, Trygve: *In the Cause of Peace.* Macmillan, 1954.
Low, Sir Francis: *Struggle for Asia.* Frederick Muller, 1955.
Maclean, Fitzroy: *Eastern Approaches.* Cape, 1949.

Selected Bibliography

Moraes, F.: *Report on Mao's China.* Macmillan, 1953.

Nicolson, Harold: *King George V.* Constable, 1952.

Niebuhr, Reinhold: *The Irony of American History.* Nisbet, 1952.

Panikkar, K. M.: *The Future of South-East Asia.* George Allen & Unwin, 1943.

Purcell, V.: *The Chinese in South-East Asia.* O.U.P., 1951.

Ranga Iyer, C. S.: *India—Peace or War?* Harrap, 1930.

Seton-Williams, M. V.: *Britain and the Arab States, 1920-48.* Luzac, 1948.

Snow, Edgar: *Red Star Over China.* Gollancz, 1937.

Van Dorn, H. A.: *Twenty Years of the Chinese Republic.* Hurst & Blackett, 1933.

Vlekke, B. H. M.: *Nusantara: A History of the East Indian Archipelago.* Harvard University Press, 1943.

Wei, Henry: *China and Soviet Russia.* Van Nostrand, 1956.

Wint, Guy: *The British in Asia.* Faber, 1947.

—— *Spotlight on Asia.* Penguin Special, 1955.

—— (with Calvocoressi): *Middle East Crisis.* Penguin Special, 1957.

Woodman, D.: *Republic of Indonesia.* Cresset, 1955.

Yutang, Lin: *My Country and My People.* Heinemann, 1936.

Zinkin, M.: *Development for Free Asia.* Chatto & Windus, 1956.

In addition to books and authors listed above, material was also gathered from journals, periodicals, and papers too numerous or miscellaneous to mention. But the following undoubtedly deserve separate notice:

The Bandung Conference speeches.

British Government White Papers, such as

Cmd. 9853: *Suez Canal Conference (selected documents).*

Cmd. 9856: *Exchange of Correspondence between the Suez Committee and the President of the Republic of Egypt.*

Chatham House publications, including the annual *International Survey.*

Foreign Affairs (published in New York).

India News.

Many pamphlets, such as P. A. Menon's Address, when Indian Ambassador to Thailand, on India's Foreign Policy; the full text of Khrushchev's speech at the Twentieth Party Congress of the Communist Party, and others; as well as articles in *The Political Quarterly, Soviet Studies,* and other more specialized or regional journals.

APPENDIX

ASIATIC GROUPINGS

(Non-Asiatic Powers are included in brackets)

ARAB LEAGUE (inaugurated 1945)
>Egypt
>Iraq
>Saudi Arabia
>Lebanon
>Syria
>Jordan
>Yemen
>
>(Libya joined in 1953
> Sudan joined in 1956)

BAGHDAD PACT (1955)
>Turkey
>Iraq
>Persia
>Pakistan
>
>(United Kingdom
> United States)

COLOMBO PLAN (1950)
>Ceylon
>India
>Pakistan
>Malaya
>British Borneo
>Vietnam
>Cambodia
>Laos

Burma (joined 1952)
Nepal (joined 1952)
Indonesia (joined 1953)
(Australia
 Canada
 New Zealand
 United Kingdom
 United States)

SOUTH-EAST ASIA DEFENCE TREATY (1954)
 Siam
 Philippines
 Pakistan
 Protocol covering: South Vietnam
                     Cambodia
                     Laos
(Australia
 New Zealand
 France
 United Kingdom
 United States)

SOVIET SOCIALIST REPUBLICS
 Russia
 Uzbek
 Turkmen
 Tajik
 Kazakh
 Georgia
 Azerbaijan
 Kirghiz
 Armenia

('The Soviet Union is a federal State, formed on the basis of a voluntary union of sixteen Soviet Socialist Republics.' The other seven S.S.R.s—all in Europe—are Ukraine, Byelorussia, Lithuania, Moldavia, Latvia, Estonia, and Karelo-Finland.)

OTHER COMMUNIST COUNTRIES IN ASIA
 China
 Mongolia
 North Vietnam
 North Korea

INDEX

ABADAN, 15, 150, 224
Abdul Hamid II, Sultan, 3, 4
Abdul Rahman, Tengku, 199
Abdullah, Emir of Trans-Jordan, later King of Jordan, 17, 23, 142, 157, 224
Abdullah, Sheikh, Kashmir, 193-4
Abyssinia, 24, 146, 233
Acheson, Dean, U.S.A. Secretary of State, 167
Aden, 238, 246, 249
Afghanistan, 12, 23, 97, 153-4, 187, 217, 232, 242
A.F.P.F.L., Anti-Fascist People's Freedom League, 189
Ahmed Fouad II, 158, 226
Ahmed Pasha, 26
Alaska, 97
Alexander, A. V., of Hillsborough (later Viscount), 178
Alexander II, Czar, 99
Alexandretta, 13
Alexandria, 125, 141, 247
— conference, 25, 141, 143
— protocol, 141
Alexis, Russian Patriarch, 126
Allenby, Field Marshal Viscount, 18
Alma Ata, 103, 105
American Immigration Law, 1924, 51
Amman, 23
Amritsar, 33
Amur River, 97
Ananda Mahidol, King, of Siam, 94, 213
Anglo-Egyptian Agreement, 1954, 158, 226
— Treaty, 1936, 158
Anglo-French Convention, 1896, 93

Anglo-Iranian Oil Co., 110, 152, 224
Anglo-Russian Agreement, 1907, 109, 150
Ankara, 7, 9, 13
Annam, 88, 89, 200
Anti-Comintern Pact, 1936, 54, 74
Antioch, Syria, 126
A.N.Z.U.S. Pact, 138, 172, 204, 220
Aqaba, Gulf of, 158
Arab League, 24, 141, 143, 154, 159, 223-4, 226
— nationalism, 24-5, 141, 154
Armenia, 5, 15, 19
Asaf Ali, 216
Asoka era, 180
Assam, 41, 81, 85, 186
Assuan High Dam, 247
Asterabad, 109
Atlantic Charter, 129, 133
Attlee, Clement (later Earl), 124, 179, 190-1
Auchinleck, Field Marshal Sir C., 25
Australia, 36, 50, 116, 120, 172, 204, 220, 239, 248
Azad, 194
Azerbaijan, 109, 151

BAGHDAD, 5, 16, 109, 148
— Pact, 138, 149, 227, 250
Balfour Declaration, 19, 20, 24, 157
Balkans, 4, 108, 126, 130
— Pact, 138, 221
Baluchistan, 186
Bandaranaike, S. W. R. D., 114, 118, 193
Bandung Conference, 193, 228-41; communiqué, 237-9; impact,

Index

Index

Index

Hanoi. 200
Hart, Sir Robert, 87
Hashemites, 17, 23, 142, 148, 224
Hassouna, Abdul Khaliq, 145
Hatta, Dr. Mohammed, 208–9
Hebrew University, Jerusalem, 21
Hadjaz, 17
Hindus, 29, 36, 40, 178, 181–2, 193
Hirohito, Crown Prince (later Emperor) of Japan, 51, 165
Hiroshima, 56, 131, 164
Hitler, Adolf, 3, 54, 75, 108, 124–5, 148
Ho Chi Minh, xii, 89–90, 114, 200–5
Holy places, Palestine, 140, 156
Holland, see Dutch East Indies
Hong Kong, 41, 43, 55, 76, 79, 87–8, 202
Hukbalahap, 210
Hungary, 246, 249–50
Hussein, Alai, 224
Hussein, Sherif of Mecca, 17–18
Hyderabad, 181, 184

IBN SAUD, xii, 17–18, 113, 142
India, 27–42, 176–86, 193–4, 223, 228; aftermath of partition, 180–4; A.I.C.C., All-India Congress Committee, 41; amalgamation of states, 181; British rule, 27–42; Independence, and partition, 1947, 179–80; India Act, 1935, 39; India Councils Act, 1909, 30; Indian Army, 23, 27, 39, 40, 153; Indian Civil Service, 23, 27, 40, 82; Indian reforms, 35–7, 180–6; Kashmir, 185; Montagu-Chelmsford Reforms, 1919, 33–4; Princes, 30, 38, 180–1; Round Table Conference, 1930–4, 38–9; Simon Commission, 1927, 37
Indo-China, 55, 80, 88–90, 199–205; see also France, Bao Dai, Ho Chi Minh, Laos, Cambodia, Vietnam, etc.
Indonesia, 135, 205–9, 217, 247; see also Sukarno, Hatta, Sastroamidjojo, etc.

Institute of Pacific Relations, 113
International Bank, 224
International Court of Justice, 224
Iran (Persia), 12, 23, 109–10, 130, 149–52, 224, 234
Iraq, 12, 18, 19, 23–6, 142, 147–9, 234, 247; see also Feisal, Fertile Crescent, etc.
— Petroleum Company, 148
Irgun, 26, 154
Irwin, Lord, see Halifax
Islam, 9, 17, 24, 99, 118, 142, 180, 233
Ismet Inönü, 10, 13
Israel, 154–8, 217, 219, 234, 241–2, 248, 250
Italy, 5, 12, 24–5, 146

JAFFA, 21, 24, 156
Jakarta, 208
Jammu, and Kashmir, 185, 187, 193–4, 240
Japan, 31, 43–57, 71–8, 84–5, 121–2, 138, 164–5, 171–3, 251
Jarring, G. V., U.N.O. mediator, 194
Java, 79, 90, 207
Jehol, 54, 73
Jerusalem, 19, 21, 126, 224
Jewish Agency, 21
Jewry, 19, 117
Jhelum River, 27, 193
Jinnah, Mohammed Ali, xii, 38, 178, 187
Johore, 81
Jones Act, 1916, 92, 210
Jordan, 19, 23, 157, 231, 234, 246
Judaism, 19, 117–18
Junagarh, 181

KAESONG, 169
Kaganovitch, L. M., 103
Kagawa, T., 52
Kalinin, M. I., 104
Kamchatka, 108, 123
Kandy, 228
Karachi, 180
Karaganda, 103
Karansinghji Bahadur, 194
Kars, 14

Index

Index

Patriarchate, Russian, Alexis, 126
—— Sergius, 126
Peaceful co-existence, xii, 116, 222, 242, 244
Pearl Harbour, 55, 173
Peel Commission, 156
Peking, 47, 48, 67, 74, 136, 162, 204, 219, 240
Penang, 79, 196, 199
Perry, Commodore, 43, 45
Persia (Iran), 12, 23, 109–10, 130, 149–52, 224, 234
Pethwick-Lawrence, Lord, 178
Philippines, 55, 80, 92–3, 210–12, 235
Phumipol Adulyadej, 213
Pibul Songgram, 94, 212–15
P.K.I. (Partei Kommunist Indonesia), 207
Poland, Poznan riots, 246, 250
Port Arthur, 47, 48, 78, 120, 136
—— Said, 248
Portsmouth, U.S.A., Treaty of, 48
Portugal, 184
Potsdam, 56, 109, 124, 131, 166
Prajadhipok, 94
Prasad, Dr. Rajendra, 184
Punjab, 33, 186
Py Yi, Emperor of China, 54, 61
—— Head of State, Manchukuo, 73

Quezon, Manuel Luis, 92, 211
Quirino, 211
'Quit India' resolution, 41

Radcliffe, Lord, 182
Raffles, Sir Stamford, 80, 86
Rajagopalachari, Chakravarti, 182
Rance, General Sir Hubert, 189
Rangoon, 81, 191, 204
Rau, Sir Benegal, 171
Razmara, 224
Refugees, 157, 170, 181–2, 187
Rendel Commission, 199
Reza Pahlevi, Muhammed, Shah of Iran, 152
Rhee, Syngman, 114, 166–8
Rhodes, island, 5, 12, 24, 157
Ribbentrop, J. von, 108
Ridgeway, General M. B., 169

Riza Khan, 110
Rommell, General, 125, 226
Roosevelt, F. D., President, 26, 120–4, 128–9
Rowlatt Bill, 33
Roxas, 210
Rozhestvensky, Admiral, 48
Russia, 48, 120–39, 240–6; Planned Society in Central Asia, 102–9; power, 124–6; relations with China, 163, 174–5, 240, 242; strategy, 132–5
Rykov, 107
Ryukyu Islands, 172

Saadabad Pact, 12, 14, 145–54
Saigon, 200
St. Petersburg (later Leningrad), 48, 100
Sakhalin, 48, 56, 120
Salonika, 3, 7
Samuel, Sir Herbert (later Viscount), 20
Samurai, 44
San Francisco, 14, 172
Sao Shwe Thaik, 190
Sarawak, 79, 81, 88
Sarnath lion pillar, 180
Sarraut, Albert, 89
Sastroamidjojo, Dr. Ali, 209, 220, 228
Satyagraha, 33
Saudi Arabia, 18, 26, 142, 151, 217, 231, 250
S.E.A.T.O., 138, 173, 188, 211, 214, 221, 242
Seiyukai, 51, 54
Senanayake, D. S., 192
Senegalese, 22
Senussi, 225
Seoul, 168
Serot, Colonel, 157
Sèvres Treaty, 5, 8, 11
Seychelles, 246
Seyid Idress, Head of the Senussi (later King of Libya), 225
Shameen, 65
Shan States, 82
Shanghai, 46, 53, 72
Shantung, 49, 71, 78
Shariat courts, 99

Index

Index

U AUNG SAN, 189-90
U Nu, 113, 190-1
Ukraine, 108, 120
U.M.N.O., United Malayan National Organization, 197-8
United Nations, 110, 120, 130, 149, 155-7, 168-71, 217, 238
— Charter, 121, 155, 221; mediation, 130, 166, 168, 171, 194, 207, 249; membership, 192, 217, 238; 'police force', 249; Security Council, 171, 214; U.N.R.R.A., 128-9; U.N.S.C.O.P., Special Committee on Palestine, 155; Veto, 121, 171
— States, 92, 110, 115, 120, 126-127, 138, 151, 156, 164-75, 203-205, 220, 249
Untouchables, 36
Ussuri River, 97
Uzbek, 103

VAN MOOK, DR. H. J., 207-8
Versailles, 5, 17, 19, 35, 50, 147
Veto, 121, 171
Vichy France, 90, 199-200, 212
Vietminh, 203, 214
Vietnam, 89, 199-205, 236
Vyshinski, Andrei, 107

WAHABIS, 18, 142
Wallace, Henry, U.S.A. Vice-President, 77
Wang Shih-chieh, 77
Warsaw Pact, 139
Washington, 50, 55
Wavell, Field Marshal Earl, 25, 42, 178
Weihaiwei, 87
Weizmann, Chaim, xii, 19, 157, 234
Wellesley province, 79
Whampao military academy, 66
White Russia, Byelorussia, 120
Wilson, President, U.S.A., 5, 120
Willingdon, Marquess of, 39

YALTA CONFERENCE, 26, 120-7, 217
Yalu River, 48, 169
Yandabo, Treaty of, 1826, 81
Yangtse Kiang, 54, 74
Yemen, 141, 217, 237, 249
Yenan, 69, 77, 78
Yilma Deressa, 233
Young Turk revolution, 3, 4
Yuan Shih-kai, 63-4
Yunnan, 76, 213

ZAHEDI, GENERAL, 152
Zhdanov, 135
Zhukov, Marshal G. K., 135-6
Zionism, 19-20, 25, 118, 143, 154-8